## Praise for *Every Shot Counts*

"Carlos' relentless work ethic, passion for the game, and commitment to excellence have made him one of the most respected players in the league. With *Every Shot Counts*, I hope that you'll be as inspired by his journey as I've been."

**—Shaquille O'Neal**

"In a world of energy-drainers, Carlos Boozer exudes positivity and resilience, especially in the face of intense challenges. *Every Shot Counts* captures the heart of a true champion."

**—Grant Hill**

"I love that Carlos is sharing his full story for the first time with *Every Shot Counts*. If given the chance, I'd coach him over and over and over again."

**—Coach K**

"Carlos is as present on the pages of *Every Shot Counts* as he is in real life. Do yourself a favor and read this book."

**—Jayson Williams**

# EVERY SHOT COUNTS

## A MEMOIR OF RESILIENCE

## CARLOS BOOZER

HANOVER
SQUARE
PRESS

HANOVER
SQUARE
PRESS™

Recycling programs
for this product may
not exist in your area.

ISBN-13: 978-1-335-45499-7

Every Shot Counts

This publication contains opinions and ideas of the author. It is intended for informational and
educational purposes only. The reader should seek the services of a competent professional for
expert assistance or professional advice. Reference to any organization, publication or website does
not constitute or imply an endorsement by the author or the publisher. The author and the publisher
specifically disclaim any and all liability arising directly or indirectly from the use or application of
any information contained in this publication.

Hanover Square Press
22 Adelaide St. West, 41st Floor
Toronto, Ontario M5H 4E3, Canada
HanoverSqPress.com
BookClubbish.com

**Printed in U.S.A.**

To my mom and dad, Carlos and Renee Boozer

To my kids, Carmani, Cameron, Cayden and Bloom

And to my entire family, which includes my friends who've become family...thank you

In loving memory of Chris

# EVERY
# SHOT
# COUNTS

# FOREWORD

*Genuine.*

It's the first word my mind travels back to again and again when I think of Carlos Boozer. It's not a word I use lightly, and it permeates through everything that I say about Carlos, from his amazing personality to his family. I coached over two hundred players at Duke University over forty-two years, with Carlos being one of seventy-three NBA selections. And if given the chance, I'd coach Carlos over and over and over again.

You never know if what you hear about a prospective player is true until you visit his home. I can weigh his physical attributes, but I don't get a sense of the player's background and character until I meet him and his family. The second I walked into the Boozers' Juneau apartment, I sensed their love. I can always tell these types of families from the way they relate to my answers. As our conversation unfolded, I gathered how much this family had sacrificed to get Carlos to this moment. Like me, Carlos Sr. also came from a military background, another boon for a coach looking for disciplined candidates. Leaving the Boozer family that night, I saw clearly that Carlos, whether he knew it or not, had already been the member of a well-oiled team for years.

*We hit the jackpot with this kid*, I thought. *We have to get him.*

Well, Duke got Carlos and I can tell you that we benefited greatly from it. Carlos could play inside, outside, facing toward or away from the basket. He could hit free throws. He set high standards for himself, but was always willing to listen and course correct. Most eighteen-, nineteen-, and twenty-year-olds don't have this maturity. Carlos absorbed and applied.

Carlos was an exceptional player, but he was also an unselfish teammate. He was confident in his own abilities, but he showed equal assuredness in his teammates' capabilities. During our 2001 championship run, Carlos did everything in his power to come back from a foot fracture, and his extraordinary play in the Final Four was a huge part of us winning.

When I was asked to coach the 2008 US Olympic Men's Basketball team, I didn't hesitate to pull Carlos onto the roster. He fulfilled a role on that team where, if needed, he would be ready. From preparation to execution, Carlos was a force multiplier on that team, and an amazing contributor to our gold medal–winning performance. I trusted Carlos completely.

After his successful NBA career, I wasn't surprised to run into Carlos during the 2022 NCAA Tournament, when he was covering Duke's Final Four appearance for ACCN and ESPN. I say I wasn't surprised because Carlos could be good at anything. He's a people person with a genuine interest in others that always shines through.

As Carlos's sons pursue their own basketball careers, they'll benefit greatly from having a father who's gone through all this, who loves them and will give them the guidance that is needed to become as successful as they can be.

Carlos has a beautiful heart. No disrespect to his parents, but Carlos is like a son to me. I love that Carlos is sharing his story with *Every Shot Counts*, so others can see what I mean. I know it will celebrate the Boozer family, because Carlos's success is not about just him. It's about his family—and that's a beautiful thing.

—Mike Kryzewski (Coach K.)

# CHAPTER 1

## CHRIS

I've never told anyone this before, but my best friend died in my arms—and it was all because of basketball. It's a day I've kept tucked away in a corner of my mind for over thirty years, like the carefully folded contents of a weathered trunk, buried behind cobwebs and cardboard boxes in the farthest corner of an attic. Until I started writing this book, I hadn't spoken about what happened to anyone, including my parents and siblings. It's a guarded memory I've only revisited in moments of solitude on my road to the NBA, and I debated dredging up the past when my family has always been about moving forward. Still, what happened changed the course of my life, as well as theirs, and I can't possibly tell my story without it.

When it happened, Chris was seven and I was six. We were two inseparable bundles of energy who lived in neighboring tenement buildings in the crime-ridden Washington, DC, projects in the late 1980s. We'd met in kindergarten and our families had become familiar enough to know that where they found one of us, the other was most assuredly there, as well. We walked to school together in the morning and left together each afternoon for the corner bodega, where we shared a $2 turkey, cheese, and mayo hero in thick white deli paper we'd unwrapped barely out of the door. Then, it was off to one of the half dozen courts sprinkled within walking distance of our complex, where we played basketball until dusk warned us to get home.

Chris and I were consumed by basketball. My father had placed the first rubber globe in my hands the year before, and one never seemed to leave them after that. That's why Chris and I got along so well—he was just as eager as me to spend all of his time on basketball. If we weren't out on the courts, we were watching NBA games on TV. Wherever we were, we talked about the sport invented by a college gym teacher in 1891 to keep football players occupied during winter months. We hashed up which teams were playing well and which ones weren't. We hypothesized matchups as if the players were super-heroes wielding their individual powers against one another. And in a way, they were.

In mid-1988, the Los Angeles Lakers were on their way to back-to-back championship titles, but it was Michael Jordan, whose Chicago Bulls team didn't even make the playoffs, who stole the spotlight. By the time the regular season ended, Jordan was the leader in scoring and steals, while also winning Defensive Player of the Year and the regular season Most Valuable Player. He was the first to win of all these accolades in the same season and his feat hasn't been matched to this day.

Two months earlier, Chris and I had been glued to the screen in my family's living room, mesmerized by the feverishly back-and-forth NBA All-Star game, where Jordan was crowned game MVP. Yet, it was the dunk contest that had us buzzing like we'd each downed a two-liter soda. In his final turn, Jordan ran the length of the court and launched himself from the foul line to the basket—a full fifteen feet of jaw-dropping air time. An eagle, wings outstretched, screeching across the sky. Jordan was flawless and awe-inspiring. Like many of our peers, Chris and I knew we were going to play in the NBA together some-day. We had no doubt. All we needed to do was practice every day, which was how we found ourselves after school at the local court, trying to hang with the older kids when we could barely graze the rim with our shots.

It was a typical humid day and the black asphalt sizzled the bottoms of our kicks, daring us all to lose our balance. Some of the players had been there all day, and with our drenched T-shirts clung to our backs, the setting sun a welcome sight.

Chris was a better player than me. He had excellent ball han-dling and dribbling skills and was quick and crafty like Jordan himself. Even at that young age, I was envious of Chris's natu-ral talent.

Working our way up the court, I watched Chris do his thing. He nailed a beautiful crossover dribble and the older kid defend-ing him lost his footing and fell onto his backside. It's called an ankle-breaker and it always gets a strong response. This time was no different. As the players hooted and hollered, the other neighborhood kids watching shook the chain-link fence sur-rounding the court.

"Dammnn! He broke you up on that one," I heard someone say behind us. I couldn't help but smile because I knew, if any-one on this court was going to make it to the NBA, it would definitely be my best friend, Chris.

On any other day, the older kid would have brushed himself off and jumped back into the game, plotting his revenge in the paint. On any other day, Chris and I would have walked home together afterward, side by side, happily reliving the amazing crossover.

This was not any other day. Chris had unintentionally shown up a gang member. The older kid got up, walked calmly back to his bike, brandished a small black handgun from the backpack hanging from the handlebars, and aimed it directly at Chris.

The shot echoed across the court and most of the kids scattered for cover, fearing they'd be hit next. Shouting and panic abounded in the gunshot's echo. Standing only a few feet behind Chris, the bullet could have hit me, but my best friend revealed its path when he fell awkwardly backward onto the blacktop, clutching his stomach. I watched in shock as the shooter got back on his bike and calmly peddled away. Nobody tried to stop him. Nobody dared attract his attention again. None of us wanted to die.

I ran to Chris and fell to my knees, propping his head and torso against my chest. I instinctually placed my hands on Chris's, but the blood kept coming, pooling into his gray T-shirt and gushing down in all directions like an erupting volcano. It smelled like pennies.

Ambulances don't arrive immediately in the hood, but I prayed that someone had run off to call one. Chris moaned and gasped for air as we waited for the EMTs. Tears streamed down his face. He was in a lot of pain and I could see the sheer terror in his eyes.

"We're getting you help," I told Chris over and over. I couldn't think of what else to say. The older kids from the neighborhood slowly huddled around us, all of us witnesses to Chris's final moments on Earth. None of them offered to help. I looked around at them, but they were all strangers, as Chris and I were to them. But they were just kids, too, frozen by what they were watching. As Chris's blood seeped down his midsection onto the blacktop, the huddle surrounding us seemed resigned to gawking, as if Chris's fate were already a forgone conclusion. He continued to moan and mumble words I couldn't understand, then started to gurgle on his own blood, deep down in his throat. His eyes rolled back as he made a final exhalation. His chest stopped rising and falling underneath my hands. He was gone.

A powerful pair of arms emerged from the crowd and yanked me out of the circle, away from Chris, who I'd laid flat to the ground. My father ushered me over to my mom and darted back

into the circle, a clear path parted for him. We watched him grab
Chris's limp wrist for signs of life. I turned into my mother's warm
body, seeking refuge. I already knew he wouldn't feel a thing.

Chris's father arrived not long after. He ran to Chris's body,
and knelt by him. His urgency was gone when he scooped his
son up and gingerly carried him toward the parking lot, just as
the ambulance pulled up, a half an hour after it was called. The
flashing red lights blurred in my teary eyes.

"Go wait in the car," my mother instructed and I complied.
Out the car window, I watched my parents approach Chris's
dad. They exchanged a few words and my parents walked back
toward me. My red, sticky hands clung to the back seat, smear-
ing its fabric with my fingerprints.

I don't remember the ride home or what was said, if anything
at all. My mother cleaned me up and put me to bed, retiring to
the kitchen table with my father as she'd done on most nights. I
looked at my big sister, Natasha, sleeping peacefully in the twin
bed next to me. I watched the shadows and light dance under
our bedroom door and strained to hear my parents, but couldn't
make out their muffled voices. I reluctantly drifted off to sleep,
my eyes still stinging from the tears.

"I had a dream last night and God told me what we're going
to do next," my father told Natasha and me the next morning
at the kitchen table. We'd been summoned out of bed earlier
than usual. Mom bounced baby Charles on her lap.

"Did God tell you to wake us all so early in the morning to
tell us?" Natasha asked through a yawn, propping her head on
her elbow.

There was no mention of Chris. Natasha had likely been
spared the details for the moment, but I expected them to bring
up Chris that morning. My parents, however, seemed focused,
energized. I was confused, but I wasn't going to bring up Chris
unless they did. Maybe this was my parents' plan to protect and
keep us moving forward.

"Well, when God speaks directly to you like this, you best take it seriously," my father said sincerely. He had total belief in what he was about to impart to us. "I dreamt about a beautiful place with mountains and trees and lakes and fish you can pull from them that are as big as you both," he said, as if he was reading about a magical land from a children's book. Natasha and I exchanged curious glances.

"Alaska," he continued, his body rising from his chair because he couldn't hold back his excitement any longer. "The Boozer family doesn't pass up an opportunity and that's what this is. We're going to Alaska!"

"What?" my sister balked. Eighteen months my senior, Natasha wasn't pleased by the sudden news.

"Your aunt Vicky and uncle Gerald live there and tell us all the time how wonderful it is," my mother quickly added. Aunt Vicky was my father's sister, who'd married a serviceman stationed there.

"Is it far from here?" I asked, trying to surmise if this adventure would keep us days or even weeks away from DC.

"It's on the other side of the country," my pragmatic mother answered. "About three thousand miles. It's going to be quite a drive." She got up with baby Charles, muttered something under her breath about giving two weeks' notice at her job and left the kitchen behind my father. Chris wouldn't be discussed this morning. I silently took my cue to keep my mouth shut.

I looked at Natasha, who was pouring herself a bowl of Fruit Loops. She had no idea what had happened the night before, but my parents' silence on the matter discouraged me from confiding in her. With no knowledge of the shooting, Natasha didn't sense the undercurrent of urgency in my parents' decision. But I understood on some level that we were leaving because I was in danger. My best friend's death was among a record 388 murders in DC in 1988 and the reason it was dubbed "the murder capital of America"—a moniker it wouldn't shake for many years to come. The rampant rise of intravenous drug use in the late 1980s spread like wildfire through DC, making it a pushers' paradise. It overflowed with potential customers, disenfranchised and desperate, susceptible to heroin's quick relief.

The gangs controlled the drugs because they ruled the streets. They decided people's fates and you did everything not to cross them. While Chris and I had zero affiliations, that didn't matter when it came to perceived retaliation. *You get one of ours? We get one of yours*—that was the code of the streets no matter what age. The specifics of allegiances were secondary. It also didn't matter that there were half a dozen basketball courts within walking distance of my family's apartment and too many interchanging players for me to recognize the shooter that day, or even remember identifying aspects of his appearance. We didn't know if he'd gotten a good look at my shocked face, either. All we knew is nothing slid by in the hood and gang vendettas could volley back and forth between sides for years. My parents didn't know how far down the rabbit hole this would go, nor were they willing to wait around and find out. I figured wherever we were going, we weren't coming back here.

Recalling the night before, had I dreamt that both my parents hugged me extra tightly and a tad longer before bed, then gently told me not to tell anyone about what had happened? Either way, I figured my parents would tell Natasha what happened themselves when the time was right. As Natasha crunched away, I folded up Chris's death, tucked it into my little trunk and pushed it into the attic corner for safekeeping.

Natasha put a bowl in front of me. "I hope you like living in an igloo," she said.

In only a couple weeks' time, my family's belongings were packed up, ready to stuff into the van my father had purchased for the trip. Our apartment was bustling with neighbors until the day before we pulled away. No one spoke about Chris in the open, though the adults whispered in hushed and somber tones away from us kids. The neighborhood was shaken up and fraying at its ends, but that was a constant here. Even without my involvement in Chris's death, our family had plenty of other reasons to go. The three years we'd lived in DC had been a struggle.

My father was born at DC General Hospital and lived in his grandfather's six-story house on an acre of land until age five, when his mother remarried and they moved back into the city. Earl Boozer wasn't a kind man to my father and favored his own children to his new stepson. During my father's junior high years, Earl, an air force mechanic, moved the family into military housing, just outside a base in Tachikawa, Japan. My father went to high school in Atwater, California, where he regularly made the local newspaper as both a football and basketball player. He went on to earn basketball scholarships to Howard University and Salisbury State University, though Earl chose my father's path and sent him to Salisbury. My father didn't last the year. But by the next fall he enrolled at the University of Maryland and got a job at McDonald's, where he met my mom, Renee.

My mother, who'd grown up in southeast DC, in a three-story brownstone with a sizable backyard, was also attending the University of Maryland. An only child until age twelve, her life was full of love and encouragement. She wasn't an athlete, but she had an expert touch with animals. Even as a young girl, she cared for turtles, birds, and other small creatures.

Renee's father was also a mechanic in the US Air Force, and she too had lived for a year near the military base in Tachikawa, Japan—the same place my father spent his junior high years. The parallels felt fortuitous.

My father enlisted in the military and my parents got married. Natasha and I were born on a US Army base in West Germany, where we lived until I was three.

We had relatives in DC on both sides, so it made sense to return there once my father's military service had ended. However, my step-grandfather, Earl, didn't want to meet Natasha and me; we were unceremoniously turned away at the door. Disappointed, but undeterred, my father found us an apartment and took on three jobs to begin building a life for us. During the day, he picked up money from retail stores to deposit at the Federal Reserve. He drove a cab in the evenings, then headed to his overnight security detail at the Navy Yard. We hardly saw him in passing.

When my mother wasn't working, she kept Natasha and me occupied at the YMCA or the public library, where we always stayed until closing. In warm weather, she took us to one of the surrounding parks in DC, Maryland, and Virginia. The parks were bustling with mothers pushing baby strollers and owners walking their dogs, but the city's underbelly always loomed. One day walking through the park with my mother and sister, I saw a man sitting on a bench, eyes closed, his body slightly slumped over to his side. He wore layers of dirty, disheveled clothes, including two coats—too many for such a warm day.

"Is he sleeping?" I asked my mother, just as white foam bubbled out of his mouth and slid down his chin. She sternly jerked us away.

The man was overdosing, likely from heroin. It's possible he died alone on that park bench. DC averaged two to five overdose deaths a day. You could walk down any street in my neighborhood and see discarded drug syringes strewn along the sidewalks among food wrappers and empty beer bottles. It was the country's epicenter for heroin use.

For all of their industriousness, my parents still struggled to make ends meet. Our lowest point as a family came when we couldn't afford a rent hike and we had to move out. My father checked us into a hotel, where we stayed for a few days before jumping to another hotel. My father paid for our room day-to-day. However, he didn't make it back in time one afternoon, so my mother packed up our belongings and took us out into the street. In a time before cell phones, she had no way to communicate with my father, and without money, her choices were limited. Night was closing in, so she looked around and spotted an apartment building a few doors down. She didn't want us to travel too far from the hotel, as our father would be looking for us. My mother waited until someone came out so she could grab the open door and usher us in. We trudged up a few flights of stairs until we reached the top landing. My mother pulled on the door that led into the apartment hallway. It was locked. She took a few pieces of clothing out of one of our bags and laid them out on the cold, dirty tile for a makeshift bed. She told us to lie down and tried to soothe us with calm words. After a few minutes of silence, I realized we were sleeping in the stairwell that night and my father wasn't coming. It was terrifying.

I woke the next morning to my mother packing away our belongings. Judging from the dark rings under her eyes, she hadn't slept for a second. She'd watched over us, keeping alert should that door open or someone venture up the steps. My mother took us to the navy hospital, where she worked in the accounting department. From there, she used the office phone to reconnect with my father, who'd been panicked and felt horrible that he'd let his family down. We remained homeless for a couple more weeks as we bounced between hotels.

In West Germany, we'd lived in a three-bedroom house with a fireplace. In DC, we were sleeping in stairwells. I'd overheard my father telling my mother that he was thinking of re-enlisting. He was already looking for an exit, so, when God showed up in my father's dreams and pointed to Alaska, that was all he needed.

The Boozer family pulled away from Washington, DC, in mid-May 1988, our lives crammed into duffle bags and cardboard boxes stuffed in the back of a cream-colored Dodge with a sliding door that slammed so violently it could take a limb off. As soon as rubber hit the road, our parents were waxing about Alaska and what it would have to offer us. My parents were incredibly optimistic people, who looked at change like it was an opportunity to be seized and conquered. Their confidence eased me into the trip and my thoughts away from DC.

I listened to my parents and watched the scenery gradually change outside my window. The farther we drove away from the city, the longer the stretches of green grass along the highway became—more than I'd ever seen in any park I visited. We stopped at exits for food and bathroom breaks; each time my dad would unfold a cumbersome paper map across the van's front hood, tracing the path he'd made with a black magic marker before we left.

By nightfall, the wilderness grew more lush, the exits signs more sporadic. That first or second night, we stopped at a motel and rented a single room with double beds. Occasionally my father drove through the night without us stopping, no doubt fueled by his determination to get his family to a safe place.

Michael Jackson's "Dirty Diana" played at least ten times a day on the radio, as my mom worked the dials to land on a clear signal. My parents were cheerful. Hopeful.

"Do you know how I met your mother?" my father asked Natasha and me over his shoulder. "We both worked at the same McDonald's."

"Did you make the cheeseburgers?" Natasha asked.

"Yes, and fries. Your mother worked the fry station."

"And your father had just broken up with another girl who worked there, too," my mother interjected, her lips curling up in a slight smile. "One day, I'm at the fry station and your father walks in looking fine as heck in a red three-piece suit, a matching fedora, and a red and green walking stick he'd made in shop class. He walked up to my fry station and said, 'Baby, I love you.'"

Natasha and I giggled. "What did you do?" she asked.

"I ran away down to the basement and hid from him until he left!" she shyly admitted, looking over at my father.

"But I wasn't ready to give up," my father said. "When I saw

her a couple days later, I asked her out on a date right there before she had a chance to run!"

"A Funkadelic's concert at the Capital Center in Landover,
Maryland," my mother said. "After the concert was over, we
walked all the way to my apartment and we stayed up talking
until the sun came up."

"I married your mom and then we didn't see each other for a
year," my father added. "I went off to Korea for basic training,
and she waited for me."

My father said it with such reverence. There was never any
doubt from Natasha and me that our parents were completely
in love. The way they looked at one another. The way they
laughed together. Their adoration for one another only spread
to us, through the time and attention they gave.

Passing through middle America, we stopped at a rest area on
a glistening lake nestled in the woods. My mom and Natasha
went off together to the restroom with Charles in tow.

"Come here, Carlos," my father said, ushering me over to
picnic area with barn-red tables. He was holding a black cylin-
drical stick in each hand. They were connected by a dangling
metal chain. Nunchucks. I'd watched my father wield them
many times, but he'd never asked me to join him before. I was
finally getting my chance.

"Should I show you a couple of things?" he asked, pulling the
chain tight with a clack. I nodded enthusiastically. From his time
in Japan as a child, my father had cultivated a great respect for
the culture. I'd peeked at my father's small, but impressive sam-
urai sword and costume collection in his closet. Bruce Lee was
hailed as a god in our house and we watched his kung fu films
with great fervor. When my dad twirled his own nunchucks at
full speed, I thought he looked like Bruce himself.

"See that flick of the wrist," he instructed patiently, trying
to slow down the figure eight motion so I could mimic him. I
eagerly took the martial arts weapon in my small hands. It only

took a few seconds waving the handles around to bump one into my elbow with a pain that shot straight up to my shoulder. With a yelp, I handed them back to my father.

"Ah, I think I'm cool on nunchucks, Pops," I said, rubbing my elbow. My father let out a soft chuckle.

"It takes some practice, but we've got time," he said, always a consummate teacher. "Now, onward to Alaska!"

The ten-day, 2,800-mile-plus trip held many firsts for this six-year-old DC kid. I saw green pastures littered with cows, neatly tended rows of corn in endless fields, and dusty red walls of rock that reached up to the clear blue sky. We stopped at the Grand Canyon and I inched forward and looked down into the abyss, gripping my mother's hand tightly.

I felt metal bend and give underneath our van as we pulled off solid land onto my first boat, a ferry, from Bellingham, Washington, toward Alaska. As the ferry jutted through the sea, I stood by its edge with my family, the breeze off the water cooling my face. And for the first time since Chris died, my thoughts weren't with what I'd left in DC, but with what lay ahead.

# CHAPTER 2

## JUNEAU

Seagull shrieks announced our ferry's arrival in Juneau, Alaska, on May 31, 1988. You can only access the city by boat or air. No roads connect it with mainland America. Our first glimpses of the secluded location were breathtaking. Hedged against snow-capped mountains with the Pacific Ocean lapping its front, Juneau was a picturesque city of thirty thousand people.

"It was a gold mining town in the late 1800s," my father told us, as we drove off the ferry and followed the directions given by our aunt and uncle. "It also has a wharf," he added. "We'll be eating the best seafood of our lives."

Natasha and I looked at each other. Neither of us knew what a wharf was and I'm not sure either of us had eaten seafood before. I silently prayed Juneau had a McDonald's.

I marveled at the miles of untouched forest, rows of what looked like oversized Christmas trees. We were driving to our new home, a three-bedroom apartment at Gruening Park, a monstrous twenty-building, subsidized community in the least-expensive part of town. Our aunt and uncle, who lived in the complex across the street, had organized quite a welcome. Our neighbors bustled in and out of the apartment carrying bed frames, mattresses, a living room set, a TV, pots and pans, dishes, some toys, and even a crib for Charles. And clothes. We were given boxes of clothes for every season, everything donated with a smile. My parents were both surprised and overjoyed. Starting over wasn't easy. There were times on our cross-country trip, mostly when they thought we'd fallen asleep, where my parents argued and fretted over how we'd procure some of the very items that later walked through our door. To this day, it's the only time I can remember my parents ever accepting charity. They prided themselves on being independent hard workers, but even my six-year-old self could read the obvious relief on their faces, which put me more at ease, too.

"What's this for?" I asked my mother, picking up a puffy coat all three of us kids could have fit in at once.

"You'll see soon enough," she said wryly, racing off with her hands full to put this or that away.

My parents said we'd hit the ground running and that's just what we did. They both found jobs right away; my father as a Federal Express delivery man and my mother with the Office of General Counsel for the Forest Service under the Department of Agriculture. With my parents off to work, we were left with a sitter, who spent most of her time tending to Charles. It was easy enough to start playing in the backyard and gradually migrate toward the woods, its dense trees ringing the apartment's parking lot.

The forest behind Gruening Park became Natasha's and my own private world for the next few years, a place of endless untouched evergreen trees that we could sprint through, screaming at the top of our lungs, without anybody caring. We were free to do what we wanted, so we sought out adventures, big and small. We explored every crag of hilly rock that rose and fell into the mountain range in the distance. We stained our fingers purple picking and eating wild blueberries. We stumbled upon streams and watched families of deer drink from them, but always ran from bear cubs without question, knowing that the mother must not be far away.

But our favorite spot was a grassy clearing not too deep into the forest, about a half mile from the apartment, where we found an old tire swing weighing down a large-branched tree. Once we mastered climbing the tree to get to it, we sat inside the vertical rubber tube together for hours, swaying back and forth while we shared our deepest secrets. Natasha and I looked out for each other, which is one of the reasons we were so close. We knew we could depend on each other. My sister was my very first best friend. Other than my mother and father, she's known me the longest of anybody on the planet.

"I kissed Geraldine," I confessed to her at our favorite spot one day. Geraldine's family lived in Building J, ours in Building D. I'd wanted to kiss her for a little while.

"And you can't tell anyone," I added hastily, when her mouth rounded. She nodded in agreement and I knew she'd keep her word.

"What did it feel like?" she asked.

"Mushy," I answered. She seemed satisfied with my assessment, as did I, until I thought about it more. I broke the silence.

"Natasha, does that mean she's my girlfriend now?" I asked. She laughed.

"No, Los," she finally said. "She's not your girlfriend until you hold hands. Everybody knows that."

I leaned back on my side of the tire, and closed my eyes, content to have a big sister who was so wise.

Natasha and I had stumbled on paradise and we understood the only way we could screw it up would be to get home after our parents. Respect the time clock and all would be well. That went fine for a few years, until one afternoon, while running back, I heard Natasha yelp behind me. She was eleven; I was nine.

"I'm stuck," she said. I turned around expecting her leg to be entangled in brambles, vines, or even a tree branch. Instead, she'd sunk down to her knees in thick gray mud and it looked like she was still descending into its pit. She thrashed about, attempting to free herself, but she only seemed to be sinking faster.

"Come on, Tash," I said, stretching to grab her arm, but her body stayed as stiff as a metal pole when the mud reached her waist.

"Pull me again," she pleaded. I yanked and she didn't budge. The mud was now up to her armpits. I had to do something fast. I lay flat to the ground and extended my arm out to her. In one quick motion, I tugged her toward me. She moved slightly through the sludge, so I pulled her again exactly the same way, at the same angle. She created a path forward until we had enough momentum to pull her out to her waist, then we clawed her the rest of the way out, both of us covered in sticky residue. Quicksand.

"What did you do to yourselves?" my mother asked, as she toweled us off. She seemed just as surprised to learn we had quicksand in Juneau—and not far from our apartment—as we were. My father, ever the disciplinarian, put the fear of God in Natasha and me that day. We were still allowed to explore the forest, but we never went near quicksand ever again.

My father took to the wilderness even more than Natasha and I did, and we went hiking with him during the day, then camped under the stars. We traded in bursting fire hydrants for fresh streams and lakes. Towering metal buildings were replaced with mighty evergreens, spruces, and pines. The endless cement sidewalks ceased; I now felt stone and earth under my bare feet.

My father was enchanted with Juneau and all its wilderness activities. He immediately bought a $5 pole, got access to a boat, and started fishing. Juneau's waters were rich with some of the largest king salmon in the world, and we needed food. If he had to get up early some mornings to catch fish for his family, he was going to do that. My father loved to fish, so I don't think he ever thought it a burden. He found it therapeutic to be on the quiet waters alone, but sometimes he would get sleepy on the drives. My mother made him promise to take someone with him and he agreed to have friends accompany him. When friends weren't available, which was often, I got a shake in the middle of the night.

"Hey, you want to go fishing?" he asked, leaning over my bed.

"Dad, what time is it?" I fired back, too tired to keep my eyes open.

"Three in the morning," he said, as if that wasn't a crazy hour to be up and about.

I moaned my rejection of his invitation and rolled away, but my father wasn't having any of it.

"Well, guess what?" he said. "You're going fishing."

"Yes, sir," I said, shaking off the grogginess to join him.

"The early bird gets the worm," he'd say, as we climbed into his truck and drove down to Auke Bay or another body of water depending on the time of year.

My father shared a silver sixteen-foot skiff with a few men. It had a red wraparound stripe and a 250-horsepower motor that you started with a strong pull of its cord, like a lawn mower. We cast our lines. Then, we waited. The water was as still as a mirror. The only sounds were the steady buzz of insects and the occasional flap of birds' wings. My father and I enjoyed the silence. He'd close his eyes, so I would, too. It felt peaceful.

When my father and I fished in the Gastineau Channel outside the city in April or May, he knew the salmon congregated at a certain bend in the waterway, which made it a prime location. The whales came so close to our boat that we heard the air blow out of their spouts.

"Sometimes the northern lights dance and the rays will shoot out at you where you can almost touch them," he'd tell me, pointing to the horizon. "That's when I know God is looking at me."

Other times, we chatted softy. My father was a fan of factoids, like myself. "You know, the biggest king salmon in the world was caught just down that way," he said once, pointing in a general direction. "One hundred and twenty-six pounds. That's the number to beat!"

My father had our fishing trips precision-locked based on the time of the season, the locations he picked, and the tide times. He lived by the military motto that "if you're fifteen minutes early, you're late." He liked to be out on the water, fully settled, an hour before the change in tides.

"We catch fish when the tide changes because they're finicky and there's new food available, so they gobble up as much as they can, along with our bait," he explained as we worked our lures onto our hooks.

I was fascinated by my father's attention to detail and procedure because it brought results. On average days, we'd catch three to four salmon, enough meat for two weeks' worth of dinners. On our best days, we'd catch as many as ten to twelve salmon at about forty pounds each, pulling them from the water as fast as our bodies let us. Timing was everything. We'd be hauling our bounty to the car as the other fishermen were just pulling their cars up to the water.

"Look, Los," he'd say. "We got here first and took all of the best fish. The more you sacrifice, the more you can achieve."

Any surplus from our trips would go into a deep freezer my father purchased, the meat lasting us for months. And these weren't just any salmon you'd find in a grocery store's butcher section. This was king salmon, considered the most delicious and sought-after kind because of its moist, smooth texture.

"Fish symbolize prosperity and fortune, which is why we thank the fish before we eat them," he told me one morning after we'd caught a good haul. My father appreciated the native culture in our area and was eventually made an honorary chief of the Tlingit tribe, through, of all things, his local basketball league.

"We pray the night before for the fish or a moose," he explained. "After we kill it, we honor it. With a moose, you eat its heart and liver first."

My father also became a hunter. Two times a year, he and three buddies took an Alaska Airlines flight and then a float plane out into the wilderness, where they'd rent a Forest Service cabin for a week of legal hunting. They usually caught a single moose, which was more than enough; full-grown adults weighed 1,200-1,600 pounds. They spent days hacking the moose into moveable pieces, then would get it to the butcher, who would make burgers, sausages, and steaks. They used the same system when they hunted bears, too, giving away any spare meat they couldn't freeze to our neighbors.

I enjoyed everything my father caught, including moose, deer, bear, and fish. This DC kid had no problem going all Grizzly Adams with his diet. My mom found a few cookbooks that worked and our meals, including the fish, were covered for six to seven months. This was a huge help for our family. I respected that, though I didn't take to hunting the way I did fishing with my father.

Around age twelve or thirteen, he took me into the woods to start teaching me how to properly handle a gun.

"Just concentrate on that soda can straight ahead," he said, handing me his 30-06 hunting rifle.

I looked down at the deadly weapon in my hands. I thought of Chris every day, but this brought me right back to his shooting, how the shot rang out like a firework, how he stumbled back abruptly from the bullet's power. Once you see a life extinguished, you understand the magnitude that even a little pressure on the trigger can carry.

I'm sure lots of kids would've been elated to go out shooting with their fathers. But I'd witnessed a murder. I didn't want to kill anything. My father no doubt understood this, but his intention was to introduce me to gaming, which was an important part of Juneau's culture. He wanted me to fit in. I brought my eye to the scope as my father instructed and squeezed the trigger. There was a hard thwap to my right eye and my body jerked backwards from the buckshot's retraction, giving me a black eye. Over time, I learned how to be firm and strong with a rifle, but I never joined my father on his hunting trips.

I didn't have an affinity for hunting, but I was game for sports of all kinds, which is where my father and I truly connected. Though we never brought up Chris again, I wasn't steered away from playing basketball or any other sport. Around age eight, I asked my father to teach me about basketball and no matter how tired he was after his shift that day, he'd find some time to shoot with me or throw a baseball around. My father also enrolled me in as many youth sports programs as I wanted.

Those first summers in Juneau seemed endless. In part, they were, as the sun wouldn't set until late evening. The longest days of summer lasted almost eighteen hours. The golf courses were still teeming with players at 10:00 p.m. The streets along the wharf stayed open just as long, as tourists milled about in the sea air.

"They call it the midnight sun," my mother told me. "We should enjoy it while we can. Winter will be different. Besides, you know what the end of summer means?"

Natasha and I knew she meant going back to school.

My parents were determined to make this a fresh start, especially with our education, which they deemed highly valuable. My father left college after his first year to join the army as a way to support my mother and save up for a future family. My mother didn't complete her college degree, either; yet both my parents were saddled with student loan debt. My parents were determined that any and all children of theirs would graduate from college, preferably without lifelong debt, which was another reason we'd left DC. Alaska had one of the strongest educational systems in the country, while DC schools were overcrowded and underattended to. We'd have a better shot at exceeding in the classroom, which would set us up to earn much needed academic scholarships down the road.

Natasha and I were enrolled in a private Christian school; my parents had been saving for this purpose since DC. Our family was Baptist, attending church every Wednesday and Sunday, but that didn't matter. It was a quality school and that's all my parents cared about. Regardless, Natasha and I stood together, terrified in our school uniforms, on our first day.

I followed Natasha up the school bus steps and gazed up at a sea of white faces—all of them staring at us, as if we were aliens. I took Natasha's lead and slipped into the seat next to her toward the front.

"Do you think there'll be other kids like us at school?" I whispered.

"I don't know," she said. The bus was quiet, so we finished the ride in silence, not wanting to draw any more attention to ourselves.

I followed Natasha off the school bus, dreading what was about to happen next. Natasha, a year ahead of me, went off to a different classroom. She gave me a reassuring look before steeling herself for whatever she too would have to weather.

The plight of being the new kid is something we can all relate to. But in DC, our appearance matched everyone else's. Here, we stood out. No one had our nappy hair or spoke like us. Nobody had our swag. I don't think I spoke for the first couple of weeks, as to not draw any more attention to myself. It was uncomfortable to feel so isolated. The first kid to approach me had played against me in kickball during recess.

"You into sports?" he asked. I thought I had a friend for life right there. What a lifeline that was! Caleb Ziegenfuss didn't care what I looked like and he became my first good friend after Chris. It took the first part of the school year for me to gain acceptance from the rest of my peers, if they accepted me at all.

The temperature took a sharp dip in September, and each day my mother added another layer of clothing over our uniforms. Thin jackets quickly made way for puffed coats. Right after Halloween, Juneau had its first snowfall. Our sneakers were promptly replaced with boots as heavy as cinder blocks. Natasha and I must have been carrying around an extra twenty pounds each. I was outraged with our cumbersome ensembles until the cold really hit us, when the temperatures plummeted into single digits for entire months.

Alaska was a level of cold that I'd never experienced before. I'd seen snow in DC, but I'd never seen snow like this, where it fell all day, all night, all week. I think there was a ten-day stretch where not a drop of snow melted. School was canceled and we took to the hills in our oversized coats and Frankenstein boots for sledding and snowball fights. As it got colder, the sun seemed to take less of an interest in us.

One morning, I woke up and it was still pitch-dark outside. I rolled over, thinking I'd woken too early, but the alarm clock read 6:00 a.m. We ate breakfast and drove to school in the dark. The sun finally appeared around 9:00 a.m., only to disappear by 3:00 p.m. We had six hours of daylight. That's all we got that day.

Juneau was so frigid that there was an ice field twelve miles away carrying multiple bona fide glaciers. How many other US states have a single glacier, let alone many? Yes, Juneau's winter was harsh and long, pushing through a springtime that never came at all. However, summer brought our surroundings back to life that June in full force.

We'd made it an entire year in Juneau, and watched nature bursting free from every nook and cranny. The animal population seemed to think it had just as much of a stake in Juneau as humans did, so we learned to coexist. Birds perched on windowsills and critters scurried across the sidewalk. From our school bus stop, Natasha and I watched raccoons or the occasional grizzly bear rummaging through garbage bins. We learned to identify the two types of inhabiting bears—black and brown (or grizzly)—and what they ate, human or otherwise.

But for all "America's Last Frontier State" offered us—and it was a lot—Juneau was foreign to us in another essential way. They call Washington, DC, the "Chocolate City" for a reason—Black people made up the vast majority of the population. Juneau's population was DC's photo negative—predominantly white folks and some Native Americans. We went from looking like everyone else to looking like nobody else. Initially, we got a lot of stares from people who'd rarely seen a Black family in their midst. I stared right back—I'd never seen so many white people together in one place.

I had my first brush with racism at age eight. We were waiting outside the school to open, when a white kid poured a carton of chocolate milk over the head of a Black classmate.

"Oreo! Oreo!" he chanted at the girl. "Half Black and half white." I didn't know the girl, but I found myself moving to her aid, pushing the bully away from her. A fight ensued, my first, yet not my last over skin color.

When I told my parents what happened, they were proud. "You knew it was wrong in the moment and you stood up for that poor girl," my mother said, as we pulled into the McDonald's drive-through for my reward. "You did the right thing."

My parents weren't always pleased with the decisions I made in the name of social consciousness, though. At age ten, the Boozer children transferred to public middle school and it was as if I was starting all over again. The only difference was that I'd distinguished myself as an athlete at our Christian school and my reputation had preceded me. In my new school, athletics begot popularity and kids wanted to be my friend. Most of my classmates were excited that a skilled basketball player had transferred to their school.

Not everyone accepted me. The N-word was slung at me in the hallways and at recess. In seventh grade, I was pushed from behind in the hallway and turned to face a much taller and heavier classmate.

"Listen, I'm minding my own business and going to class, but if you use the N-word again, I'm going to put you on your ass," I seethed. At this point, a good crowd had formed around us, anticipating action.

My classmate looked at me and said the word again, enunciating each syllable tauntingly. So, I did exactly what I told him I would. I swung, hitting the left side of his face, which sent him careening to the floor. A teacher separated us in seconds and we were both sent to the principal's office. My parents appeared, as did my classmate's parents. Nobody looked pleased.

I calmly explained what happened, knowing there were at least fifteen kids I could name who would corroborate my story. I was suspended for two days. The other kid got a week.

"Did you have to punch him?" my mother asked over her shoulder during the ride home. "Did it make you feel better to see him hurt?" She wasn't mad at me as she asked it, so I really stopped to think about it.

"No, ma'am, it didn't make me feel any better," I told her honestly. My parents urged all of us children to think about the short- and long-term consequences of our actions. I got some short-term satisfaction leveling that kid, but I got suspended from school for it. My parents encouraged us to think long-term.

"Two wrongs don't make a right," she said, the final word on the matter.

I've hesitated sharing these early impressions because racism exists everywhere, from Juneau to Washington, DC. Still, when you're one of five Black families among a 30,000-person population, there's no hiding from the double takes.

After our first year in Alaska, we flew back East to visit our relatives for an annual Fourth of July family barbeque.

"Why do we have to fly in three planes to get there?" I asked my mom, myself a novice to the frugality of connecting flights. In the years to come, no matter our financial situation, we never missed our annual DC trip. We scraped pennies together because getting there was that important to my parents, even as our family grew over the next few years. In January of 1990, my sister Nakeisha was born and Natanya followed in August of 1992.

On our first trip back to DC, thirteen months following Chris's death, I asked my younger relatives what had happened to the shooter. I was told he'd fled the city and hid for months, but had recently been seen down at the courts again. Anger boiled inside me. Even at age seven, I understood that a great injustice had occurred. My best friend had been gunned down, but this kid had peddled off into the sunset scot-free. He'd have opportunities to pursue a career, fall in love, and have children. Chris wouldn't. I thought how unfair it was that Chris's mom would mark each year wondering what her son could have accomplished. My parents and I hadn't spoken about Chris since the night he died, so I had no one to confide in. Swallowing my bitterness, I took this new piece of information, folded it up neatly, and tucked it into my trunk, out of sight.

Washington, DC, had been an uncaring city for us, which made our appreciation for Juneau grow. My first few years there were mostly the shiny side of the coin, where Natasha and I swayed back and forth in our tire swing, our heads tilted back, staring up at the clear blue sky and the clouds drifting by. That's how I remember it.

# CHAPTER 3

## THE EMBRACE

I thought I was going to play in the World Series someday. I imagined myself atop the mound, nodding subtly to the catcher before contracting my left leg up to my body, extending my right arm and releasing my hand in one fluid motion, sending the ball rocketing to his waiting glove. I would be just like Seattle Mariner pitcher Randy Johnson, a menacing, six-foot-ten lefty with a devastating fastball and a fear-inducing slider.

My father threw with me nearly every day after work and we hardly missed a televised game. I joined the city league and began to play locally with the other kids. And I watched the Little League World Series devoutly on ESPN2 every summer. My goal was to get to that series.

At age eleven, I was one of fifteen kids selected to represent Juneau's All-Star baseball team. We played through spring into summer and made it all the way to the regional championship game. We were two games out from representing Alaska in the World Series in South Williamsport, Pennsylvania, that August. Only two wins away.

However, two things happened around that time that made

me reevaluate my baseball aspirations. One was Michael Jordan, which we'll get to a little later. The other was that game. As the starting pitcher that day, I'd struck out two batters and thrown the other out at first. We were off to a good start, until I got up to bat. I was a strong batter. When I heard and felt the familiar clang of metal connecting with cowhide, I shed my bat and sprinted for first base with everything I had. In my periphery, I could see the third baseman scoop up the ball and launch it toward my destination. In a split second, the first baseman tagged me with his glove and I was thrown out at first. My coach met me at the dugout entrance, just a few feet away from my teammates.

"Why didn't you run harder?" he asked. He seemed mad at me. "You could have made it."

"Sorry, Coach," I mumbled and dejectedly climbed down the steps to take my seat on the bench. I'd given it my all.

"Brower, report to the bullpen," my coach announced. Brower was our second pitcher; my coach intended to sit me out. When it came time for our team to take the field again, I was left behind. I tried to shake off my disappointment and cheered for my teammates throughout the second inning, thinking this was only temporary and surely I'd return for the third.

At the bottom of the third, when I didn't take the pitching mound again, I heard my father's voice booming from the spectator stands to the right of me. "What are you doing, Coach?" he yelled, much less jovial than his usual self. My coach didn't even look my father's way. Not once. He didn't acknowledge me, either. I sat out the rest of the game in silence, fighting back tears that eventually gave way as it became clear that we weren't going to win the game. No Pennsylvania. No World Series. I was heartbroken—not that I didn't get to play, but that my opportunity to help my team win had been taken away and I had no idea why.

The teams lined up to high-five and congratulate each other

on a good game, but my eyes were glued to my father, who emerged from behind the chain-link barrier and approached my coach with purpose. The conversation had already ended by the time I joined my father, who put his arm around my shoulder and walked me off the diamond. "You didn't do anything wrong," he said unprompted, answering my thoughts. "Sometimes things just go the way they go."

As we passed the dugout, I watched my coach fielding questions from the local press. "Why didn't you play Boozer?" I clearly heard one of them ask, but I was out of earshot before I could hear his answer.

In the days that followed, I replayed what had happened in my head, again and again, trying to uncover some clue as to why my coach did what he did. Had I done something before the game to make him angry with me? My answer came in the form of Michael Jordan soaring across our television screen during the 1993 NBA Finals. As soon as MJ appeared, it didn't matter anymore why my coach did what he did. I'd never play baseball again.

I'd competed in every sport available to me, from baseball to track-and-field to cross-country running. I excelled at all of them, but my heart truly belonged to basketball, from the day my dad placed that orange globe in my four-year-old hands. There was a mano a mano factor that stoked my innate competitive fire. I felt completely alive when I stood across from an opponent, my mind thinking, *Am I better than you? Let's find out.*

I'd gotten more of a thrill from basketball than any other sport and as I watched the TV screen, I suddenly understood why. There was something happening every second in basketball. The players never stopped. I found my eyes chasing the ball through clever passes, tight dribbles, slick jump shots, and dynamic dunks. I knew right then I wanted to be a part of that world.

"Pops, I want do that," I said, my eyes still fixed on this marvelous player who made everything look so effortless and, dare I say, poetic. Jordan took off into the air with his famous straddle jump. Slam dunk. My father and I smiled simultaneously.

"That's *all* you want to do?" he asked, emphasizing the "all."

"Definitely. I want to play in the NBA."

"Not even baseball?" he assessed, one eyebrow cocked slightly. Scottie Pippen to Jordan again with the breakaway, climbing to the basket on invisible steps. Floating. Another slam dunk, this time two-handed for emphasis.

"Do you see Jordan?" my dad asked, seizing the moment. "Three NBA championships in a row and probably one or two more before he retires," he said. "Jordan was cut from his junior varsity team as a sophomore. The greatest player of all time cut from his JV team. Given a 'no' and sent home. Now, it could have ended there for him, but MJ had something special that made him come back and try out again the next year."

"What was it?" I asked, hoping for some way to acquire this magic MJ pixie dust.

"It's something inside of you that keeps you going, keeps you moving forward, no matter what," he said, getting more serious. "Los, there are millions of kids that want to play in the NBA like Jordan and very few make it. Very few."

I turned to my dad. "I will do whatever it takes," I said. I couldn't describe it to him, but a switch inside of me had flipped on.

"Do you know what the word *embrace* means?" he asked, scratching his moustache. "That's a pretty strong word. *Embrace*. You're going to have to love everything about basketball—even the stuff you hate about it. From endless practice drills to stinking like high heaven, to feeling so sore you don't want to get out of bed each morning. I'll take the time to teach you how to play the game, but you're going have to work. Nothing will be handed to you."

"Embrace and learn," I repeated. "Got it."

"You have to earn becoming a basketball player," he finished. "Take the time to be this."

My basketball career started with that conversation. Imagine if I'd gotten shot down in that moment? It happens to a lot of kids, not necessarily because their parents aren't supportive, but because they lean more on the side of practicality. Though they could have easily told me to pick another career goal, my parents' pragmatism still left room for me to dream big. Professional basketball was an incredibly narrow career path. I'd basically told my parents that I wanted to be the next Beethoven, and they asked what type of piano I needed. They took my dreams seriously. They took me seriously. My parents were willing to go broke to provide me with the necessary tools, and that was the same for all of my siblings. Natasha began singing lessons, while Charles followed me into basketball. As long as we put the work in, they were on board.

The very next day—with my father's words still ringing in my ears—I raced home and barreled through my math, science, and history homework. Then, I waited by the window for my mother's car, clutching the living room curtains. Once she gave my homework her approval—usually around 5:30 p.m.—I'd leave with my father, just home from work himself, for the thirty-minute drive to Auke Bay Elementary School. This became our standard routine for the next five years. Nearly every day. Rain, sleet, or snow—and we experienced plenty of all three because we practiced primarily on an outdoor court. We'd pull into the parking lot and I'd be out of the car before my dad had time to turn off the engine. I'd slosh through the slush across the black-top to the court—that sound of my rubber soles squeaking clean still gets my heart pumping to this day. My sneakers and socks were usually soaked through, but I didn't care. It was time to get to work. We practiced two hours and were home in time for dinner with the rest of the family at 8:30 p.m.

On Sundays after church, my entire family came to the school and my younger siblings kept busy on the playground with my mother, while my father and I put up shots. When we couldn't get to the school, I practiced shots on a half-court, located on our apartment's property. I was so serious, I let my other sports coaches know I wouldn't be returning to their baseball and track-and-field teams. I wanted to dedicate all of my time to basketball. My parents had gone all-in on me, which was already affecting my siblings' lives, as well. They placed a lot of faith in me at age twelve, and I had to make it happen on my end, which meant focusing my time and efforts on one sport. Basketball also happened to be my father's favorite sport and the one he had the most knowledge of. A basketball always felt right in my hands and that feeling reminded me of Chris. Not a day went by where I didn't think of him, and in a way, he was there with my father and me from that first practice, watching us.

"Do you know how I started playing basketball?" my father asked during one of our earliest practices. "When your Grandpa Earl was in the air force, we lived in Japan. That's where I went to junior high. I was one of the taller kids. One day, the school decided to start a basketball team and the coach asked me to join. Talk about falling hard."

At six-foot-three, I thought my father was a giant, especially compared to my wiry five-foot-nine frame. I only hoped I'd grow to his height.

"I'd also like to show you some new things, because I don't think you'll be playing at guard forever," he added. I'd fancied myself a Grant Hill–esque player, fast and powerful like the ball-hammer guard, but I could be open to learning a new position.

My father had been a versatile athlete, running track and

playing football at the varsity level. Yet, he loved basketball the most. He'd played all the way through high school, and though his hoop dreams were marred by a football injury and a family more likely to sabotage than support him, my father kept playing while he attended the University of Maryland. During a pickup game, he befriended Terrapins guard Brad Davis, who introduced him to Coach Lefty Driesell. Impressed with his skills, Coach Driesell utilized my father as a practice player for two years.

My father had always been active, with a get-up-and-go attitude in seemingly endless supply. For the last few years in Juneau, I'd watched him play weekly in the over-forty league, where he was a dominant guard. He was fast, quick, athletic, and could jump. And he practiced—sometimes I followed my father to the gym and retrieved his balls for him.

Having served for a decade in the US Army, my father also had a great respect for discipline. As a staff sergeant, he'd been placed in charge of a team that assembled remote launch pads for short-firing Hawk missiles, the predecessors to Patriot missiles. He was the conductor of a timely operation that took precision, which had only come from repetition.

I felt in capable hands with my father, as we began with the basics. "Let's start with some dribbling," he said, passing me the ball, chuckling and shaking his head. "Couldn't have fallen harder."

Our first practices began with me simply making twos from a single spot five times in a row, which could take a twelve-year-old quite a bit of time to conquer.

"Every shot counts!" my father would encourage me, when he'd sense my resolve begin to wane.

We worked on ball handling and shooting to make sure I developed a good touch. I threw countless free throws and ran sprints. We went full court; we went one-on-one. Somedays, my father took the brunt of things by simply rebounding and feeding the ball back to me, so I could work my shots. He never said no. Never.

My father wasn't just a former player; he was a student of the game. He scoured the public library for drill books and gleaned coaching insights from greats like John Wooden and Bobby Knight. My family couldn't afford a home computer, so he snuck onto the one at work, eyes scanning over his shoulder as he printed out pages to bring to the court that evening. As my father taught me the fundamentals, he also kept an eye on the NBA and how it was always evolving. Was there a certain type of player that could add something that was missing? What on-court traits would said player need to have? He followed the trends, but also looked to the future with the studiousness of a Wall Street stockbroker.

Sometimes we discussed the NBA, analyzing each team as we practiced together. Other times we didn't talk at all. As I got older, we'd talk about my grades, girls, and all the other fun stuff that comes with adolescence. My father even managed to slip the "birds and the bees" talk in at one point.

Like two hikers climbing up at an arctic mountain, my father and I also endured the elements together. We practiced outdoors each day, but the court's metal roof—its only real protection—did little to keep it dry during the harsher seven or eight months of the year. Sleet and snow flew in sideways through its surrounding fence and left a white dusting everywhere. We brushed it aside with brooms we kept in the car trunk. When it was windy, I could feel the chill right down to my bones. My fingers throbbed. I slipped. I fell. But I always got back up. During short daylight hours, we practiced by the light of the fluorescent floods provided by the school. In the flickering dim light, I started to get a feel for the dimensions of the court no matter where I was.

Early on, I realized that basketball could be an outlet for my emotions. This would be incredibly helpful in high school, as my confrontational skills needed work. I tended to internalize conflict, whether I'd gotten into a fight or earned an iffy grade that put my basketball dreams in jeopardy. But when I put up shots all that bottled-up emotion poured out. There was no school. Those thoughts fell away. It was only basketball.

At school, I learned more about the special conviction it would take to become a professional basketball player. My English teacher instructed us to write an essay about what we wanted to be when we grew up. I crafted my love letter to the NBA, pointing out where my talents resided and what areas I needed to work on. I handled that essay with immense care and poured a lot of my personal pride into it. I put it all on the line.

The next day, we read our essays aloud in front of the entire class. One classmate described wanting to become a teacher; another wanted to try their hand at photography. I couldn't wait to share my life's dream with my teacher, as my classmates already knew I was a baller. My name called, I made my way up to the front of the room, cradling my paper like the significant personal document that it was. I turned to face my classmates. My teacher was also seated among them, in the front row's right corner. I could spy him in my periphery. I took a deep breath.

"I want to go to the NBA," I began confidently. "I want to play against the best players in the world." I then went on to give the many reasons why a twelve-year-old boy would want to play in the NBA. When I'd finished, the entire class clapped their approval. Most of them had seen me play some type of sport, so they knew there was some weight to what I had just declared in front of everybody.

"Carlos, you should be more realistic about your future," my teacher said. I turned to look at him; my bubble suddenly burst. "Think about working at the gas station or Kmart, or something like that."

My cheeks flushed red and hot. I felt like I just stood there frozen for a moment, my classmates looking back at me, no one quite sure how to react. My teacher broke my trance by telling me to take my seat and called on the next student, as if nothing errant had been said at all. I sat through the rest of class making a list of all the tasks I would do to prove my teacher wrong.

A big part of my father's plan to get me to the NBA was to immerse me in as much basketball as he could. He wanted as many irons in the fire as possible. He began taking me to open-gym nights at the high school, sometimes four times a week, if we could swing it, run by the high school basketball coach, George Houston. Getting to practice inside was always a luxury.

My father also coached me on a team through the parks and recreation department. It was there that he stumbled upon an opportunity to make me an even better player. I'd had a horrible game on that day in particular, only scoring 10 points. We'd lost resoundingly. Every time I'd attempted my normal routes to the basket, the defense pushed me to go left, which I was totally unequipped for. It was a very effective strategy and my father was impressed. He shook the coach's hand in defeat so emphatically, I thought he might tear the guy's arm off.

"The coach told me you were very good," my father said the next day at practice. "But that's only going right. I think we can do something about that. Come here, Carlos."

He unbuckled his pants' belt and wrapped it between my right arm and my waist, pulling it tight. My right hand rested on my thigh, completely immobile. "We're going to try everything left for awhile, so you won't have any weaknesses," he said, passing the ball to my floppy left hand, which I barely caught. "Let's dribble!"

I might have dribbled left-handed up and down the court one hundred times that day and my left hand felt like Jell-O afterwards. But over the next three months, I learned how to pass left-handed, tip the ball in left-handed, and attack the basket from the left. A part of the court I'd never used suddenly became an option and options create opportunities.

When my father said I was going to do everything left-handed, he meant it. At home, I ate my cereal and brushed my teeth with my left hand, while my whole family got involved policing me. After two months, my father decided it was time to practice without the belt.

"Let's see what you got!" my father said, taking a wide defensive stance. I bounced the ball with my right hand, but quickly transferred it to my left hand, breaking loose past my father toward the basket, where I finished with a left layup.

"Alright now! Wait till the college scouts see you!" he hooted in approval. "Let's go again!" My father was as excited to get another crack at me as I was to get past him.

It felt like that moment you learn to ride a bike, when difficult suddenly becomes normal and you can't ever believe there was a time you didn't know how to ride a bike. It's as if I'd been trying to lift something very heavy, and it suddenly became light. Leading with my left hand opened up a whole new avenue for me. I could go either way now and was no longer a one-dimensional player.

Our practices rolled into the summer before high school, and something miraculous happened. I started stretching overnight. I'd wake up with little aches in my knees and back as my bones lengthened. That summer, I grew a few more inches to five-foot-eleven. My parents seemed totally unsurprised.

"Your grandfather was six-foot-six, wasn't he?" my mother asked my father one morning, as they eyed my vertical progress over breakfast. "And your mom was very tall, as well."

"And my cousin," my father added, taking a sip of his coffee. "I think he was six-foot-eight. And Uncle Luscious! We can't forget Uncle Luscious! He was six-foot-seven!"

"How come nobody told me?" I asked.

"Well, you never asked," my mother answered succinctly.

As it turns out, I come from a long line of gigantic people and was the last to know about it. I was so hooked on basketball at that point, though, that I would have still pursued it, no matter my height. But don't get me wrong. I welcomed every inch. The taller, the better in my eyes. Each inch brought me closer to that rim.

As I sprouted like a cornstalk that summer, my father looked online for what my next step might be. He found the West Coast All-Star "Double Pump" Camp, out of Carson, California, which would be held on the Cal State-Dominguez Hills college campus. I wasn't sure what the "Double Pump" name had to do with basketball until my father told me that the camp had been founded by two twin brothers, David and Dana Pump.

"This is where all the best basketball players on the West Coast go," he said. "We're going to put you in the fire and see how you do."

My mother flew with me to the camp; my plane ride was a mix of excitement and anxiety. When we arrived at the campus, I insisted we go to the gym first, so I could check out who'd I'd be playing against. But after watching a few minutes, my confidence crumbled. The gym was teeming with players between eighth and eleventh grade and they all looked bigger, stronger, and more athletic than me. And the way they moved—I'd never seen guys like this before.

A six-foot-something monster caught a pass right in front of me, dribbled once, spun into a leap and sailed all the way to the net for the dunk. The way he pieced together a sequence of multiple moves—that was straight-up NBA-style play. It was nasty and definitely something I'd never seen in person before. This kid couldn't have been older than sixteen or seventeen—that's as old as they took players at this camp. How had he learned to do that?

His name was Richard Jefferson and he'd go on to play for the University of Arizona, then in the NBA for seventeen seasons. He won a championship with LeBron James in 2016. Richard was only the first player I noticed. I scanned the rest of the court and there were nine other Richards pulling moves just like he had.

Another player whizzed by, this one managing a crossover on his man, passing the ball between his legs, then behind his back and finishing by clearing a seven-foot defender clean. That was six-foot-three Baron Davis, who'd play two years for UCLA before moving on to the NBA for seventeen seasons, as well.

*This is the real fucking deal*, I thought to myself. I'd never felt so intimidated.

"Mom, I don't want to go," I told her, as we unpacked at our motel room later. I was shaken by what I'd seen. She sat me down on one of the beds.

"Carlos, you wouldn't be here if you weren't good enough, if Pops didn't think it," she said calmly. "I see all the work you put into this. Have faith in that. Take stock in it. I guarantee you're the only player out there that's frozen his butt off on numerous occasions to get in practice time."

I smiled at my mom. She was right, of course. There was really only one way to see if I could hang with this group, and I could feel my curiosity overcoming my fear.

"This is an opportunity," she added, "and we don't pass up on opportunities, do we? We face them head-on."

I knew my parents had scrimped and saved to pay for this camp. My father was keeping his word. He was doing everything he could to make me a better player and get me on the road to the NBA. I decided I wouldn't squander this chance. I reported to my assigned team, while my mom took her place in the stands with the other parents. On the opposite side of the court, there were a lot of men in a rainbow of different colored polo shirts holding clipboards, some furiously writing, as they eyed the players.

"Who are they?" I nudged one of my teammates.

"Those are the college coaches," he said. "It's what we're here for." Great. In my fear over keeping up, I hadn't thought about who would be watching.

I had nerves all the way up to the jump ball in my first game. But then it was just basketball, the thing I knew the most in the world. Muscle memory kicked in and my worries disappeared. I was in the moment, passing to my teammates and hitting my jump shots, with both my right and left hands. I realized I wasn't the best player out there, but I was also far from the worst. I could hang and had a really good time in the process. I would go back to Alaska with my head held high.

On one of the final days of camp, I'd put in a solid day's work on the court. I scored 15 points and had 6 or 7 rebounds.

"You looked good," my mother commended me, as we gathered my gear, climbed down the stands, and headed toward the exit.

"Wait!"

My mother and I turned around to find an Asian man with a goatee racing toward us.

"I'm Darren Matsubara, but everybody calls me Mats," he said breathlessly, holding his hand out to me and then my mother. "I watched your son play today and he's good. My assistant coach told me you're from Alaska and I just wanted to tell you I think that's great. You know, our team motto is 'It isn't where you're from, but how you play.'"

"We'd love to get him a scholarship somewhere," my mother said. We both saw the slight twinge in Mats's face before he answered.

"I think he might be able to get a scholarship," he appraised honestly. "But tell me, has he committed to anyone yet?"

"Committed?" my mother took a beat to contemplate, then it hit her. "Oh! You mean committed to a college? Oh, you must have looked at the program."

"I did," said Mats, opening his directory to the *B*s for Boozer.

"That's a typo," my mom corrected, pointing to the *Jr.* by my name. "The *Jr.* got separated from his name. It's not his grade. He's only twelve years old and a freshman this fall."

What a difference one letter made in this excitable stranger's face. His eyes widened as if he'd unwrapped the correct bar of Wonka chocolate and found the Golden Ticket.

"He's twelve," Mats repeated, looking me up and down. "Well, that changes everything. I would love for Carlos to come play for my AAU team in Las Vegas next weekend. It's a big tournament, sponsored by Adidas. All the biggest coaches from the biggest colleges attend."

Mats pulled a business card out of the Adidas bag slung over his shoulder and handed it to my mom.

"And they give out lots of free gear, like shirts and shoes," he added, looking to me, probably knowing how much it would entice me. "How would you like to play some travel ball, Carlos?"

"That sounds great," I answered instinctively. I was sold and ready to sign on the dotted line. Just hand me the pen! But my pragmatic mother took over the wheel before I could say anything else.

"We'll discuss this with my husband and get back to you as soon as possible," she said evenly.

"Fair enough," Mats answered, nodding his head, "but do me a favor and don't tell anyone else you're an incoming high school freshman. I want you to play for my team."

He winked at us with that last line.

"Who was that guy?" I asked my mother, as she ushered me away.

"I don't know, but we need to find a pay phone," she declared, with a bit more purpose in her step.

I watched expectantly as my mom relayed our interaction with Mats to my father, feeding a coin into the phone every few minutes as he looked up *AAU* and *travel ball* on his work computer. We were supposed to fly back to Juneau the next day and changing that flight to drive to Las Vegas was going to cost money my family really didn't have. But as my mom spent more time on the phone with my father, I started to realize that they were hashing it out and I might just get to go. I jumped up and down with excitement.

"Your father wants to speak with you," my mom said, handing me the receiver.

"Hey, Pops!" I said.

"I heard you did great!" he said in his soft, reassuring tone. "I'm really proud of you."

I felt good about how I'd done that day, but was nervous with anticipation, waiting to hear if I'd get to play in Las Vegas.

"This Big Time Tournament in Las Vegas," he continued. "It's next-level stuff. You ready?"

"Oh yeah, I'm ready," I purred. My confidence was riding high after a week at camp.

"Well, I think you're ready, too," he finally revealed. "Let's roll the dice and see what happens!"

My mom rented a car and we drove five hours from the Los Angeles area to Las Vegas, passing through the flat and desolate Death Valley and over a mountain, where a twinkling of neon lights welcomed us out of the darkness. It had been a little over a year since I'd first declared my NBA dreams to my father, and here I was in Las Vegas about to do the thing I loved to do best.

As my father explained to my mom, *AAU* stood for the Amateur Athletic Union, a nonprofit, multisport organization created in 1888 to highlight young amateur athletes. The AAU's basketball program was extravagant and well organized. My mom and I checked into our reserved room in the pyramid-shaped Luxor Hotel and Casino on an entire floor that had been blocked off for all the players. Our room was almost as big as our entire three-bedroom apartment back home. And it had its own little refrigerator, neatly hidden behind one of the TV stand's doors. The best part was sponsors paid for it all!

The next morning, I reported to Mats at the Big Time Tournament gym. I'd be playing for Mats's Elite Basketball Organization (EBO) travel team. We all huddled around him as he gave out last-minute instructions, but my gaze floated over to the court. I'd had the same reaction the previous week after seeing the West Coast Camp's talent. It was overwhelming. There were players dunking and hitting threes and crossing over one another to where bodies were flying every which way. This was a style of basketball I'd never seen before growing up in Alaska. But this time I wasn't intimidated. I was charged up to test myself against them.

We played against giants like Lamar Odom, the aforementioned Davis and Jefferson, Chris Burgess, and Elton Brand—all who would go on to the NBA, though nobody knew it at the time. Luckily, our team also had some heavies (and future UCLA stars), including six-foot-seven small forward Matt Barnes, who'd later play four years for UCLA before he headed to the NBA for fourteen seasons. Our guard, Ray Young, was another high school phenom. Ray would also attend UCLA, then play in the NBA's minor leagues, the Canadian Basketball Association and the European circuit. Small forward Jason Kapono was our three-point wizard. You'd be hard-pressed to find a place on the court where he couldn't pop one off. After his UCLA stint, where he led in scoring all four years, Jason became the first NBA player to lead the league in three-point percentages for two consecutive years. He also won a championship ring with the Miami Heat in 2006.

By the end of the weekend, I'd gotten a chance to watch and play with some of the best basketball players I'd ever seen in my life. The pool of college coaches watching seemed larger, as well, than what we'd seen at the Double Pump Camp.

"Got plans for next summer?" Mats asked me, putting his arm around my shoulder after our last game.

"You know it," I answered coolly, as my mind quickly tried to calculate exactly how many days remained until then.

When we returned from Las Vegas, my father eagerly came out to the parking lot to greet our car, waving around a brochure of some kind, as if it were the winning lottery ticket. He handed it to me through the car window. I looked down at two beaming students holding books, smiling at one another, mid-climb down the steps of a lavish building with white columns. They looked very happy.

"What does that say?" my father asked, flipping it over and pointing to the mailing label.

"Carlos Boozer Jr.," I read aloud.

"It's a college brochure, Los," he said. "Your first college brochure."

After the California and Las Vegas tournaments, I was already receiving interest.

"Well done," my father said, nodding to my mother.

I might have slept with the college brochure under my pillow that night, that's how jazzed I was by the development. But a few days later, another brochure stuffed our mailbox, six inches thick. And then another one. In fact, college brochures didn't stop coming to us for the next four years. My father placed a small plastic bin in the corner of the kitchen to keep these brochures until we could go through them. That bin eventually became a thirty-gallon plastic garbage can, which he moved into the living room. Two bins eventually joined that one until all three were brimming with brochures—quite a visual to walk by in the morning on my way to school. I was wanted. That's for sure. I was officially on my way.

# CHAPTER 4

## MATS

It started with a tennis ball. I was ten years old when my father took the fluorescent lime-green sphere out of his pocket and tossed it to me.

"Pops, you want me to try tennis?" I'd asked, rubbing my fingers over its fuzziness and the two white seams that separated it like a baseball. I was already playing baseball, basketball, and running track. I hadn't thought about tennis before, but how different could it be from baseball? My father had played tennis in high school, as well.

"I want you to dunk it," he said, nodding to the hoop, which is how I began my quest for the slam dunk, a move every basketball hopeful strives toward, but few master. My dunk had humble beginnings. At first, I could only release the ball high enough to teeter on the rim. If I got lucky, it would fall in. And while this was before my snow-swirled basketball practices, when baseball was my main focus, I always saw my mastery of the dunk as a personal challenge, should I pursue basketball or not. That's the way my little brain worked.

When I was able to tip the tennis ball in with certainty, my father swapped it out for a bigger, sleeker-touch volleyball. Then, we moved on to a women's basketball (at 28.5 inches, it's one size smaller than a men's 29.5-inch) and then finally the size 7, official NBA-size version. And yes, we drilled it with both my left and right hands. It was a gradual progression that took a couple of years, but I completed my first dunk sometime during the winter of eighth grade. On that evening, the court's floodlights took a little longer to come on because the pipes were frozen. As they flickered awake, I warmed up the way I usually did, with a dribble down court. I always envisioned myself dodging, crossing over, and generally disrupting invisible defenders, as I zigged and zagged toward the basket, planning to finish with a layup. However, as I approached, I decided to jump as high as I could, stretched my right hand to the rim and flicked the ball in.

My father did a double take. "Do that again!" he yelled excitedly. I started again down the court at full speed, but my timing was off and the ball hit the backboard. Bursting with adrenaline, I tried to re-create my dunk throughout our practice, but I grew too tired as the night rolled on.

"Don't worry." My father beamed. "It's like riding a bike. Once your body figures it out, it knows what to do. Muscle memory. I bet you'll hit it again tomorrow."

My father always knew the right thing to say and do—he took me to McDonald's to celebrate, then we raced home so I could tell my mother.

It's a major moment when a basketball player learns to dunk. The words *exhilaration* and *power* come to mind, but all I kept thinking was I could do something that the majority of adult men in the world couldn't—and I was only twelve.

I was eager to utilize this new skill with my new teammates on the varsity basketball team at Juneau-Douglas High School. I was the second freshman to ever make the squad and I couldn't have been more elated. By now, my looming six-foot-five frame and basketball experience in and out of the state had preceded me, but I just wanted to be as good as I could be. I wasn't fazed at all when Coach Houston told me I wouldn't be a starter. He'd already seen me practicing at open-gym nights and team tryouts and had a good handle on what I was capable of. I'd watched him coach a ton of high school games. Coach was detail oriented and did his preparation. He didn't have a wife or kids. He was married to the game. I trusted that he'd do right by me.

Our team was made of upperclassmen, including four senior co-captains, who'd all played together for multiple years and fit one another like a glove. I would need to meld to this team, not them to me.

Co-captain Josh Lockhart was our best player and the first to make the varsity squad his ninth grade year. Josh was also my favorite player, a smooth-operating guard with speed and a good shot who made everything he did look oh-so good. As a thirteen-year-old freshman, I watched what the eighteen-year-old senior did and emulated it. If he ran extra sprints after practice, I ran extra sprints after practice. If he shot for an hour after practice, I did the same. I welcomed his work ethic.

Though Josh was my favorite player to watch, I wanted to be James Johnson, our starting point guard, who cruised around town in a blacked-out 5.0 Mustang. Chad Carrie was a tough mother. The team's most physical player, Chad didn't take any crap from anyone. Robert Casperson, our fourth senior co-captain, was the glue that brought us all together.

Our travel schedule wasn't typical of a high school squad, where you play teams in your own geographic area and can usually find a rival within a fifteen-minute radius. Juneau had only one high school, so our away games were truly *away*. We took overnight boats and ferries south to play teams in Sitka or Ketchikan, laying our sleeping bags out on the benches or floor. These vessels also had small arcades with two or three games. I'd step into that small room and into another world, stretching my quarter for twenty minutes on *Pac-Man* or *Galaga*. Other times, I'd go outside and watch the waves part as our boat cut through the water. It reminded me of the quiet mornings I'd fished with my father.

We took two-hour flights to play teams in Anchorage and Fairbanks. I always claimed a window seat, so I could see us passing over the Earth below. We were usually hosted overnight by the rival players' families, which made for some funny encounters. During introductions, the parents always looked at me, then their son, then back at me again. Who was this giant standing next to their child?

I was fortunate to play with this particular varsity team because they were so willing to take me under their wing. They could have iced out the gigantic man-child, but they didn't. Throughout the season, they taught me how to play the right way. They knew I was the most talented kid on the team, so they challenged me every day to be better, to stretch myself further. We weren't a championship team, but I gained much more than a title. These four guys laid the foundation that lived on in me throughout my high school career. They set the tone for me for the next four years.

My parents continued the same edict they'd put in place for me and my siblings years before. Our education came first and if our grades faltered, extracurricular activities, like sports, would quickly fall to the wayside. Natasha had her sights set on becoming a singer, so her vocal lessons hung in the balance. Charles had started playing basketball, as well. We all had skin in the game and never doubted our parents' seriousness when it came to academics.

Still, I came home with a D-minus in math after my first semester and they were ready to pull the plug. Coach Houston pleaded with my parents to relent—just for basketball. My parents hastily agreed, but I was only to attend school, basketball practice, and after-school tutoring with my math teacher, Mr. Carlson. No hanging out with friends. No television. Straight home from practice. It was enough to scare me straight. I'd come perilously close to losing what I loved most. I wasn't going to do anything to jeopardize another summer of travel ball. Mats had kept in touch with my father the entire year. They were two peas in a pod, discussing basketball—and my future in it—together.

A week or two after school let out, I flew down to Fresno to join Mats and the EBO traveling team for a summer of playing all around the country. Mats managed two teams, ten boys on each, with one of the teams being his more seasoned squad. That was twenty teenage boys, all together, all at once, 24/7, on the road. You would think this would be a recipe for disaster, but Mats had an organized system that got us where we needed to be on time and in one piece. That included a support staff of two or three assistant coaches, as well as four to six interchangeable parents to chaperone at any given time. Separately, my parents even chaperoned a few trips.

Mats was the EBO team president, its general manager, and coach. I also thought of him as our ring master, who kept us on this demanding travel-ball-team schedule no matter what. Only a man with a genuine love for the sport would want to give up his summer to be with a bunch of teenagers and Mats was that man to a tee. He'd played in high school and college, then made it all the way to the NBA Summer Pro League as a free agent, where he told us soberly that he'd realized he just wasn't good enough. But Mats's love of basketball ran so deep that he pivoted to coaching, where he found an equal, if not superior passion to when he played. He was coaching at Fresno City Junior College, when he decided to start a much-needed AAU team in the Northern California area.

The AAU's spring-summer basketball program was already well established when I joined in 1995. There were about one hundred twenty sponsored teams from coast to coast, some of them backed by big names like Adidas and Nike. There could have been anywhere from five hundred to one thousand independent, or nonsponsored, teams in the mix, as well. A lot of American boys play basketball.

Some of the more competitive teams included the New Orleans Jazz, Atlanta Celtics, Chicago Fire, and the Long Island Panthers. The EBO was also considered a strong team; our name lacked a geographical reference because we came from everywhere. Brett Nelson was from West Virginia. Bobby Nash hailed from Hawaii. I came from Alaska. It was truly what Mats had first said to my mother: "It doesn't matter where you're from, but how you play."

Our summer schedule included regional tournaments and camps all over the country, where we played as many as four or five games a day. The Adidas ABCD camp in Teaneck, New Jersey, and the Big Time Tournament in Las Vegas were two of our bigger tentpole, national events. They attracted the highest level of talent, as well as the most college scouts looking to fill their rosters. In between those events, we attended a variety of camps and smaller tournaments to prime ourselves. Sometimes we played together as a team, while other camps were individual-only, where we split up to play on different teams.

It was a packed summer. We sat through long bus rides and hauled our gear through airport waiting lines, squirming to find comfort in stiff terminal chairs, sometimes for hours. I must have inherited my father's love of traveling, because I didn't mind a bit of it. Traveling didn't agitate, tire, or even bore me. I was excited because we were on our way to a new destination to play more basketball. I usually put on my Discman headphones and zoned out to Biggie's "Ready to Die" on repeat to pass the time.

Mats's genuine love for what he did made him incredibly personable, but he also took what we were doing seriously. He really wanted us all to play college ball. He really wanted us all to make it to the NBA.

"We're here for business," he told us in our first motel lobby. "You're trying to get a scholarship. We're not here on vacation, but we're going to have fun, we're going to play basketball, and we're going to play video games and we're going to do normal kid stuff, but I'll tell you what you won't be doing. You're not going to be running wild."

We all nodded our heads in acknowledgment as Mats ran down the "house rules" for our stay.

"Curfew is the time when you need to go to sleep to be ready for tomorrow," he said. "But I will say this—if the coaches and I are coming back from dinner, after washing your uniforms for hours, you better make sure we don't see you."

My roommate that summer, and every summer afterward, was Joe Gilliam. "Gil" and I were real rebels. We liked to pool our money together and hit up Carl's Jr. or McDonald's—whatever was in walking distance. That was the very short depths of our rebelliousness. When we weren't in our rooms occupied by some type of sport on television, the team mostly migrated together as a group, in our matching EBO shirts, when we went out to eat, swam in the pool, or went out to see a film. There was no sneaking in alcohol or drugs on the side, and that was probably to Mats's credit. He picked the *right* kids for the EBO team, ones who wouldn't squander this chance with boneheaded decisions. There were only twenty EBO spots and Mats was so organized, he probably had a list of alternates on speed dial.

Held in late July, the Big Time Tournament in Las Vegas conjured up an extra level of excitement in all of us. How could it not, being in the entertainment capital of the world? Pull away any window curtain and your eyes would blur from a circus of flashing lights. The air seemed charged with something.

With great wisdom, Mats booked us in a hotel off the Strip, away from the casinos and other distractions. We still jumped on the beds and had water-gun fights, chasing each other through our adjoining rooms. At the pool, we vied for beach chairs that would give us a perfect view of the bikinied guests.

But by the next morning, the mood among us changed. Mats ushered us all in through the gymnasium's back entrance, as had been his custom all summer. He liked our teams to head straight to the locker room, away from the stressful standing-room-only crowd waiting in the gym, littered with college scouts.

"We're going to focus, we're going to play, and then we leave," he said with an encouraging smile.

On the court, we all became laser-focused. Collectively, we understood that this time was vital and fleeting. We had forty-eight minutes to show scouts what we had. Almost all of us wanted to go to college and then on to the NBA. We were a like-minded group of guys just going through life together, figuring it out at the same time.

At the West Coast All-Star Double Pump Camp, the ball tipped off the rim and I jumped up before everybody else, grabbed it with two hands and slammed it down for a dunk. The backboard immediately exploded, the shattering of tempered glass and the crash of the metal rim sending a shockwave through the gym. Every head turned my way.

*I'm in big trouble,* I thought. *How am I going to pay for this? More accurately, how are my parents going to pay for this? Was I going to be kicked out of camp?*

Across the gym, I saw the Pump brothers, David and Dana, eying me. They were the founders of the camp and hard to miss; they were red-headed twins. One of them, and I was never sure which one, gave me a subtle, but affirming nod. The other camp members crowded around me like I'd just hit triple cherries and coins were pouring out of the machine.

"Whoa, check out grizzly bear over here, breaking the board," one player hooted. I was drenched in praise, although I kept picturing how I'd explain all this to my mom, along with the astronomical price tag it would take to replace the equipment.

Instead, as word spread through the AAU about the fourteen-year-old Sasquatch from Alaska who'd taken down the board at the Double Pump camp, I became an urban legend.

"Yo, that's him," I heard a player whisper to another at a camp I attended a few months later in LA. I had bragging rights for the rest of the year. Debating its coincidence, my father and I also noticed the bigger Division I colleges, like Michigan State, UCLA, Kansas, and Kentucky started sending their brochures our way.

"The backboard break heard around the world!" my father joked.

Up until that summer I was a shy kid. I was playing with some of the nation's best young players and they all had an air of confidence, as if to say, *Yeah, we're all going to make it to the NBA. Why wouldn't we?* I wasn't prepared the first time a teammate hooked in a shot and bellowed "Facial!" like a wolf howling at the moon. It was okay, I realized, to scream and shout in an effort to get the ball into (or away from) the basket. I was discovering a new freedom of expression. My father had always been very vocal when he played, constantly communicating with his teammates. Sometime during that summer, my inner voice came out of me like the roar of a grizzly bear. When I returned to Juneau, I had a new sense of who I was. I was fully committed to something and knew what direction I was heading in. I was taking the time to become a proper basketball player. My first full summer of travel ball also gave me a taste for basketball culture. Our team laughed themselves to tears cracking jokes and slagging each other on our bus rides, but when we hit the court, playtime was over. We were a unit of serious basketball players. And the closer we got off the court, the better we got together on it. I loved both sides of this dichotomy.

I was also starting to get noticed more. There was a brief discussion about me leaving Alaska, as a few lower 48 prep academies wanted me to come play for them. High schools with fancier basketball programs were promising to develop me prop-

erly. Mats even offered to have me come to Fresno my sophomore year, if I really wanted to get out of Alaska. However,
neither my parents nor I liked the idea of me moving away. I
didn't want to give up Coach Houston or Alaska, which we'd
made our home. I didn't want to disrupt my parents or my
younger siblings' lives by uprooting myself or them. Mats seemed
happy with our choice. We all agreed I could still make it to
the NBA, but I'd be traveling some weekends to the lower 48
states during the school year for tournaments and camps. There
would be no way around that if I wanted to keep myself in the
running for the top colleges.

Returning to school, I wore Adidas gear from head to toe,
carrying a stack of CDs that hadn't been released in Juneau yet,
which upped my cool factor by 1000. Juneau always got new
music at least six months behind the lower 48, so I'd put on the
latest Tupac album as we warmed up, then would race to the CD
player to turn it off when we saw Coach Houston enter the gym.

"How tall are you now?" Couch Houston asked me on our
first day back to practice.

"Six-nine, Coach," I proudly answered.

"You grew four more inches since last season," he said, shaking his head in happy disbelief. "And I see you signed up to
take swimming with me?" I had planned to take the class with
Natasha, as I hadn't learned to swim yet and thought it was time.

"I have something else in mind for you, Los, something for
that man's body you're walking around in," Coach Houston
said, leading me to the auxiliary gym behind our locker room.
He pushed opened a metal sliding door on a hinge, revealing a
compact area with a weight bench, some dumbbells of various
sizes, and a couple other weightlifting machines.

"Carlos, if you add weight-training to your routine, I guarantee it will take your game to new heights. We're going to put
some muscle on those big bones of yours." I still leaned toward
the willowy side, so I wasn't averse to that at all. Sometimes

my teammates would join me, but a lot of the time I was lift-
ing alongside the football squad. I'd never been introduced to
weightlifting before this and I might not have been, if not for
Coach looking out for me. When he told me it would help me
get to the NBA, that was all I needed to hear.

"You know, as the team's best player, I'm going to look to you
to be a leader," he said, as I fumbled with a pulley. Up until that
moment, I hadn't thought myself the best player on the team.
My brain didn't contemplate basketball in those terms. I'd always focused on getting better, blinders on.

"What do you mean, Coach?" I asked.

"I'm going to be leaning on you to be more vocal out there,
to communicate and coordinate with your teammates," he said.

"What about the juniors and seniors?" I asked. I couldn't see
myself bossing around more experienced upperclassmen.

"You're going to have to lead by example first," he said.
"You're going to play hard, which will make them play harder.
You're going to put up so many extra shots in practice, that they'll
be dying to get that loose ball to you. And then once you start
doing that, they will follow you."

I absorbed what Coach was saying to me. This was my invitation to step up.

"So, you think we'll get to States this year?" he asked, immediately lightening up our discussion.

"We're going to win States," I corrected. We'd lost in the
semifinals the year before and I'd dragged around that loss like
a sack of bricks the entire summer. Every time I'd wanted to
slow down just a tad or let up slightly, I thought about that semi-
final game. I was hungry—no, ravenous—to win that State title.

In our isolated, tight-knit community, high school basketball games drew big crowds. On game day, our gym burst at its
seams with fifteen hundred spectators—every bleacher seat or
corner to stand in filled. There were a couple of times that the

fire marshal closed off the gym altogether when we'd reached capacity.

I knew a lot of our spectators were coming to see the tall skinny kid who could dunk. There were red and black 4s, my jersey number, painted on faces and shoulders everywhere I turned. On the road, I was even more a novelty, and I tried not to disappoint. In Ketchikan, I nailed a windmill dunk on a fast break and the place went bananas. That was a definite rarity in Alaska.

My sophomore year saw a real jump in my abilities. My stats rose as I grew more confident in my movements. Every team we faced had a hard time defending me, especially when I switched hands and went left. I officially became the scourge of the league among players and coaches alike.

That's not to say I didn't have any "off" days. I had my fair share, and I came up with my own methods to raise a lagging performance. At halftime during one of our closer games, I left my team in the locker room and plunked myself in front of the bathroom mirror, summoning a pep talk I knew would fire me up.

"Do you want to work at the fucking gas station?" I asked myself out loud. "Or do you want to be in the NBA?"

Suddenly, the feelings of my underwhelming first half fell away. I was only focused on the playing time left and how I was going to go out there to dominate. We won that game by 25 points.

"Man, you're a beast!" my teammate said after one of my better games. "The Beast Unleashed!"

I thought about the mighty grizzly bear, raised up on its hind legs, claws drawn and ready for attack. The nickname suited me. I felt like I became a beast in the paint, someone different than the Carlos who walked the halls of Juneau-Douglas High School.

We became 4A State Champions in 1997, a first for our high school. Stores hung congratulations signs in their windows and we had an all-school ceremony to commemorate our achievement. Afterward, Couch Houston called me into his office.

"You've been named a Parade All-American," he said from behind his disheveled desk of folders and paper. Couch waited a few seconds for my reaction. "Do you know what that means?"

Floats and waving beauty queens came to mind. Coach understood my silence.

"It means they've ranked you among the top twenty high school players in the country this year," he said, sitting back in his chair. "Only Langdon has done it before."

Trajan Langdon was an Alaskan legend, who led East Anchorage High School to the 1994 Alaskan State Championship. Langdon became the first Alaskan player to attend Duke University, which boasted one of the cream-of-the-crop college basketball programs in the country. He was thriving under the tutelage of Coach Mike Krzyzewski, widely considered the No. 1 coach in the country. An NBA career seemed likely, which would make Trajan the first Alaskan resident to achieve the honor. I aimed to be the second.

"You did well this season," Coach Houston said. "Now, go play your summer ball, but please, whatever you do, do not get injured. I need you in one piece next season."

I didn't have to wait for summer. The AAU schedule dovetailed with the end of the high school basketball season, so the tournaments resumed and the scouts were out looking again by April. This year, I'd been invited for the first time to the Midnight Madness event in New Jersey, as national a showcase as there was in the program.

"I think he should do it," Mats told my father. "It will give him exposure on the East Coast, in case he decides to go to college out there. You know, get his footprint out there. Everyone's going to be curious to see how the kid from Alaska plays."

My father agreed, so I left school for the airport on a Friday, played in the tournament and earned MVP, then flew back on the Sunday red-eye flight. I was expected to and did attend school Monday morning. I can't say my brain was firing on all cylinders, but my body was present.

Now a state champion, I returned to Mats and my EBO team chomping at the bit for another summer of travel ball. We were all pleasantly surprised to find out that our new sponsor, EA Sports, had delivered a few Nintendo systems to our motel. We held competitions all summer with *NBA Live, Tecmo Bowl* and *Mike Tyson's Punch-Out!!*. Our coaching staff joked about our "built-in babysitters," but athletes and gaming go hand in hand because we like competition in any form. When our chaperones would finish their checks for the evening, to make sure all twenty of us were tucked safely into our beds, we'd get right back up and play until 3:00 or 4:00 in the morning. Huddled around the screen one early morning, I couldn't help but think how much Chris would have enjoyed this unexpected boon alongside me. We came to play basketball, but also got to geek out on videos games—a fourteen-year-old's perfect summer.

I'd been playing with Mats's older squad for a year and everyone seemed encouraged by my progress. I was gaining control over my man-sized body, even while I continued to put on muscle mass. Following our last tournament of the summer, Mats told me I'd done well.

"This next season will be for all the marbles," Mats said. "And I think all the big schools—all of them—will want you."

"Thanks, Coach," I answered.

"I have a feeling coming from Alaska, you're going to get some extra exposure from the press and the coaching rumor mill," he said. "That and you'll be a six-foot-nine junior who can do it all."

We laughed together, but I think we both knew that we were on the precipice of something bigger.

"I remember they used to say that every player wants exposure to maximize their opportunities," Mats said. "But don't forget, if you're not taking care of business, if you're not resting, eating right, and putting in the practice hours, exposure can turn into exposed really easily. Take care of yourself, like you have been doing. Keep to that path."

I thanked Mats again for discovering me, which he did, because my mother and I were almost out that gym door when he approached us. I thanked him for all the long calls with my father, letting him wax on and on about basketball. I thanked him for giving me my break.

"You know how you can repay me?" he asked. "Make it to the NBA."

"No problem," I said, knowing that was a debt I was going to repay.

# CHAPTER 5

## THE BEAST UNLEASHED

"I have a six pack!"

I stared into the bedroom mirror, T-shirt held up to my chest, torquing my body at different angles, as I investigated.

"Yeah, you have a six pack," I heard Charles mumble from underneath the pillow he was burrowed under. "You also have a big mouth, so shut it. It's too early," he moaned.

"But Janet loves my abs," I boasted. "Don't you, Ms. Jackson?" I asked my childhood crush, hanging on my wall. She was sandwiched between posters of Tupac, Denzel Washington, and Jordan with his trophies. My brother Charles had no respect for my discovery, but I knew something was afoot.

I couldn't stop inspecting the changes, astonished at what I saw. In very little time, I'd morphed from a tall, skinny, but skilled player into this full-grown man amongst boys. My weight finally caught up with my six-foot-nine frame and I filled out to about 235 pounds. No players in Alaska came close to my new measurements.

My calves were slabs of steel from a summer of weightlifting. My arms were bigger and sturdier, suddenly proportionate to my always enormous, E.T.-fingered hands, improving my grip and coordination even more. But overall, I felt stronger. Much stronger in every step I took. I'd turned into this unstoppable animal, finally fully grown into my moniker: The Beast Unleashed.

There really was no hiding now as I walked down the hallways. Everyone knew who I was, even before I knew them. I was the skyscraping sports star being courted by the big basketball schools. I gained instant popularity with the student body, which put me more at ease with my classmates. I amassed a core group of six friends that enjoyed the normal teenage trappings of Juneau. As upperclassmen, we took McDonald's runs at lunch and loitered around the strip mall, the smell of fried eggrolls heavy in the air from the Chinese restaurant. I stared in the windows of Footlocker, dreaming of the day I could afford one of the expensive snowboards on display.

I dated throughout the rest of high school. Juneau's one-screen movie theater got every film at least a month after its release, but the dark was what we were after. Alaska's ample camouflage also afforded occasional encounters. "Just around this rock," I told one girlfriend, as we sought out some privacy in the wilderness. I turned the corner and immediately put my arm out to halt her behind me. Maybe twenty feet in front of us stood a pack of wolves, feasting on a deer carcass. I hadn't had much experience with wolves, but the Alaskan rule of thumb with wild animals was to leave them unbothered.

"Back out slowly," I whispered softly, never taking my eyes off the pack. We negotiated our escape step-by-step and with a tense branch snap here and there, we created enough distance to turn around and run as fast as our feet could take us.

"I can just see the headlines," my girlfriend said with a smirk afterward. "STAR BASKETBALL PLAYER MAULED BY WOLFPACK IN MAKEOUT MISHAP."

I continued to apply myself to my studies, but found ways to combine objectives. I took American Law to chase a girl and was pleasantly surprised to find out that I liked to argue. Every two weeks, the class held a trial. I never wanted to be the judge or part of the jury. I always angled to be one of the lawyers. I spent hours in the library reading legal cases, noting who won and why. The closet nerd in me, who could store decades of basketball statistics in my brain, was down to debate anybody. I had a Rolodex of wild legal information in my mind. I'd come to class with cases to support my claims, which always impressed my teacher, Mr. Lienhart.

"Are you sure you want to go to the NBA?" he quipped. I appreciated his faith in me.

Over the winter break of my junior year, it was time for me to make some decisions. My father and I stared at those three thirty-gallon drums brimming with college brochures, now housed in a corner of the living room. It had seemed like yesterday that my excited father had met my mother and me at our car when we returned from California, holding that first brochure with pure joy.

"Time to get down to the nitty-gritty," he said. "You know we could just toss a bunch in the air and pick randomly?"

"That would make our jobs easier." I sighed.

For better or worse, I had to whittle my college choices down to ten, which was the maximum number of schools that could send a basketball recruiter, usually the head coach, to Alaska to meet me, per NCAA regulations.

"Maryland," he said, as he passed me the ball later on the court, continuing our conversation. Sometimes we did our best thinking out there, lost in the easy repetition of our movements.

"St. John's," I answered back. "I like the coach."

"Of course," he said. "And UCLA, Arizona, and Kentucky."

"Duke," I added, as I let go of a shot that kissed the rim, then bounced away.

"Shoot from a higher angle," my father corrected me, retrieving and passing the ball back to me. I tipped my wrist slightly higher.

"A little more," he coaxed and I adjusted. "Stop. Good. I think we have our ten semifinalists."

"I think we do," I concurred, releasing and sinking the shot.

The college courting process (pun not intended) usually coincided with the athlete's December-to-April junior year season, so the coach could come to his hometown, eat a meal with the family, take in a home game, then sit down with the parents and son for the living room pitch.

"How many are coming?" I asked my father once enough time had passed for the coaches to properly answer. Those ten colleges made up my absolute dream list of schools and four of them employed my Mount Rushmore of basketball coaches. That quadruplet included Coach K, Kansas's Roy Williams, Syracuse University's Jim Boeheim, and St. John's Mike Jarvis. If my Rushmore had a fifth coach's face, it would've been John Thompson, from Georgetown University. I didn't make that public at the time, but Thompson was my dark horse selection. Honestly, I would've felt privileged to play basketball at any of the ten schools, although I didn't expect every college to send someone, especially the East Coast institutions. That would entail six-hour cross-country flights, then a few hours of connecting flights and/or the ferry to Juneau—a heavy day's travel. It just seemed like too much commitment for some of these big coaches to come see me. Alaska just wasn't a hotbed for high school hoops.

"They all accepted," my father answered.

"Syracuse is coming," I said, a little incredulous. He nodded.

"And Connecticut. And St. John's," he said, each name bringing more delight to his face.

"Even Duke?" I asked. "Coach K will be sitting on our couch in our living room?"

"Coach K will be sitting on our couch in our living room this fall," he parroted back.

*Damn, I must be going places*, I thought. I felt extremely honored that these colleges would consider offering me a free education to play ball for their school. It seemed like an uneven exchange, for whoever offered me a scholarship would change the trajectory of my life, and hopefully my family's, too.

The visits began and suddenly Kansas Jayhawks coach Roy Williams was sitting in the Boozer living room in one of the chairs we'd dragged over from the kitchen table. I sat on the loveseat, while my parents were together on our plain beige couch. My younger siblings were shooed off to the back bedrooms and asked to be quiet. These were little kids, though, so occasionally their sounds would echo down the hallway. Coach Williams wasn't fazed when a loud screech interrupted us. He smiled.

After a decade as an assistant coach at UNC, Coach Williams took the helm at Kansas in 1988. Under his tenure, the team had qualified for the NCAA tournament every year and made it to the 1991 Finals. As he described the program, Coach Williams gave off a player's vibe, much like I'd observed with the NBA coaches on TV. He channeled a youthful energy that didn't seem too far removed from the players. I could tell that he'd be very approachable and probably fun to play for. St. John's coach Mike Jarvis also had the player's vibe, and he was Black. I loved his gritty backstory—which gave me clues as to the type of person I'd be playing for.

Georgetown's John Thompson had a "father figure" vibe, which put me and my parents at ease. Where Jarvis exuded youth and energy, I saw the appeal in Coach Thompson's older comportment.

Bill Guthrie, who coached the University of North Carolina Tarheels, also made the trip. A couple of weekends later, Ken-

tucky coach Tubby Smith came. Sometimes, they brought their
assistant coaches, as well.

It felt like that scene out of 2009's *The Blind Side*, where every
major college football coach to ever exist comes calling for quiet
offensive tackle, Michael Oher. I'd watched these coaches on TV
for years. I'd studied them, dissected their coaching styles—and
now they were sitting across from me and my parents in our
living room. All ten schools were offering full scholarships and
boasted players who'd gone on to play in the NBA. If I could
take snapshots representing a scrapbook of my life, this moment
would be among them—that's how palpable the experience was
for this fifteen-year-old.

The majority of the coaches talked about what their programs could do for me and how good the team would be when
I joined it. They talked about their campuses and the facilities
and the support staff that would be working with me. Sometimes my cute little sisters wandered into the room, distracting
their speeches, but they weren't the ones the coaches should have
been watching. My father listened intently to each pitch, then
pounced with his own line of questioning, poking and prod-
ding for weaknesses. Sometimes, I think he got a kick out of
tripping these big-time coaches up.

"I'm not handing my son over to just anybody!" he'd pro-
claim to our household, after our guests had left. No one could
argue with that.

In 1999, the NCAA guidelines were clear that college athletes were considered to have amateur status, and couldn't accept
payment in any form, or they would forfeit their scholarship eligibility. That included gifts, monetary or otherwise, no matter
how big or small. There was a clear line drawn in the sand on
accepting incentives and the harsh repercussions should one get
caught. Though college basketball was a multimillion-dollar
business, it would take another twenty-plus years for student
athletes to finally get a slice of the lucrative pie of college sports.

That didn't stop a few colleges not among my ten choices from trying to sweeten the pot in exchange for my commitment. The offers never came from the head coaches or in front of my parents. I can't even say that the coaches were aware of what was being offered to me, but I received substantial under-the-recruiting-table from about six or seven colleges. I don't know if some of their identities might shock you—there's no manual for this kind of stuff. I do know I was always caught off-guard when it happened, no matter who it was.

The first time it happened, I was on the phone with a college recruiter and I thought I'd misheard him.

"What did he say?" my father asked me after I got off the phone. My brow furrowed from confusion.

"I think they just offered me a two-bedroom apartment off campus and told me I don't have to go to classes," I said, noting how ridiculous it sounded out loud. I must have misheard.

But not a couple weeks later, another recruiter nonchalantly offered me the same exact deal. Still another mentioned that a brand-new 1999 Jeep Cherokee—the hottest whip of that season—awaited me in their parking lot, should I choose their fine institution. Another college representative offered to relocate my entire family along with me and set both my parents up with jobs. Still, another college cut to the chase and offered a lump sum of $300,000. All of the colleges offering these prohibited perks said I'd be among their starting five.

I never felt good when I got off these calls and when the time came, those colleges were the first ones I crossed off my top-ten list. Both of my parents had worked two jobs at times to help me get to this point and this wasn't what they'd envisioned for me from their sacrifice. Short-term versus long-term. I had to make a choice. I decided I had no interest in jeopardizing my college status. I also wasn't looking for handouts and I didn't want to owe anyone anything. I wanted to work my ass off for everything I earned. It was the only way I knew how.

During my junior season, Coach Houston kept my head from inflating like a helium balloon. We were the defending state champions with a good chance to repeat. Often, we'd be up 25 points or more and I wouldn't play the fourth quarter at all. The testosterone-fueled savage in me wanted to score 20 more points, like a madman. I had this kill-or-be-killed attitude that was hard to turn off. Thankfully, Coach was a lot wiser than me and had enough humility for the both of us. He had a deep respect for the sport.

"What's the point?" he'd ask me, when I'd badger him to put me back in the game. "We're going to win the game no matter what and we don't need to embarrass them. Have you heard of a graceful loser? Well, you can also be a graceful winner."

Instead, Couch Houston gave me something else to do during those endless fourth quarters.

"What's your teammate doing wrong there?" he asked me. I looked to where he pointed to one of our guards, unable to grasp what he was suggesting.

"I don't know," I said.

"You may be on the bench, but you haven't checked out of the game. You never check out," he said. "Do you want to be a better player? Learn your teammates' positions and you'll be able to communicate quickly if they're out of place on a play. If you earnestly learn what they do, they'll listen and respect you because they'll know you did your homework."

The light bulb blinked on over my head. One thing I was going to have for the rest of my career was teammates. It was a simple suggestion, but one that increased my basketball IQ tenfold because I was suddenly looking at the game from other players' perspectives. Coach didn't know the full benefits of his advice until one of our point guards got suspended and I stepped into the position a few times without our team skipping a beat. I loved playing guard and imagined my style after Detroit Piston Grant Hill.

Having the country's top college coaches watch you play sure does give you motivation. We won our second, back-to-back state title and I was named Parade All-American once again, still in line with what Trajan Langdon accomplished five years earlier. I didn't meet all ten coaches before my junior year ended, as a couple would make their visits early during my senior year. Noticeably absent from this group was Coach K, but he popped up in my life sooner rather than later.

The summer before my senior year was my last chance to showcase myself to recruiters and Camp ABCD, held on the Fairleigh-Dickinson University campus in Teaneck, New Jersey, was a big one. It had been founded in 1984 by Sonny Vaccaro who, in a former life, signed Michael Jordan to his first sneaker deal. This is the event that discovered Kobe Bryant, Tracy Mc-Grady, Jermaine O'Neal and a hotly talked about up-and-comer who was only a few years behind me named LeBron James. ABCD was an invite-only event, which anticipated four hundred college coaches attending over the week. For high school ballers, this was a red-carpet affair.

It was during the first game, as I casually looked over to the sidelines, that I saw him for the first time. Coach K was there and he was watching my game with particular interest. On my top-ten list, Coach K was my No. 1.

I'd first laid eyes on Coach K while watching the 1991 NCAA Tournament with my father. We'd just gotten cable television, so we saw Grant Hill, Christian Laettner and Bobby Hurley lead one of the best Duke teams ever to the national championship, 72–65 over Kansas. Hill, my favorite player at the time, handled the ball like a master, bringing it up-court and sharing the offense running plays, but what stuck out to me was Coach K on the sidelines, jumping up and down at the buzzer. I watched him erupt with such overwhelming emotion that he had to expel it by hugging every single player on the team.

"Wow, that has to be an amazing feeling," I said aloud. I wanted to feel like that one day. I wanted to be part of a close team. I wanted to win a championship. I wanted to experience that victory hug.

Coach K didn't stop until he'd embraced the entire squad. Then, he went in search of his coaching staff, managers, and his wife, holding them all.

*This guy has so much energy,* I thought.

As I'd watch more Duke games with my father, it was difficult not to notice Coach K's full-blown bellowing throughout, his fists raised and clinched every time Duke got onto the scoreboard. He was so invested in the moment, it was as if he was the team's sixth player, working from the sidelines.

*Oh shit!* I thought, quickly looking away from him. I stole another brief glance to confirm it. Yes, the country's winningest college basketball coach of all time was definitely watching my game. I told myself not to get too excited, that he wasn't necessarily watching me. I cautioned myself to calm down and to get my head back in the game.

But then, I thought some more about it. *Should I want this guy to notice me?* If I hoped to attend Duke, I thought I should kick myself into hyperdrive, taking command of the game with one slam dunk after another. I made sure I dunked with my left hand enough times to show it was no fluke. In a massive effort, I scored 37 points playing against my top-tier peers.

The tree of my efforts bore fruit a few weeks later when Duke assistant coach Quin Snyder called my parents on behalf of Coach K, to schedule his visit to Juneau that fall.

"Coach K really enjoyed watching your son play at the ABCD camp," Quinn told them. I was glad I hadn't held back. Coach K was coming to Juneau, which was such big news for the area that the local newspaper wrote an article about it.

Once I got used to the idea that Coach K had traveled over two thousand miles to sit in the Boozer living room, I tuned into what he was saying as best I could, trying to keep my nervous energy from making me lose focus. Luckily, Coach K has a way of pulling you in, especially when he speaks in a softer, more gentle tone than the volcanic coach we see on TV. I was fascinated by it.

"I'm not sure I'll even play you," he told me. It wasn't a boastful statement meant to put me in my place. Coach K had the No. 1 team in the country, with four of his players on their way to becoming first-round NBA Draft picks. If any of the coaches could make such a claim, Coach K was the one to do it.

"Nakeisha! Natanya! Quit hanging on Coach K!" my mom instructed. Even my adorable, attention-assassin sisters couldn't shake Coach K's evenhanded pitch.

"We've got six All-Americans on the squad," he said. "I'm not guaranteeing a spot to anybody. If you want to start, prove it on the practice court every day. Prove it in the games, that you belong in that spot."

Coach K was speaking my language. When he left, I realized that of the ten coaches, he was the only that left me without a single question, whether it was about curriculum, or the practice schedule, or my family coming to visit me. Coach K was the only recruiter who covered everything.

"Now, that's someone I can leave my son with," my father commented succinctly.

After Coach K visited us, I had the difficult task of whittling ten choices down to no more than five for campus visits, per NCAA guidelines. I decided to visit only three campuses with my parents.

Our first stop was St. John's University, which was an hour's subway ride from Manhattan. Even more appealing was that I'd be a two-hour drive away from Natasha, who was attending Westminster Choir College in Princeton, New Jersey.

I'd really been impressed meeting with Mike Jarvis. A Black coach with a rare thirty-year tenure at the college level, Jarvis had coached New York Knicks legend Patrick Ewing into the NBA and the St. John's squad had made it to the NCAA Tournament's Elite Eight bracket the previous season, with a handful of members returning. They were in a prime position to get far in the NCAA tournament during my freshman year.

After my parents and I took in a St. John's game, I ended up at the album release party for rapper Method Man with a few of the current players at a nightclub called The Tunnel. I had just turned sixteen years old, but was whisked onstage with the Wu-Tang Clan legend in front of a couple thousand rowdy fans.

"This here's Carlos Booozer," Method Man beamed into his microphone, leaning on that vowel good. "Carlos is going to play for St. John's next year, aren't you?" I couldn't do much in that moment but nod my head.

However, I wasn't quite set on the Red Storm. We visited UCLA that December, where the familiar rush of warm air hit our faces as we walked through the airport's sliding-glass doors. I quickly shed the much-needed winter jacket I'd worn that morning leaving Juneau.

These final college visits followed the same general format over a weekend. The coach always tried to connect a recruit with a current player he already knew. My UCLA host was Baron Davis, who I'd played against over three summers on the AAU summer circuit. I followed Baron to classes in his shorts and flip-flops, across UCLA's sprawling campus, the sun warming our backs. We ate lunch with my parents in the cafeteria, then Baron excused himself to prepare for a game that evening against UNLV.

My father and I entered the Pauley Pavilion to take our seats and I did a double take. Directly behind our seats, I recognized Grant Hill and Jaleel White, aka "Steve Urkel"—sans his Coke bottle glasses and red suspenders—from the TV series *Family Matters*. The three-time NBA All-Star for the Detroit Pistons acknowledged me first with a quick greeting. Hill, a Duke alum, was in LA for a few weeks, preparing for his sixth NBA season, totally unaware that I'd tried to pattern a good part of my high school game after his.

UCLA's finest selling point, though, was the fact that three of my EBO teammates had already committed to the Bruins team next fall. To have four players on the same team, who'd spent years cultivating their game and personalities together, was a potent consideration. There would be a familiarity both on and off the court that could make my college basketball career that much smoother. It could be my surest path to the NBA. UCLA was geographically closest to my family in Juneau, as well.

I knew I wouldn't make up my mind until I visited Duke University in Durham, North Carolina, home to one of the sport's biggest, if not its greatest, rivalries in college basketball.

I had a team of hosts to tour Duke's campus, which included Elton Brand, Corey Maggette, and of course, fellow Alaskan resident and legend Trajan Langdon. These were all players I'd been watching on TV for years, showing me around and taking me under their wing. I felt an immediate sense of comradery among them.

On game day, my parents and I walked into Cameron Indoor Stadium for the first time and it felt as majestic and magical as I hoped it would. I gazed up at the Duke-blue championship banners and jerseys hanging from the rafters, honoring retired greats like Grant Hill and Bobby Hurley. The Cameron Crazies, a raucous group of coordinated fans in blue-and-white-striped polo shirts, were already seated behind one of the baskets, poised to break the enemy's concentration. The school band sat at the other end of the court, jamming out some tune when it suddenly stopped. A chant began to circulate the oval structure until the crowd was cheering in unison: "We want Booz-er!" over and over again. It only took a few seconds for my parents and me to understand what they were shouting. The continuous four-syllable eruption came from all sides and echoed into the rafters. It was like walking into the biggest birthday party ever thrown and hearing "Surprise!"—and although the attendees that day were strangers, not family and friends, I still felt like they loved me already. I felt wanted. It sent a chill up my spine. How had they coordinated this? I looked at my parents. My father was giddy and my mother had tears in her eyes. To be in Cameron, the backdrop of some of the greatest college games ever, felt surreal.

My parents and I were shown to our seats, only a few rows off the floor. Once again, Grant Hill occupied a seat behind us and rose to greet us. "Not a bad place to go to school," he nudged me with a smile.

Cameron sat around nine thousand spectators—compact for a college basketball arena, but an amazing live experience. Every play vibrated through you like a subwoofer stereo. Duke had that same intoxicating atmosphere that had lured me into the sport at age twelve, watching Jordan defy gravity with my father—except now we were in the thick of this crackling air. I felt closer to the NBA just by stepping foot in Cameron. By the end of the weekend, it seemed like a no-brainer to me. Everything felt right. I knew I wanted to become a Blue Devil. I wanted to become a part of this strong, longstanding frater-nity of winners.

While attending college to play ball was a forgone conclusion, I still played my senior year with full gusto. I averaged 35 points and 15 rebounds a game to packed gymnasiums. Picking spots on the court where I'd drilled for years outside in the snow, I shot with about 75 percent success from the floor.

My senior year wasn't flawless. Our first loss came down to the wire, with a couple plays that I personally felt responsible for. We should have beaten that team, too, which made that one especially sting. After the game, a couple of sportswriters were waiting to speak with me, but I was so angry and upset with myself, I walked right past them out the door without even ac-knowledging them. I didn't feel like talking to anyone.

Instead, I went home that night and seriously reflected on my performance, replaying each wrong step I made over and over in torturous rewind. Someone else went home that night and thought a lot on my performance, as well. One of those shunned sportswriters wrote a scathing article about me for the local newspaper that everybody read, claiming I was a sore loser—all because I hadn't felt like speaking with him. I was already heartbroken over the loss, and the story pushed the dagger in a few more inches. It was the first negative article that had ever been written about me.

The truth was I didn't know how to handle the loss. We hadn't lost that much during my entire high school career. A range of emotions coursed through my seventeen-year-old mind and body that I couldn't handle. If I had spoken with the writ-ers, they would have known that I felt I hadn't done enough, hadn't stolen enough rebounds or scored enough points. They also would have learned that I felt I'd let my team and my coach down. Instead, the reporter saw a brooding, entitled teenager ignoring his efforts.

The next day, Coach Houston asked me to stay after practice. He could see how downtrodden I was and I knew he would bring up the article.

"Listen, Los," he said, sitting next to me on our bench. "I understand you have superhigh expectations for yourself, which I admire. I'm not going to sit here and tell you what or what not to do. You make your own decisions in that way.

"But answer me this," he continued. "If you had spoken with those reporters, they would have known how bad you felt about the loss, right?"

I nodded my head yes.

"And when they couldn't talk to you, one drew his own con-clusions about you," he said. "Los, some writers are going to be positive and others will be negative about you, but it's better for you to represent your own words and thoughts. Don't leave it up to others. If you have an opportunity, speak on it, you know what I mean? Even if it's to tell them you're bothered by how you played and can't talk that much right now beyond that."

The article and the talk that followed made me realize I'd put a tremendous amount of responsibility for my team's success on my shoulders, to the point where I didn't know how to deal with loss and all the emotion that came with it. I would have to grow thicker skin, for this was a small glimpse of what I might encounter with the media in college and, hopefully, the NBA.

That scathing article aside, I felt overwhelming support from the people of Alaska. At my last appearance in Ketchikan, we won the tournament, and the gym gave me a standing ovation when I was named MVP. As I went to leave with my team, there was a large group of parents with their kids waiting for me to sign their basketballs and shirts.

"Go ahead without me," I told my teammates, as I began to sign my name to whatever was waved in my face. "I'll catch a ride with my parents."

A table and chair appeared, as if out of nowhere, and an orderly line formed. I looked around at all the smiling faces that could have been home that night, tucked into their warm homes, watching *Martin* or *Friends*, but they'd chosen to come watch me play basketball. I was overwhelmed by their appreciation and if I could've kept playing in Alaska, I would have surely done it for them.

We didn't win the state title again my senior season, but I finished my high school career with a 95–12 record and over 2,500 career points. I was named to *USA Today*'s All-American first team, as well as a *Slam Magazine* All-American. I was also an all-state choice for four years and the state Player of the Year three times. Probably most prestigious at the time, I was also named to the McDonald's All-American team, ranking me among the

top twenty high school players in the country that year. I was
the second player ever to qualify from the state of Alaska, behind
Trajan Langdon in 1994, and my family and friends watched
me play its championship game on ESPN that March. I sizzled
with 22 points and 11 rebounds.

After making calls to Coach Jarvis and Coach Lavin, I announced my commitment to Duke University's class of 2003
on April 3, 1999.

"Looks like it's time for another road trip," my father said,
when I graduated from high school that June. He'd promised
Natasha a car to drive around in New Jersey, so we packed my
things into a blue Ford Taurus, and took off midsummer for
a final father-son road trip. We stopped at the Grand Canyon
again, stayed in generic motels sprinkled along the highway, and
feasted on fast food. Like our talks in the boat and on the court,
we discussed anything and everything.

"Los, you remember that time we went fishing on the channel?" he asked. We both grinned. I knew exactly what he was
referring to. I was twelve years old, and we'd been in our trusty
sixteen-foot skiff, my father trying out a $300 luxury purchase
fishing pole. This badass pole was balanced on the metal brace
closest to me, so I watched for it to dip as the fish began to nib-
ble at the bait. I waited as I'd been taught because pulling the
line too quickly could give the fish a chance to slip its intended
meal right off the hook.

Suddenly, the entire pole dipped underwater. I stood up and
pulled frantically, but the pole was out of my hands, tearing
from its metal brace and plunging into the water.

"Why didn't you grab onto it?" my father screamed, angry
until he saw the hole where the metal brace had been pulled
clean from the boat's lip. Whatever grabbed the bait needed
the strength and girth of a shark to pull that brace out. Anger
melted to fear, as he realized whatever had done this damage

was substantially bigger than our boat. A lost $300 fishing pole was the least of our worries.

"Moby Dick didn't have anything on us that day," my father laughed, and I did, too. I never took for granted how lucky I'd been to have so much time with my father, far more than what was usual for a child with two working parents and four siblings. Our relationship wasn't perfect. There were times when I missed my curfew and he handled me accordingly. But overwhelmingly, my father, and my mother for that matter, gave me the chance to dream without limits. Some of my friends had dreams, too, but not the parents to support them like mine did. You don't get to pick your parents, so I was especially grateful for what I got.

"You know, you'll have to get up and go to class," he said, in half jest, breaking our silence. "You know you're going to have to do that on your own? Your mom's not going to pop out of the closet to check your homework, either."

"Yes, sir. I'm aware," I answered. "I'm responsible for myself now." This wasn't a foreign concept to me because my parents had prepared me well.

When we arrived in Princeton over a week later my sister hugged me heartily. "I'm only a drive away," she reminded me. My protector until the end.

My father rented a car for the final day's drive south to Duke, pulling into the campus parking lot that afternoon. The motor sputtered to a stop before he turned his head and asked me.

"Ready to level up?"

# CHAPTER 6

## DUKE

They come by themselves or in pairs or in groups.

"Tickets? Anybody got tickets?" asks a middle-aged man at the corner of the crosswalk, like he's outside the gates to the Super Bowl stadium. There are no takers.

The cement path starts on the campus outskirts, winding its way to its final destination. To the left, a lone runner is out on the track, in the mix of shadow and light, privately fighting his own physical limits. Farther ahead, Wallace Wade Stadium craters thousands of feet down into a bowl that holds forty thousand on sold-out nights. The path takes a sharp turn to the left, past buildings with immaculate stonework and craftsmanship typical of the turn of the century. There is a hazy pink glow in the distance, a beacon of light that everyone gravitates toward.

The path widens, as does the number of people—many clad in "Duke" blue—until it comes to stairs that descend into the front square outside Cameron Indoor Stadium. Spotlights bounce off Cameron's facade of black, gray, orange, and rose stones—all cut by hand from a seventy-two-acre quarry Duke purchased in the '20s to build the university. The cobalt blue stained glass

windows adorning the building's wings are more reminiscent
of a medieval castle than a basketball arena.

According to legend, Cameron Stadium was built to satisfy a
bet between Duke's ultracompetitive founders and the founders
of Princeton University. To win the right to host the first home
game of the next season, Duke built a lavish 8,400-seat stadium
(few housed more than 4,000 at the time) in a record nine months,
before the New Jersey institution could complete theirs. Duke then
shellacked Princeton 36–27 under Cameron's roof in January 1940.

Cameron has been called the "crown jewel" of college basketball venues and named among the top-ten sports arenas nation-
wide. Yet, despite the enormous demand for more seating,
Cameron Stadium will never expand past its maximum 9,400
spectators. Season tickets are handed down from generation to
generation, like priceless family heirlooms. Family members
drive fourteen hours to meet up and watch games at Cameron.
Tickets aren't squandered. And eight miles down the road, the
UNC Tarheels have challenged Duke with what is arguably the
biggest ongoing rivalry in college basketball. It's a rivalry that
has drawn US presidents to its games. A Blue Devils fan, or a
Tarheels fan for that matter, would probably give up a kidney
before they give up their Duke-UNC seat. They don't call it
"Basketball Country" down there for nothing.

When I finally had the opportunity to explore Duke's 8,600-
acre campus, it looked even better than what I'd remembered
from my visit with my parents months earlier. The sports fields
and buildings were clustered closely together so the teams could
overlap with support facilities. Outside of that area, Duke was
undoubtedly one of the most beautiful settings I'd ever seen—
and I lived in Juneau for a decade. The campus was a meld of
old and new architecture, the former evident in so many buildings with the uniform "Duke stone" facade, as well as ornately
chiseled archways. Through one of these entrances, I ducked
into the very modern student center and grabbed a slice of pizza

from the food court. Then I took the concrete steps up to Duke's church, peaking my head inside a miniature version of St. Patrick's Cathedral. Farther up the sidewalk, "the Quad" offered a long stretch of grass, surrounded by fraternity dorms, where students congregated to sit, eat, and talk. I kept walking, passing down a throughway street to Sarah P. Duke Gardens, a 55-acre masterpiece of landscaped and wooded areas. Exotic fish swam around the Terrace Fish Pool, the Gardens' center attraction. In either direction, a series of five-mile-long trails revealed sitting cloisters and gazebos. Duke Gardens had its own plant collection and even its own rock garden. Still, it was the colorful flowers—roses in the fall and tulips in the spring—that drew my eye. Flower beds smattered the Gardens' landscape, releasing a floral scent that overloaded my senses. I looked out across the small lake, breathing in the scent of tulips woven between stonework. It became one of my favorite places to visit early on.

Coming from Juneau, Duke might as well have been Times Square. I was one of 6,125 freshmen accepted to the class of 2003, joining students from every part of the world—the future doctors, judges, and CEOs of companies. I was meeting an assortment of people with different motivations and aspirations. Wanting to learn more about people in general, I declared sociology as my major.

I'd put in a request to share a room with Jayson Williams, who I'd met a couple of months earlier at the McDonald's All-American game in Ames, Iowa. Jay, who'd been named the National Player of the Year for both his athletics and academics, had helped tip me toward selecting Duke. His enthusiasm for basketball matched my own and I wanted to surround myself with people who had a similar drive. So, Jay and I'd made a plan to arrive on campus a few weeks early to get in better shape. We desperately wanted starting positions and took Coach K's recruiting credo to heart.

"Did you do any of the conditioning exercises from that book they gave us?" Jay asked, when I picked him up at Greensboro

Airport, an hour away from campus. Senior Chris Carrawell had lent me his car, and he must have been secretly trying to kill us. The AC was busted on a sticky hundred-degree afternoon typical of North Carolina summers and my body folded into the deep bucket seats like a flip phone.

"Nah," I answered honestly, as Jay sunk down into Chris's sweltering jalopy. Between high school graduation and prepping for college, I hadn't had the time to crack open the strength and conditioning tome the coaching staff sent us.

Jay gave me a look that let me know he hadn't quite made a dent in the conditioning book, either. If his last few weeks at home following graduation had been anything like mine, he'd probably only had time to pack. But the fact that he'd shown up early told me I had someone to challenge and push me.

"That's why we're here early," I said. "The more you sacrifice, the more you can achieve." The words were my father's, but they felt fitting.

From the start it was the easiest of friendships. We had a lot in common. Like me, Jay had gotten a heap of media attention during his high school years, especially when he'd adjusted his game to become a top passer. The six-foot-two New Jersey native was the No. 1 prospect from the East Coast, while I'd been his counterpart from the West. Jay was an intellectual guy, the president of his high school chess club and a self-professed nerd. He'd been raised to value academic excellence and family, like I had. Jay stayed low-key about the attention he'd gotten, something he'd try to preserve as his star rose at Duke. I respected his humility and he seemed to mesh well with my laid-back personality off the court. Jay had been an only child, and I was delighted to gain another brother so far from home.

Jay and I were excited to take advantage of the extra time we'd get in the gym that we'd call home—at least for the next year. As part of Duke's early matriculation period, we had access to the campus, so in the first week, we took advantage of

having a proper track to run on. After one run, we were heading back to Cameron's locker room when Jay and I fell into a
quick 2-on-2 game. Without thinking, I pulled a spin move to
face the basket—while still in my track shoes. I came down on
the unstable footwear and felt my ankle twist, but not thinking
it serious, I left it until the next morning. Sliding out of bed,
I felt excruciating pain. My foot had blown up to the size of a
toaster, and never having been injured seriously like this before,
I didn't know that was a telltale sign of a broken bone.

I called David Henderson, the assistant coach in charge of the
squad's "big men," and he set up an X-ray, which revealed that
I'd broken the fifth metatarsal bone in my left foot. The good
news was Duke had ample experience with basketball injuries
like this and I got expert care quickly at its adjunct hospital, one
of the best in the country. I was in surgery two days after the
injury, where a screw was placed in the bone to merge it back
together. I was sent back to my dorm in a cast. The bad news
was my rehabilitation period was estimated at eight to twelve
weeks—and our season opener was exactly eight weeks away.

This was my first sports injury ever, and I hadn't done it biking or running or doing any other activity. It came from doing
what I was best at, and suddenly I felt vulnerable. I'd never experienced uncertainty before with my body. Coach K and Grant
Hill encouraged me to concentrate on rehabilitation, but I felt
frustration, especially when I watched from the sidelines during
practice. I'd worked my ass off to make this team and I wanted
to be out there.

My college basketball career got off to a rough start hobbling
around on crutches, but the rest of my college life hit the ground
running. During the first week of classes, I returned to the dorm
room to find our answering machine's blinking light with a
message. I pressed Play, expecting to hear Jay's mother or mine.

"Hi, Carlos," a woman's voice said. "I got your number from
the directory. My name is Cindy. I was wondering if you'd like

to meet up and hang out?" She left her phone number to call her back.

Since she'd gotten my number from the student directory, I assumed she was a Duke student, too. I wasn't certain what to do, so I did what Coach K told us on our first day.

"If you have a question, if you need help, call one of us on this card," he said, holding up a wallet-size laminated square at least fifty names deep with everyone affiliated with the Duke basketball program, from the coaching staff to the players to the front office. I called one of the senior players on the team.

"She wants to hang out with you?" he asked. "So, what are you still doing on the phone with me? Call her back. And welcome to college."

I hung up and dialed Cindy, who told me everyone called her CeCe. She asked me if I was free that evening. I was intrigued by her directness.

"Well, I'm on crutches," I told her, still unsure how she knew who I was.

"I know. I saw you in the bookstore," she said. "I'd love to get dinner and just chat."

CeCe was a senior attending North Carolina Central University, five minutes down the road, but had been in Duke's bookstore with a friend the same day as me.

"Ah, a stalker," I said, which got a laugh. I tried to remember if I'd seen any cute girls lurking around the shelves, but my mind drew a blank. I liked the sound of her voice, though. "Sure, let's meet up."

CeCe picked me up in her car and drove me to her townhouse a few minutes from campus. At first glance, she had a beautiful caramel complexion and an athletic build. She was tall, too, at five-foot-eleven. I wasn't surprised to find out that she ran track and played volleyball. But the night kept getting better for me. CeCe cooked me dinner: a medium-well steak, creamy mashed potatoes, and collard greens. The meat melted in my mouth like butter. I'd never had a girlfriend cook for me before and this was a real meal. My favorite meal, in fact. She told me what it was like to grow up in Durham, while I regaled her with tales of my time in the Juneau wilderness. CeCe was especially interested in my family's dynamic. Four years older than me, she was mature and responsible, while I was on my own for the first time. We talked through the night, then laughed over breakfast at the local Waffle House. CeCe had a soft voice, and the more we spoke, the more I realized that her boldness in the bookstore was out of character. It made me like her even more that she'd taken a chance. When she dropped me back off to my dorm the next morning, I tore through the door on my crutches and attacked the single set of stairs to my room to call my mother.

"Mom, I found the one," I said confidently.

"What about the ten other girls who called here last week looking for you?" she asked. My mother was exaggerating, but there may have been one or two still lingering around.

"Nah. That's all over," I said. "I've found the one."

To call it a "whirlwind romance" might not capture how quickly CeCe and I fell in love. I'd never wanted to spend time with someone as much as I did with CeCe, to where a day away from her felt like months. Being on crutches didn't slow me down too much. I attended my classes and reported to practice every day with my team, where I tried to soak up what I could from the sidelines. Sometimes that time went to studying tape on rival teams or toward the weight room for an upper-body workout. Every remaining second gladly went to CeCe. I started to see her every day in the cracks of time left in between. It didn't matter the hour. After my classes were finished for the day, I'd head over to CeCe's place. After late-night practices, she'd pick me up around 11:00 p.m. and have me back on campus for 7:00 a.m. practice the next morning. I spent so little time in my own dorm room, that I'd occasionally find a teammate sleeping in my bed, after Jay gave them permission to crash there.

Once I shed my crutches, I took CeCe to Duke Gardens, where we strolled through its colorful rose garden—her favorite flowers—and shared our future dreams together.

Through rehab and physical therapy, I was able to lose the cast and crutches in six weeks, which gave me two weeks to assimilate with a team that had already been gelling without me. I'd watched Coach K beat up my teammates from the sidelines and now it was my turn.

"Carlos Motherfucking Boozer," Coach K barked at my first practice, setting a feverish pace I wasn't accustomed to. "If you don't get your ass down the court faster, I'm going to put my foot up it." For my entire freshman year, I would have sworn my middle name was Motherfucker.

"Boozer!" Coach K yelled. "Get into fucking position. Why didn't you pass there? Did you have to hold on to the fucking ball just so you could make that shitty attempt at the shot yourself?"

Tough practice? All those times I played outside in Alaskan blizzards suddenly seemed warm and inviting by comparison, like puppies licking your face. But I knew what I was getting into. I'd watched Coach K, red as a tomato, blow his stack from courtside in nearly all of the Duke games on ESPN. He'd get angry at his players or the referees, toss his clipboard or a towel or a bag of ice onto the court, and scream his frustrations to the basketball gods. Coach K had played for the army team under coaching legend Bobby Knight, which surely shaped his own hard-nosed approach. The man held nothing back.

After practice, Jay and I helped drag each other back to our dorm room, where we both collapsed onto our beds. Jay had been at this for six weeks and he was wrecked. What hope did I have?

"Bro, I'm not as good as I thought I was," I said, as muscles I didn't even know I had screamed at me in revolt.

"It's been that brutal every day," Jay said, without moving an inch. "I think Coach aims to kill us before October."

"Brutal? That was straight-up hell," I managed, just getting the words out before I fell fast asleep.

I woke up the next morning in deep need of a reality check. I went into the bathroom and stared myself down in the mirror, like I had in high school, but this time, I turned my left shoulder toward its reflection, and stared at the fresh tattoo I'd gotten in nearby Durham when I'd first arrived. It was the first of nearly twenty tattoos I'd ink up and down my arms, legs, and body over the years. This first tattoo was the most important though. It was one of my own doodles of a grizzly bear. He shredded through my skin with his razor-sharp talons, smoke billowing up from the slashes, with the words *The Beast Unleashed* arching over its head. As soon as my feet touched the slick maple hardwood floor, that's who I'd transformed into—a relentless grizzly bear who tore to the net, growling and snarling all the way. Off the court, I was a nice guy. On the court, that Carlos disappeared. Shoot. Rebound. Shoot. Rebound. Relentless like a grizzly bear. The Beast Unleashed.

I'd gotten the tattoo to remind myself where I'd come from and the sacrifices I'd made to get to where I was now. I'd given up summers to play with the travel teams. I'd given up weekdays and nights for practice and games. I'd skipped weekends with friends and family for tournaments and clinics. I'd given up warmth. I'd anchored two teams to back-to-back state championships. The Beast had done all that and I'd gotten this tattoo to make sure I didn't forget it. This was my badge of courage.

"I've earned the right to be here," I told the slightly shaken seventeen-year-old staring back at me. "I deserve to be here."

"Who you talking to, bro?" Jay said, as he came into the bathroom behind me, rubbing his eyes and yawning.

"No one," I said, turning around. "Let's go wake up the rest of the guys."

The freshman players were all situated together on a single floor in the Bassett Dorm on the East Campus, and we began watching out for one another. We dragged each other out of bed in the morning by any means necessary—cups of cold water, blaring loud rap music, jumping on each other like annoying siblings. The upperclassmen, like Shane Battier, Chris Carrawell, and Nate James, were all used to the drill. They had the routine down and took care of themselves. But we were freshmen, and to survive, we had to stick together. Of course, this was also part of Coach K's master plan. Each new team went through the same thing, like pledging the most popular fraternity on campus. We were joining "The Brotherhood"—the unofficial name that the men's basketball team had gone by for generations before I stepped onto Duke soil. I had to hold myself to a higher standard now.

We all left those first practices confused, filled with self-doubt, but that was Coach stripping us down to our rawest selves, so he could build us all back up instilled with the need—no, the desire—to work together to succeed. We were all the best or we wouldn't have been there, but this wasn't high school. In a short period of time, Coach K was tasked with melding individual stars into a cohesive team of stars going for a championship.

The Duke basketball program is one of the most comprehensive in the country. You're a student athlete at an elite level, which comes with a lot of perks, but just as many pitfalls. You have to study and keep up a certain grade point average to stay eligible to play sports or your scholarship will be taken away. But then you have to actually put the time in on the court, whether it's team practice or shooting baskets on your own. There's just not enough hours in the day and Duke knows this. So, they put resources in place that you wouldn't find at your typical college.

Student managers are assigned to each player and survive a

rigorous set of interviews for an opportunity to experience the inner workings of a major college sports program. My student managers traveled with me and the team, helped with my luggage and wrote down chart-hussle plays and other stats from the bench during games. On campus, the managers cleaned our uniforms and made themselves available to the players at any time, day or night, to work out. If I was staring at my ceiling at 2:00 a.m., and there were a lot of nights I did just that, my managers would meet me at the gym to put up shots with me, watch video, or lift weights.

Once I was at practice, my coaches demanded my full attention. As one of the team's "big men," I was assigned to Coach Henderson. He and Coach K threw me a curve ball once I was back on my feet.

"Carlos, you're going to start from here," Coach K said, pulling me to the traditional center position at the top of the basket. "You're going to start here, but you're going everywhere you've always gone—and a few new places."

An animated Coach K quickly ran to each area, arms flailing, as he rattled off where my new starting position would take me. "Inside. Outside. Facing the basket. Back to the board. Shooting threes. You're going to do it all."

His excitement was infectious. I loved that he had a plan for me. He was so present, his only goal to make me a better player, so the team could win. I knew that I'd made the right choice in Coach K and Duke. This was the man, and the team, that would lead us to a national championship.

Coach K didn't like to box players into specific positions, but he had to fill out the paperwork, so officially, I'd be Duke's center, replacing Elton Brand. Brand had helped Duke to the Final Four in his freshman year, the championship game during his sophomore year and had been named National Player of the Year, but opted to leave for the NBA Draft.

"We're going to get more physical, away from the perimeter

and more back-to-the-board," explained Coach Henderson, who helped catch me up to speed. I'd been considered a big man for a while and weighed in around 245 pounds when I got to Duke. But my coaches wanted me bigger, knowing I'd need more bulk to stop players like seven-foot Brandon Haywood from UNC, who had a good 30 pounds on me. I found myself in the weight room a lot with the football team.

Mastering a new position, with different patterns and goals, was a challenge, especially in such a short period of time. Jay and I commiserated together; he'd been flipped to guard, when he'd played "the 3" or small forward in high school. Jay probably had a bigger shift to make than me, going from a solo scorer to a ball handler who now had to pass the ball more often. But again, Coach K didn't like to limit us with positions. The five he put on the court would be the best five players he had, but they'd be utilized in the best way possible. He knew what we were all capable of before we did. We just had to trust him.

"Ahh!" I screamed in frustration, as I tried to conform to this new role on the court.

"Make any sound you want," Coach K yelled from the gym's opposite end, where he was drilling my teammates. "You can howl like a werewolf in moonlight if it lights a fire under your ass!"

About a week before our first game, Coach K called me over to the sidelines. With my injury, I hadn't yet spoken to him one-on-one. I approached, slightly terrified, unsure what would come out of his mouth.

"Carlos," he said, arms crossed, his eyes still fixed on my teammates hustling back and forth. It was the first time I'd heard him speak, not growl at me. "Carlos, in life, there are levels. Say you cook for a living. Now, you might be content to go to work every day, flip some burgers, then come home, crack open a beer, and watch some TV before you head to bed, to wake up the next day and do it all over again. There's nothing wrong with that. For some people, that makes them happy."

He paused, gazing out at my teammates like a ship captain reading the horizon.

"But there are others," he continued, "who were born to create food masterpieces in the best restaurants in the world, and they seek out the best places to study, they spend hours and hours in the kitchen perfecting every dish, and then they go out into the world to work at the top restaurants or even open one of their own.

"Carlos, you can come every day and work, or you can come and work hard. You can always push yourself some more. In those moments, the ones where you work past fatigue—those are the moments you really get better. Do everything at a championship level. When you shoot, are you doing it at a championship level? Will that work in a championship game?"

I was smart enough to know not to interrupt one of the greatest basketball minds ever when he was giving me advice.

"If you work all season at a championship level, when you get to that game, you won't fail, because you've been preparing yourself for that moment all year," he concluded.

It was pretty profound stuff for a seventeen-year-old. And the competitor in me wanted to rise to Coach K's challenge. I wouldn't be a line cook. I would be a world-renowned chef, who stayed after hours to master everything from cracking an egg to perfecting the fluffiest chocolate soufflé. I started applying the championship level to my practices. I treated every shot like it was the one that would clinch the game. I started to apply this mindset to my academics and to life in general. And I began to get better.

With our opening game upon us, I might have been nervous if I wasn't so excited. The game was being televised and my parents and the rest of Juneau would be watching. I was only the second player ever from Alaska to go to Duke. I'd be lying if I said I didn't feel the pressure. I'd felt this way when my mother took me to my first travel-ball camp to face the unknown. *Am I good enough?* I told myself that I was, that the adrenaline coursing through my veins would soon be put to good use.

In the stadium tunnel, I heard the crowd's roar each time a player was introduced. And then it was my turn.

"This is for you, Chris," I said aloud. I took a deep breath, opened the curtains, and came out with a trot, high-fiving my teammates and stepping into line midcourt. That's when I heard it for the first time. I almost thought the crowd was booing me, but how could they do that when they'd never seen me play before? In the lowest registers they could muster, the crowd roared "Boooooozzz" in unison. That's how enthused Duke students (and their parents, grandparents, and the rest of the community) were about their basketball team. They knew all the players before they'd even stepped foot on the court. I felt so welcomed and lifted up by the gesture. It gave me an instant connection to the crowd. I really wanted to play my best for them.

Coach K played me off the bench for our first two games, against No. 13 Stanford, who we lost to by a single point in overtime and No. 1 UConn, who beat us 66–71. I started in our next game at home against Army. We decimated Coach K's alma mater 100–42, sending the Cameron Crazies into a frenzy. I contributed 15 points to the victory, which kicked off an eighteen-game winning streak that lasted until our tussle with No. 23 Maryland in February 2000. Maryland took us out 87–98—and they did it at Cameron. They were going to be trouble for us. Other than them, only St. John's beat us at Cameron that season.

The full scope of our rivalry with UNC was on display when we played them at home that March in our last game of the regular season. I'd watched seventy blue tents pop up in a field near the stadium before the season even started, a tradition begun by avid students in the 1980s, who camped out for weeks to get the opportunity to win tickets. This makeshift town, which appeared every season, was christened Krzyzewskiville, because Coach K had been known to stop by with a box of donuts or a pizza pie from time to time to show his appreciation.

When we beat the Tarheels, the crowd's cheers shook Cameron to its core. When Jay and I left Cameron together, we saw a bonfire on one of the lawns, then another as we approached our dorm. We saw our fellow students huddled around the blazes, singing Duke's alma mater song at the top of their lungs.

"Grown men burning down park benches for us, CBooz," said Jay. The funny thing was as soon as the season ended in April, the Duke and UNC players rendezvoused at Cameron or UNC's Dean Dome for daily pickup games, the rivalry easily tucked away until next season.

Our regular season ended at 24–4, ranking us third in our Eastern division. In Charlotte, we rattled off three straight wins, including a satisfying 81–68 victory over the rival University of Maryland, to take the Atlantic Coast Conference title. After a season under Coach K, the team's pacing was humming, while Jay and Shane were absolute scoring machines.

By winning the ACC tournament title, we improved to the No. 1 seed in our bracket in the 2000 NCAA Tournament. In Winston-Salem, we plastered an overmatched Lamar College in the first round, then beat the University of Kansas in the next game, 69-64. We were onto the "Sweet Sixteen"—our game against the University of Florida took place a week later in Syracuse, New York. We were on a roll and saw no reason why we couldn't take it all. We were only four wins away. But the fifth-seeded Gators had plans, too, which they executed better. At halftime, we trailed them, 43–33, having committed over a dozen costly turnovers.

Coach K's half-time speech could've been likened to dipping one's head in a sink of ice water. We woke up. We took the lead in the second half, but continued to miss shots that led to costly turnovers. Florida outscored us 13–0 in the final four minutes, which included four crucial free throws from one Gator's player in the final sixty seconds. Florida stopped us 78–87, advancing them to the Elite Eight. We hadn't played our best—twenty-two turnovers was a cringeworthy statistic to carry back to Durham, but Coach K wasn't upset. He was incredibly proud and was already making plans for next year on our flight home.

"What a trip you guys took me on!" he gushed.

In the regular season, I averaged 13 points a game and was selected for the ACC All-Freshman team by the Associated Press. But I was most proud of leading my team in field-goal percentages (.614), which is the ratio of shots taken to the ones you make. Thanks to my father, I'd shot from every possible spot on the court. Overall, we had a tight squad, at least that's what the Associated Press thought when they ranked us No. 1 in the country at the season's end. We hadn't made it to the ACC Finals, but were still considered by some as the best team and the favorite to take it all next season.

Jay and I had amazing rookie seasons we wanted to build on. Along with teammate Mike "Dun-Dun" Dunleavy, we accepted invitations to try out for the USA Basketball Men's National Team that summer. Only thirty college-age players were invited to try out over three days at the US Olympic Training Center in Colorado Springs, Colorado. The younger of its two squads would play in the World Championships in Brazil that July. Jay, Mike, and I couldn't think of a better way to spend our summer. But when they called out the team roster, Jay's and Mike's names were spoken, but mine was not. I stood there in the gym and couldn't hold back my tears.

My father wasn't there to console me, but I thank Jay's dad for stepping in. "You have to take this moment and use it to your advantage, Carlos," he said. "Take what you feel here today, bring it back to Duke and turn it into fuel."

Although I didn't make the summer team, I stayed on the East Coast to practice with the local talent and spend time with

CeCe. I'd become close to CeCe's family, especially with her grandmother, who hosted cookouts every Sunday. They'd welcomed me right off the bat. Still, I missed my own family.

"Guess who walked up to our pickup game at the Dean Dome today?" I asked my father after one practice. I talked to my father every day and he relished the stories I told him about the famous basketball players I came into contact with.

"Vince Carter and Jerry Stackhouse were already there," I teased. Carter was a UNC alum and the No. 5 pick in the 1998 Draft. Stackhouse also attended UNC and was the No. 3 pick in the 1995 Draft. I was rubbing elbows with basketball gods.

"Don't say it," my father said.

"Yup. Jordan," I answered.

"Stop," he cooed. "Did you talk to him?"

"No. I didn't say a word, Pops." A silence lingered between us for a moment. There was something gnawing at me, and I think my father could detect it. I kept talking, trying to distract him, and myself. "Yeah, I was too busy concentrating on defending him to chat."

My father knew something was up. "What's the matter, Los?"

"Pops, Coach Henderson is leaving," I said. "He got the head coach gig at the University of Delaware."

Of all Duke's coaching staff, I was the closest to the big-man coach. I had a good relationship with Coach K, but he hadn't been the one who'd met me on the court at midnight to burn off nervous energy and talk strategy. Coach Henderson had done that, but now he was moving on and I suddenly felt alone. I didn't know who his replacement would be, which made me feel a little lost at sea. Still, I'll never forget what my father said to me next, because he said it without hesitation.

"Hang tight," my father said. "We're coming to you."

# CHAPTER 7

## THAT CHAMPIONSHIP FEELING

For the second time in my life, my family moved across the country for me. My parents and three younger siblings packed up their lives and rented a house in Cary, a quaint city about twenty minutes outside Durham. My younger brother, Charles, now fourteen years old, and my youngest sisters, Nakeisha and Natanya, had only known isolated Juneau their entire lives; moving to the lower 48 would be a culture shock. From clothes to music to movies, Juneau naturally lagged behind the mainland.

My parents had attended nearly all my games throughout high school, and I know they'd missed watching me play live. Our returning squad had an amazing chance to win the NCAA Championship; the Associated Press had preranked us No. 1 in the nation for a fourth year in a row. With everything they'd done for me, I loved the idea of my family coming along for the ride. They'd earned whatever success came of it as much as I did.

I hadn't realized how much I'd missed my family until I had the ability to go home again on the weekends and enjoy a home-cooked meal. My little sisters, Nakeisha and Natanya, now nine and eleven years old, had grown so much in our year apart.

Sometimes, my younger brother, Charles, stayed with me at the on-campus apartment I'd moved into with another teammate, Andre Bruckner. Charles's own basketball career was coming along, so my parents enrolled him in a prominent local high school with a strong sports program and recognized academics, which my two younger sisters also attended later.

My family met CeCe, who remained the biggest part of my life outside of basketball. If I didn't have a ball in my hands, I was usually with her, eating out at restaurants like Kurama, Durham's hibachi version of Benihana, or watching movies at her place. During a bad snowstorm, Duke canceled its classes, yet CeCe got a call that day from the team office that basketball practice was still on. I don't know how they knew she was my girlfriend or how they got her phone number, but the Duke basketball program had eyes everywhere.

I wasn't the first Duke basketball player to fall in love at college, and it wasn't as if anyone tried to stop me. But I was expected to pull my weight, girlfriend or not. That's when Steve Wojciechowski entered my life. "Wojo" had actually been around as an assistant coach to the guards during my freshman year, but moved into the big-man position to replace Coach Henderson.

"It's you and me now," Wojo said, and he wasn't kidding. I think I saw him every single day up until I left Duke, that's how strong our bond became. Wojo was my spirit guide at Duke, always steering me in the right direction. I could call Wojo for advice or for midnight shot sessions in the gym. A McDonald's All-American, Wojo played four years for Duke and led the team to a 32–4 record and the Sweet Sixteen during his senior year. Coach K had been smart to scoop Wojo up right out of college. With his passion and energy for the game, he was a natural at coaching and a match made in heaven for me.

"I know you want more touches, but you don't have control over that," Wojo told me from time to time. "If you want more opportunities, focus on what you can control—making the shot when you do get the pass."

The seeds for a championship year are usually planted two or three years ahead. Our team captain, Shane Battier, made it to the 1999 NCAA Finals as a sophomore, then led us four freshman starters to the Sweet Sixteen in 2000. Without question, Shane was both the anchor, as well as the moving force behind our team—and I realize these two notions contradict one another. "This is our year!" became a frequent slogan around the gym, largely motivated by our desire to win it all in Shane's last year. Our love for Shane drove us through the summer workouts into my sophomore season.

Shane had already been voted defensive Player of the Year two times by the National Association of Basketball Coaches. He also led offensive charges and he could sink threes like a deep-sea fisherman. He was our emotional leader, able to rein us in during the heat of the moment with just the right words, whether we were at practice, in the locker room or in the huddle. Shane held us all accountable.

"That doesn't look like that championship feeling!" he'd yell at the guards when he saw them slacking off.

Somehow, Shane made himself available to us 24/7—or at least it seemed that way. Even with all of that talent coursing through him, Shane was the most selfless player I'd ever interacted with.

But there wasn't much argument that the best player on the squad was Jay, our star guard who averaged over 20 points a game his freshman year. ESPN analyst Dick Vitale hailed Jay as the second-best guard in the world behind Jason Kidd, who was playing in the NBA. So, Shane sacrificed his senior year passing the ball away to Jay and others, when he could have tried to shoot himself. He didn't care whose name made the newspapers or who was being discussed on *SportsCenter*. Shane cared about winning the championship and realized dishing the ball out gave us the best odds. Shane had me down low, Mike Dunleavy on the wing, and Jay anywhere he wanted. And if all that failed, Shane switched to his threes. Coach K had also recruited freshman Chris Duhon, a phenomenal point guard from the New Orleans area, who aided Shane with assists and defense.

"I'll do whatever it takes to win," I heard Shane say to Coach K on more than one occasion, as we geared up for his final season. "Whatever you want me to do, Coach, I'll do it."

It didn't matter who was in earshot nor what Coach K's answer might be. Shane did it, no questions asked. So, when Shane turned to any of us and asked if we wanted to get extra shots up, we eagerly agreed. No one was afraid to put in the work because the prospect of failing Shane again was too horrible to contemplate. So, every time we declared, "This is our year," what we meant was, "This is Shane's year."

We trampled Princeton 87–50 during our mid-November opener, punctuated by Shane hitting nine three-pointers in 12 attempts, a new Duke record. My parents, siblings and CeCe sat together in the Cameron crowd to watch me score 11 points and snag 5 rebounds, taking in the magical atmosphere that swept everyone up into a frenzy every basket.

We rattled off ten victories to start the season until we faced No. 3 Stanford a few days before Christmas in Oakland, California, where we lost by a point. You'd think that Coach K would be furious with us, but that was the beauty of our coach. He'd nearly burst blood vessels during the game, but if we'd given it our all, he'd easily acknowledge it. There was no lecture afterward, no terse words for coming up short. Instead, Coach K was already onto the next game. We dug our heels in harder, stayed extra hours putting up more shots and watched more tape, which won us 9 more games.

Over three days, we took out No. 7 NC State, No. 11 Maryland and No. 6 North Carolina. It was our third clash with Maryland that season, who were becoming a persistent thorn in our side. They'd been ahead 89–77 with 1:05 left on the clock.

The Maryland fans began chanting, "Overrated," and I just knew Shane would feed the ball to Jay because Jay hated that chant more than any other person on the team.

Sure enough, Jay hit a layup with 53.5 seconds left. Then, the team goaded Maryland's Drew Nicholas into a corner, Jay slapped the ball out of his hands and high-tailed it back to our basket for a quick three. It was suddenly 90–85 and everyone was up from our bench like someone had doused it in kerosene and set a match. I was screaming at the top of my lungs. My teammates were screaming. Coach K was screaming.

The Maryland crowd was enraged, especially when Jay hit another three, his eighth point in under a minute. The score was 90–88, with thirty seconds left. On Maryland's next possession, Nate James cut off a pass and in a final chaotic sequence that saw the ball touched by three Duke players' hands, Nate was the one to tip the ball in for the tying basket with 1.3 seconds left. Our come-from-behind victory, which we eventually won in overtime, was called the "The Miracle Minute." I conibuted 19 points and 4 rebounds in one of the nastiest college games we had.

The buzzer sounded and the arena exploded in anger, every Maryland fan convinced they'd been cheated. The roar was deafening, but it didn't stop there. Fans began throwing glass bottles and other items into the Duke's cheering section, elevated off the floor. The team watched in horror as our parents, Coach K's wife and the other coaches' wives came under assault. CeCe was also sitting with my parents. Without thinking, my feet started to move in their direction, but somebody held me back.

The great thing about Coach K is he doesn't mess around. He ran to the nearest security guard and within a minute, had an army of ten brawny men following him to the entrance that led up to our section. The trail of guards collected our families and escorted them to the arena floor, where they were taken backstage through one of the tunnels. They were booed at and berated until they were out of sight.

I stood on the sidelines, shaking. This was a basketball game, not a biker rally. I'd never seen disgruntled basketball fans turn like that. The threat of physical harm, especially to our loved ones, had been real and palpable. I couldn't get to my mother fast enough, barreling through the crowded court to the tunnel my family had exited a few minutes earlier.

I found my mother, father, and CeCe, along with the other Duke relatives, outside our locker room.

My mom held a kerchief to her head, bleeding from a gash. Tears filled her eyes. She was in some pain, but trying her best not to show it. My father was so infuriated that he couldn't stand still, bouncing from one wall to another like a pinball. If given the preference, I would've liked to have a conversation with whoever threw that glass bottle at her head.

Our celebration was cut short that night. We were more concerned about getting out of the gym safely and back home to Durham. We changed quickly and silently, then joined our families and security to walk together through the arena to the exit. We were all escorted to our buses, our parents and siblings now sitting among us. Pulling away from Maryland, our bus let out a sharp screech as the driver changed gears, echoing the weariness of an exhilarating, but exhausting night.

Heading into our February 1st game against No. 4 archrival UNC, we were an impressive 19–1 and 7–0 in the Atlantic Coast Conference. Despite our best efforts, though, there would be no bench-burning outside Cameron that night. We lost 83–85. Two weeks later, we dropped another one-basket game to No. 12 Virginia. That's just how competitive our conference was, where single baskets decided fates in the final seconds.

Our deepest-cutting loss came two weeks after that when we took on No. 16 Maryland at Cameron. Maryland had beaten us at Cameron the year before, so we knew they wouldn't be intimidated like other teams. It was Shane's Senior Night, marking his final home game. I injured my right foot with about fourteen and a half minutes left and limped out of the game. Shane stepped up with 31 points, but it wasn't enough to stop the Terrapins and their star scorer, Steve Blake. We lost 80–91.

I knew right away that I'd broken my foot again, though the opposite one from my freshman year. Every time I put pressure on it, I heard and felt a pop. Back in Cameron's X-ray room, the doctors confirmed a hairline fracture in my third metatarsal. I wouldn't need surgery, but I was fitted with a compression boot and ruled out of our regular-season finale against North Carolina five days later, as well as the ACC Tournament set to begin a few days after that in Atlanta.

I didn't want to believe I was out because we'd just hit our stride. I'd been the third-highest scorer, averaging 14 points that season, and the media came down hard on the rest of the squad, knocking them by predicting the team wouldn't be able to make it to the championship without me.

Coach K saw things going a different way, and after a discouraging first practice without me, he gathered us up in the locker room for a heart-to-heart talk. Everybody was downtrodden. Shane was so upset, that he threw a chair across the room. Coach K waited for us to settle.

"If you guys follow me, we'll win a national championship," he said with utter certainty. "But you're going to have to trust me. We're not going to approach this as if we're switching one guy out for another. We're going to reinvent ourselves. I've got a plan."

*I've got a plan.* Those four little words meant something from Coach K's mouth. He'd surpassed a record-setting 500 college victories earlier that season, so the man had been around the block a time or two. He'd shepherded eight teams to the Final Four and won two NCAA titles already. He'd weathered major injuries that could cripple a team at the most inopportune moment. He wasn't panicked. He was charged up. He really believed we could do it. Now the rest of us had to believe, as well.

Coach K was so resolute in that defining moment, that he went around the room, asking every player the same question.

"Do you believe in me?" he asked. He put it all on the line right there. One by one we answered.

"Yes."

"Yes."

"Yes."

"Yes."

Yeses from the whole team. There was no turning back now.

"I know you're going to bust your ass to get back," Coach K told me separately. "Attack the rehab protocol, but make sure you follow it. I need you back at full strength."

"Absolutely, Coach," I said, accepting my marching orders. "Whatever it takes."

Wojo became my rehab buddy, calming my anxiety that I wouldn't heal fast enough. In the first week, lugging my foot around in a cumbersome boot, Wojo's positive attitude kept me afloat.

"This plan has been put together by doctors and other experts much smarter than you and I," he said. "All we can do is follow it, one day at a time."

As I settled into daily physical therapy, Coach K reconfigured the team to keep our championship hopes alive. By moving freshman Chris Duhon to starting point guard and Jay over to shooting guard, we became a quicker lineup heading into the ACC Tournament. The team's dynamic now mirrored Steve Nash and the Phoenix Suns. We'd push our pace, forcing everyone to keep up with us, while flooding the basket with three-point attempts.

Winning the ACC Tournament gave us the No. 1 seed in our bracket and an easier first-round opponent in the No. 16 Monmouth University. We whipped them 95–52. Two days later, I cheered from the bench as we beat the University of Missouri, led by our former assistant coach, Quin Snyder. Against predictions, we advanced to the Sweet Sixteen without a key player.

My team was keeping our championship hopes alive. I had to heal faster and get back on my feet.

Meanwhile, Wojo and I followed the rehab plan laid out by the Duke medical team. Once I was back on my feet, Wojo meticulously adhered to the list of drills I could and couldn't do, which was updated daily by the medical staff, as they monitored my recovery. We started drills to gradually increase my speed. The team wasn't going to revert back to the way it played before my injury. I would need to adapt to their new style of play.

I was medically cleared to compete four days before our Sweet Sixteen clash against No. 4 UCLA in Philadelphia. I hadn't stepped onto the court in 20 days, but I was well ahead of the doctors' timetable to have me back by the Final Four. It was tempting to dive back into things headfirst, but Wojo was there to make sure there was enough water in the pool. "Nice and easy," he repeated, when my feet finally met the court again. "We don't want to blow a wheel before takeoff."

"How are you feeling, Carlos?" Coach K asked. "Ready to take her out for a spin?"

"Yes, Coach!" I answered enthusiastically, as we launched into our plays at the faster tempo, this time with me at center. By the end of practice, Coach had seen enough. "You're going to play on Thursday," he told me. I floated back to my dorm room.

On March 22, I was the sixth man off the bench against UCLA. I wasn't a scoring machine, but I had 6 rebounds and 2 steals. More importantly, we all left the court knowing I could work in this new lineup with just a little more practice. The final score was 76–63, led by Jay with a whopping 34 points and Shane, who contributed 24 points. On the same day, the University of Southern California took out Kentucky, to claim their spot in the Elite Eight. We would meet USC in the East Regional Final in two days.

I played twenty-two minutes in our game against USC, and although I only scored one point, I was rebounding, stealing and generally gaining crucial playtime with the new squad. We toppled USC 79–69, knowing Maryland loomed in our future. On the same night, nearly 3,000 miles across the country, the Terrapins snuffed No. 6 Stanford out, 87–73. We'd clash with Maryland, our arch rival, a fourth and final time this season.

"If we can get past Maryland, we're going to take it all," Coach K predicted. "I think you can beat them." We nodded in agreement, but we also knew how hungry and aggressive Maryland had been all season. They wanted this just as badly as we did, and they'd already had a taste of beating us.

A week later, we convened in Minneapolis for the Final Four, the pinnacle of college basketball and all its pageantry. In that extra week of practice, I'd inched closer to pre-injury form each day, and not a moment too soon. The team needed me for Maryland—more than any team we'd faced that season. With UNC we had a rivalry, but they weren't a championship team. Maryland was a championship team—and they knew it. They weren't intimidated by the Duke mystique in the slightest.

We, as a team, didn't show up for the first quarter of the game. We played terribly, with little evidence of the chemistry we'd had leading into this crucial game. We were down by 22 points after the first quarter when Shane called a timeout.

"We know these guys well," he said in the huddle. "It's going to come down to who wants it more. All those nights we shot extra hours, extra sprints we ran, time we spent watching film, it will all pay off right now. We've got lots of time."

Shane's words focused us enough to shave Maryland's comfortable lead down to 11 by halftime, and we did it in four minutes. Our passing. Our shooting. Everything started to click into place. We felt momentum building as we entered the locker room to confer with Coach K.

"If you keep playing the way you did right before halftime, you're going to win this," he said. That wasn't an opinion. It was fact.

In the second half, we didn't look back. We pushed our pace, gained more possessions and scored from them. We got hot and both teams could feel it. Our eleven-point deficit suddenly became a 57–35 advantage. With me an inside option again, I was able to score 19 points, nine of them in the final five minutes. We stopped Maryland in their tracks, 95–84.

Beating Maryland had extra significance beyond eliminating the team we'd thought our toughest rival. It didn't matter to me, but I'm sure some of my teammates' minds might have drifted back to our last game, where the crowd had accosted our family and friends. I don't think any of us were hellbent on revenge, but this game ended that throughline.

This game was special for me because I got to be a part of it. I contributed. "You came back right at the right time," Wojo told me later. "You were a real shot in the arm!"

The same night, Arizona, the No. 1 team in the Pac-10, took out Michigan State, 80–61. It would be a classic East vs. West clash for the 2001 NCAA Championship.

On April 2, forty-six thousand fans piled into the Hubert H. Humphrey Metrodome for the 2001 NCAA Championship final. Quite a few of them were Duke fans from what I saw of the familiar pockets of blue. Duke fans traveled well.

With the NBA-worthy attendance, along with the millions watching from home, the entire team couldn't help but feel nervous. The NBA scouts were watching, but once the ball went up, we knew we were the better team. We could feel it. Maryland had been the real threat all season and if we could get by them, we'd get by Arizona.

That's not to say that it wasn't a tight game. It was, especially with monsters like seven-foot-one Loren Woods and crafty point guard Gilbert Arenas. In the final two and a half minutes, we only led by 3 points. But that night was Mike Dunleavy's time to shine. He nailed three consecutive three-pointers and had a brilliant second-half run. Dun-Dun finished with 21 points. I contributed 12 points and nabbed 12 rebounds.

Chris Duhon scored our last point in the game from the foul line, bringing the score to 82–72. Once we regained possession, with only 25 seconds left, I saw the entire Duke coaching team hopping up and down like a group of rabbits. The buzzer sounded and our teammates flooded us from the bench, arms around one another, jumping up and down in excitement. Once again, Coach K began grabbing anyone within range for hugs, while a chorus of "thank yous" sang back to him. I got my hug, and I felt it was as amazing as it had looked all those years ago watching on TV. We stood together, my arm draped over Shane's shoulder and Coach K to his right, our heads tilted up in unison as the hoop nets were unfurled for presentation to our coach. Before we headed off to the locker room, Coach K called us into the final huddle of our 2001 season.

"Take this moment in," he said. "A few of you will have a shot at the NBA, but just take in this moment. You've made the history books and you've earned every bit of that."

That's how Coach K talked to us. About being happy in the moment. Carpe diem. Seize the day. And that's what we did. I'd come to Duke because I'd yearned to be a part of a team that battled all of these great teams with exceptional players and came out victorious. I absolutely had that experience.

Winning the NCAA Championship was a big deal. The accolades seemed endless. My name is forever etched into the plaque on the crystal ball trophy at Duke's Basketball Hall of Fame, which tens of thousands of fans pilgrimage to each year. The team was given a key to the city and we shook President Bush's hand at the White House. We were treated like national heroes. Yet, the best part of all of this was the knowledge that NBA coaches had watched the game.

Not long after the fanfare died down, CeCe came over to my apartment after work.

"There's something wrong with my phone," I told her, tilting my head to the counter that separated the kitchen from the living room, but hiding my face. "I can't get it to power up. I've been charging it all day."

"You mean your new phone?" she asked, placing her purse down, picking up the hardware and inspecting it. CeCe had bought me this phone—just one of the ways she'd taken care of me that I wanted to acknowledge to her now.

"Did you drop it in water—even for just a second?" she asked, turning it around before holding down the power button on its right side. I'd turned around to watch her. "I heard if you place one of these in a bowl of dry rice overnight, it will—"

CeCe stopped midsentence. She stared at the lit-up screen, which read, "Will you marry me?" in pixelated boxes. She burst out crying, while I vaulted the couch and took her in my arms.

"I'd like to get married after I get my NBA contract," I told her, wiping away her tears with my thumbs.

I reached into my tracksuit pocket and pulled out a black velvet box. It was a modest ring with a chip of a tiny diamond balanced on a thin, unadorned band. It cost $900. I would say that it was all I could afford, but that wasn't true. I had to borrow money from my father to buy it.

CeCe didn't notice how modest the ring was. We were both too young and overwhelmingly in love. In the year and a half we'd lived life together, from its most mundane to exciting moments. We wanted to continue moving forward together.

Knowing that, I finally shared the story of Chris's murder with CeCe, the first person I'd ever tell it to. I struggled to relive what had happened and describe it aloud, but I knew I had to if my future wife was to understand me completely. Afterward, I felt relieved to finally share such a secret that nagged at me daily. She gave me an emphatic hug that let me know that it was all going to be alright.

After we won the 2001 championship, some of us on the team were facing an important decision. Though NCAA regulations have changed over the years, in 2001, there was nothing keeping any of us from leaving Duke early to enter the NBA Draft. We wouldn't earn our college degrees and if we remained undrafted, for whatever reason, we couldn't return to Duke for another year. We'd be forfeiting our eligibility forever. However, we'd be punching our ticket to the big leagues a year earlier. Was there a rush? I think some of us might have feared gambling a career-ending injury during our junior year. That thought crossed my mind, as did the temptation to leave on top.

Jay, Mike, and I were high prospects for the 2001 NBA Draft. All we needed to do was let our intentions be known and we'd have been guaranteed invitations. We all flirted with the idea until Coach K summoned us during a barbeque at his Durham home that June.

"I think we can do it again," he told us, as we stood around the backyard pool, already baking in the cruel Carolina sun. "Go all the way. You all have the talent. You have a real chance to repeat."

Coach K took a long sip of soda—he never drank alcohol around us—and waited for someone to say something. I don't think any man in this country understood the current state of college basketball better than Coach K did. He knew who the movers and the shakers were, which players were entering or exiting, to what team and coach they were going, and how they'd likely fair. Coach K had the best possible handle on what next year's field would look like. He liked the way we stacked up.

Jay, Mike, and I looked at one another. We trusted Coach K. We knew he'd do anything to make us better players and staying one more year at Duke could do that.

"Alright, Coach," Jay said. "Let's do it. But win or lose next year, we move on to the NBA." Mike and I agreed.

With our pledges made, the three of us remained at Duke for our junior year. CeCe and I found our own apartment off campus and I went through a third preseason of preparation.

We kicked off our junior-year campaign with a three-game series in Hawaii. We were the Associated Press's No. 1–ranked team and it showed, as we plowed through the competition like a John Deere tractor for twelve straight games. Some of the victories were outright batterings where we won by 20, 30, and even 40 points. But that all came crashing down in our thirteenth game of the 2002 season against Florida State.

We weren't expected to lose to the Seminoles, a decent, but not stellar team with an 8–5 record. Still, it was a close game to the end, when Florida State's Monte Cummings got past Jay and scored a layup over Mike with only seconds left to take the lead. Coach K was irate from the bench, as we launched our final assault down the court to score. However, Jay's shot was blocked and Mike's attempt to rebound and shoot left the ball circling the rim before it was unceremoniously spit out. We lost 76–77.

It was a hard defeat that sent us all barreling back to Earth. We were not impervious.

"They were tougher than we were," Coach K soberly told the press, and it was a quieter than usual trip back to North Carolina. We all knew we hadn't played our best and Coach K's silence was just as effective at letting us know it.

The loss to Florida State snapped our twelve-game winning streak, but we had to pick ourselves up for a home game against Georgia Tech two days later. I walked into our locker room a few hours before our 7:00 p.m. game, and saw white index cards plastered to every possible surface. They covered the walls, the doors and even sealed our locker doors shut. The cards all said the same thing in typed black lettering: Attack.

As the rest of the team arrived, we all looked to each other for an explanation. Suddenly, the lights cut out and an assistant pressed Play on the VCR in the corner. The TV came alive, illuminating our faces. It was the film *Braveheart*, cued up to Mel Gibson's famous William Wallace speech.

"They may take our lives," the blue-painted Wallace told the Scottish troops heading into battle. "But they'll never take our freedom!"

The lights came back on and Coach K charged into the room wearing a Viking helmet. He rolled onto the floor and popped his body back up again like Willy Wonka in front of his chocolate factory, the helmet still intact.

"Attack!" Coach K screamed like a banshee. "Let's attack!" On his enthusiasm alone, we stormed out of the locker room and trounced poor Georgia Tech 104–79. They didn't stand a chance. Coach K's performance came at the right time. We rattled off eight more wins before we met Florida State again exactly one month and a day later. We buried them with a death knell score of 80–49.

We only lost two more times that season and rolled into the 2002 NCAA Tourney with a 26–3 record and the No. 3 seed. We were crackin', humming like a well-oiled machine. In the ACC Tournament, we took out North Carolina, Wake Forest, then NC State, which buoyed us back up to the No. 1 seed in our NCAA bracket. Taking out the No. 16 Winthrop was an easy affair with a final score of 84–37. We faced No. 8 Notre Dame in the second round, besting them 84–77 and qualifying for the Sweet Sixteen a third year in a row. So far, everything was moving along as planned.

In Lexington, Kentucky, we faced the No. 5–ranked Indiana Hoosiers. We were up by 17 points, but the underdogs chipped away at our precarious lead until we were down by a basket with only 4 seconds left on the clock. Jay shot a three-pointer, which bounced off the rim. I snatched the ball and reflexively hurled it up, but didn't reach the target. The buzzer beckoned Hoosier fans onto the floor. Winning with a score of 74–73, Indiana was advancing to the Elite Eight. Our journey was over and I couldn't get to sleep that night, my body fighting with my mind at the realization that this was it with my brothers.

I think of that game from time to time and it irks me because of the finality it signaled. My time at Duke was over. The experience was invaluable, and my junior year stats cemented my name in Duke's history books. In three years, I'd started 93 of 101 games, averaging 15 points and 7 rebounds. My career field goal percentage remained both a Duke and ACC record, until Zion Williamson came to Duke in 2018. I credit my father for making me shoot the ball daily from everywhere on the court. It was hardwired into me to set my feet and shoot without thinking.

Getting stopped in the Sweet Sixteen didn't seem to cool NBA coaches on any of us. As we'd promised in Coach K's backyard, Jay, Mike, and I had decided to leave college a year early for the 2002 NBA Draft.

Not long after, Coach K summoned me to his office. I thought back to our first meeting in our Juneau living room three years earlier. Coach K had more than delivered on his promises. He'd led us to a National Championship. He'd made me work harder than I ever thought I could. He'd molded me into an NBA player.

"Carlos, you're about to embark on your dream," Coach K started. "Just follow your intuition and stay true to who you are. You will have a lot of interest. A lot of people will be pulling on you for your time. For your money. Agents. Scammers. *Shark Tank*–types with zany ideas they want you to invest in, which is just as good as flushing cash down the toilet."

I knew I was going to miss this man, but he spoke again before I could tell him. I'm sure he knew already.

"Now, get out of here," Coach K ordered. "I have a championship to win next year." He busied himself with some paperwork in front of him, signaling that our talk was over. Knowing Coach, the next me or Jay or Mike, or maybe even all three were listed on the paper he was holding and were en route to Durham and the greatest coach in all of college basketball.

I rose and let myself out, feeling ready for anything the NBA dished my way, knowing I had Coach K's seal of approval.

"Oh, and Carlos?" Coach K asked, his gaze leaving the paper. "Good luck in the Draft."

# CHAPTER 8

## THE DRAFT

It was humiliating. By far, the most embarrassing moment of my life. The night that had played out in my head on repeat for the last decade, lulling me contently to sleep. Basketball hopefuls visualize the night their name is read aloud at the NBA Draft much the way some girls know every minute detail of their dream wedding.

My draft night was a nightmare.

Though we'd been invited, my family and I opted out of attending the 2002 Draft at Madison Square Garden in New York City. Instead, about twenty friends and family gathered at my parents' house in Cary to watch the Draft live on TNT. My mom laid out a spread with all of my favorite foods for our night of celebration years in the making. Sliced steak and chicken were fanned out on platters. The mashed potatoes and collard greens were steaming.

As our guests arrived, they shook my hand and congratulated me. The television blared in the background as our guests grazed from the buffet and formed their own pockets of conversation around the living room. With everything in place, all we had to do was wait for my name to be called out on live television, with millions watching along with us.

We weren't throwing darts blindfolded, though. There were some things my father and I knew going into the night, based on what positions the NBA teams needed filled for the upcoming season and the individual team tryouts that had taken place the previous month.

"The Houston Rockets select Yao Ming," NBA commissioner David Stern announced from his podium. Via satellite, the seven-foot-six juggernaut sat with his family on their own living room couch somewhere in China, smiling sheepishly when one of his miniature relatives gave him a high five. Ming getting scooped up at No. 1 had been predicted, as it had been when my teammates Jay Williams and Mike Dunleavy were selected at No. 2 and 3 in quick succession. Jay was off to the Chicago Bulls and Mike went to the Golden State Warriors.

"Alright J-Will and Dun-Dun," I toasted out loud to my friends, but internally I girded myself for at least another hour of not hearing my name. As a power forward, I was expected to land somewhere between the fifteenth and twenty-fifth pick in the latter part of the first round.

I moved behind my father, who was seated comfortably on the couch, and put my hands on his shoulders. I held tight to my Rock of Gibraltar.

"At No. 5, the Denver Nuggets select Nikoloz Tskitishvili," Commissioner Stern announced to immediate applause. A seven-foot Georgian who'd already played a pro-level year and won a championship in the Italian League, Tskitishvili was a solid choice.

"Los, we're probably going to see a bit more of this," my father noted to me over his shoulder, referring to a new NBA rule that season that would allow the teams to draft foreign athletes, but keep them overseas for a far less costly development period until they were called up. It was an appetizing way to call dibs on international players without paying them big salaries up front, and we were watching its effect on the Draft in real time. Two picks later, my father only bolstered his observation when six-foot-eleven Brazilian Nenê Hilario's name was called out as the seventh pick, sending him to the New York Knicks.

As the evening rolled on, a nagging anticipation pulled at my chest. I just wanted to get it over with already. I felt vulnerable, and a discouraging thought crept its way up into my consciousness. *Had my workouts with the NBA teams not gone as well as I'd thought?*

Coach K said the coaches had all followed up with him afterward. Still, that was no guarantee any of them wanted me. I tried to beat down my sudden doubts by concentrating on the players getting called. At No. 9, the Phoenix Suns snapped up Amar'e Stoudemire, the sole player that year to go straight from high school to the NBA. Stoudemire was an explosive, versatile six-foot-ten player who could go at forward or center—precisely the type of player GMs dream of. I would have picked him myself.

Caron Butler went to the Miami Heat at No. 10. No surprises there. Butler had two very strong seasons at UConn, the type of instant-impact player who was rarely going to see an upperclassman's season at the college level.

Picks eleven through fourteen didn't faze me, even though three of the four players selected were power forwards. Fifteen was my magic number, its pending arrival signaled by my father posturing up and telling the room to hush.

"Here we go," he said, maybe more to himself than the rest of us.

"For the fifteenth selection, the Houston Rockets select Boštjan Nachbar," Stern told the TV cameras. Nachbar was a twenty-two-year-old, six-foot-nine Slovenian who'd gained momentum in the pro Italian league over the last two years. Definitely not an obvious choice, but there were nine more names to be read before the first round ended. I *would* be one of those names.

The very next name called was Jiří Welsch, a twenty-two-year-old Czech who went to the Philadelphia 76ers. Another foreign player that nobody had heard of until tonight. *What was going on?*

My mind started doing some basketball arithmetic. In the preceding month, I'd been invited to work out for Orlando, Miami, the Clippers, and Lakers; Charlotte, Milwaukee, Golden State, Phoenix, Denver, Detroit, and Utah. Of those, I thought I'd really clicked with Utah, Miami, and Orlando, but I knew I'd be ecstatic to join any squad. Those eleven teams each held at least one Draft pick between No. 5 and No. 27, with the Lakers my last chance to be any team's first choice.

The Pistons made their second pick at No. 23, but skipped me over again for small forward Tayshaun Prince. Nenad Krstić, a seven-foot Serbian power forward, claimed slot No. 25.

The No. 27 pick was my last chance to become the top selection of any of the eleven teams I'd tried out for. And it was the Lakers. To say I wanted to play for the Lakers would have been an understatement. They had Kobe Bryant and Shaquille O'Neal, a rare combination of two dominant players in two different positions. With back-to-back NBA championships, the franchise was hot to threepeat. I was flown out that May, while the team was in the playoffs. I worked out with a couple of players, though not the stars, while Coach Phil Jackson eyed me from his office window looking over the court.

I felt my tryout went well, so my spirits were high as I entered the locker room. I took a lap around the room, greeting everybody with a dap—even Kobe, who'd arrived with a few others for practice. And then Shaq came in.

"What's up, young fella?" he asked in his unmistakable baritone.

"Yo, that's diesel right there," I said to whoever was standing within earshot. Kobe shook his head and turned back to his locker. I was starstruck. Shaq was one of my idols for his dominant play, but also for the sheer humor and joy he brought to the game. I had a Shaq poster on my wall and must have watched thousands of videos of him. Standing right in front of me, I knew this was the biggest guy that God had ever created. I wanted to play with him and Kobe because they were the best. I wanted to play against the best—even in the NBA.

Instead, the Lakers selected Chris Jefferies, a short forward. Now every team I'd met with in person had passed on me. I could only hope that some team, any team, just one team had me as their second or even third choice.

My eyes darted around the room looking at everyone's expressions, but I'll be damned if a single person looked back at me. An uncomfortable feeling hung in the air, as if the groom was being ditched at the altar and his audience was trapped, watching helplessly from the pews. I was on the most public job interview possible, getting turned down over and over on national television. On top of that, we all got to see who kept getting the job over me.

Had I missed something? Was there some glaring flaw in my game I'd never noticed about to smack me in the face like a two-by-four? Had I rubbed someone the wrong way at workouts and maybe word had gotten around? Was I just not as good as everyone told me I was?

In that moment, I selfishly thought of Rashard Lewis during the 1998 Draft. Lewis was one of those talents who'd been scouted by a few solid schools, but opted to skip college to go right into the NBA. Throughout the Draft evening, he watched as other selectees' names were called, hugged their relieved-looking parents and left them in a backstage green room for an on-camera walk to the auditorium stage. The green room held fifteen invited players plus their entourages, huddled around their banquet tables, while about twenty-six other invitees and their groups sat in the main auditorium.

The more names called, the faster the green room thinned
out until Lewis, his family, and agent were the only ones left at
their lonely banquet table. At one point, Lewis got up and left
the green room altogether with his hand covering his face. The
commentators quickly volleyed to another subject, but we players watching from home knew exactly what he was doing. My
man had to leave to go cry in the bathroom, so no one would
see him—and trust me, I got that. You don't want to make
it this far and fall flat on your face on live television. Lewis
sweated it out until the Seattle Supersonics drafted him in the
32nd slot, which closed out the first round. He and his group
were the last ones to leave the green room. Standing there in
my parent's living room, I was secretly elated that I hadn't sub-
jected myself and my family to that added drama by just staying home altogether.

Before my mind could sink further into uncertainty, my cell
phone vibrated in my jeans pocket. It was my new agent, Rob
Pelinka. While we were all sweating it out in our living room,
Rob had been plugged into the percolating back-channel network between the owners, GMs, coaches, and agents. Each announced pick set off a new wave of last-minute negotiations, as
the chess pieces moved into place one by one.

"If you go to 36, the Knicks are going to pick you up," he said
quickly, trying to ease the embarrassing sting he knew I already
felt. Rob had played in three NCAA Final Four tournaments
for the University of Michigan before becoming a lawyer and
now a sports agent. He understood the sacrifice it took to get to
this moment. I whispered the information to my father, careful that no one overheard us should something else go wrong.

"The Knicks," he mouthed silently to me, his head bobbing,
as if to say, "Not bad."

With Rob's words, I downshifted and tried to relax a little.
Six more picks and I'd be in the NBA. I could make this. The
Knicks weren't a bad place to land, a storied franchise. Walt

Frazier, Willis Reed in the '70s. Patrick Ewing and the rest of the Big Apple gang in the '80s and '90s. I'd be fist-bumping Spike Lee courtside after my big plays. Not to mention the city's culture—I envisioned CeCe and me taking in Broadway shows and eating by candlelight at a selection of the finest restaurants in the world. Maybe we'd hit up a club for dancing afterward. Yes, I could see that. I just needed to survive six more picks.

As the draft's second round started, I stayed perched behind my father, my hands still resting on his shoulders. It just didn't feel right to move from that spot until we knew. Unfortunately, the live telecast had thrown to a panel of analysts, who dove into a deep breakdown of the first-round picks, intermingled with sporadic updates on the second-round selections. There was no more live coverage of the names being read. Suddenly, we were in the dark. So, we waited.

Somewhere in those next few minutes, my name appeared out of the blue on the screen with a few others. I'd been snapped up at No. 35 by the Cleveland Cavaliers. A quick cheer erupted across the room and I felt my father pat my hand in approval.

*Cleveland*, I thought. I hadn't even worked out for Cleveland. Did teams even consider players they hadn't invited to work out? I wondered who from that franchise had wanted me enough to take a chance on me and when could I shake their hand?

Whatever the reasons, I was relieved. I'd cycled through pretty much all my emotions in just a few hours—from confidence and excitement to anger and embarrassment. When expectations are high and you don't meet them, well, it can throw a young man for a loop.

I couldn't help but feel disappointed and hurt, even as friends and family congratulated me. I'd built up an incredible resumé at Duke, and that hadn't been enough.

My cell phone buzzed again, pulling me out of those negative thoughts. Natasha was calling from her dorm's pay phone. She was crying, outwardly more upset that I'd been picked so late in the evening. I was immediately touched by her protectiveness over me.

"It's going to be alright, Tash," I told her soothingly, simultaneously trying to convince myself of what I was telling her.

"But they didn't even show your name getting called out!" she sobbed.

"And that's okay," I told her. "I am so grateful that I got picked at all. I didn't get a low number, but I got a number, just like the thirty-four guys ahead of me. Tash, I'm going to the NBA."

"Yes, you are," my father said, as I got off the phone and our last guests filtered out. "And you know, we're going to make the best of it. This is what we've been fighting for."

My dad and I sat down at the kitchen table to analyze an outcome that none of us had expected. International players had been the X factor, for sure, as the 2002 Draft set a record with seventeen foreign selections. China's Ming became the first ever player without game experience in the US to go No. 1. A good handful of these foreign players eclipsed my suddenly inadequate six-foot-nine frame, too.

"Seven foot five. Seven foot one. Seven foot." My father rattled off the heights of all these behemoths soon to invade the NBA. "You're going to have to show them you can defend these taller players."

My dad was right. Eight power forwards had been selected before me. There were obviously too many question marks in the coaches' heads around me for any of them to pull the trigger. Their guts had told them "no." I tore off a corner of notepad paper and jotted down the names of three players who'd been surprisingly selected ahead of me. I'd pull it out my wallet periodically and stare at the names to remind myself of that night and that nothing is ever guaranteed.

"All those teams overlooked you," my father said, "but that doesn't matter now. You're in. You made it. From Auke Bay to the NBA. Not bad, right?"

"Pops," I said, trying to find the words for my gratitude, but with my father, simple had always worked best between us. "Thank you."

He smiled and shuffled off to bed, leaving me with my thoughts. I had to put things in perspective. As my parents taught me, I had to look at the bigger picture. I'd been one of fifty-seven basketball players in the world to gain entry into the NBA in 2002. As I looked over the list, I noticed a few good names absent, players I would've thought better than me. It made me even more thankful to have been selected.

"Look at it this way, Carlos," Coach K said, when we spoke the next day. "You're not locked into a long contract for four, five, six years. You'll have a lot more flexibility to negotiate a bigger contract after the two years. This isn't a bad thing at all."

My father and Coach K's words helped me see that my late selection could be a blessing in disguise—something I could build on. Who's to say what would have happened if I'd been locked into a five-year contract with a franchise out of the gate? Would I have been as hungry those first few years? I know rejection gave me a new goal. I'd go out there and prove myself every night if I had to. Someone from the Cleveland Cavaliers had seen something in me. Whatever that was, I was going to pour it on.

But before I reported to Cleveland, I made a quick trip out to LA, to sign paperwork with my new agent, Rob Pelinka, a connection made through EBO teammate DeShawn Stevenson, who was drafted by the Utah Jazz straight out of high school in 2000.

"I have someone I want you to meet," Rob said, who'd made plans to attend a Lakers game. I knew it had to be Kobe Bryant, whom he also represented. Fresh off his second NBA championship, Kobe was at the top of the mountain and arguably the best player in the game.

"Hello, Carlos," Kobe said after the game, as we loitered

around in the bowels of the Staples Center. I couldn't believe my luck in signing with the agent who also repped Kobe. I suddenly had access to the best pickup game in all of LA. The next day, I met up with Kobe and a few others at the UCLA basketball court. A steady stream of NBA pros flowed in and out, including Baron Davis and Paul Pierce. I was rubbing elbows with gods.

We'd finished a pickup game and switched to King of the Court, a one-on-one ball drill that kept the winner playing and the loser packing. We watched as Kobe picked us off one by one, making shot after shot for the next forty minutes straight. It didn't matter who was on the court with him. Kobe kept connecting.

"Unbelievable," Paul Pierce muttered on his way to the sidelines. Then, it was my turn to challenge "the Black Mamba." I stood in front of Kobe, took a defensive stance and suddenly he was off. His footwork was crisp, his body movements so polished. He didn't have to be the fastest because he was so efficient. We must have gone for about twenty minutes before I was able to get control of the ball; Kobe just kept scoring on me over and over again. It happened so quickly, that I didn't have time to get embarrassed. Everyone else had been shut down, too. Eventually, Kobe rebounded the ball a final time, placed it gently down onto a court line and walked away because no one could take him out. That gym was full of future All-Stars from wall to wall. He smoked us all. He was that good.

This trip started my relationship with Kobe, a mentorship we'd revisit every summer, as he rated my and my teammate's performances that season and gave advice. I learned to block a couple hours out for these annual calls, because Kobe could talk about basketball with a depth and sophistication I hadn't heard from another player and never would. The first time Kobe and I spoke, I was in Paris for an NBA appearance. *How did I get here?* I thought, staring out the hotel window at the Eiffel Tower as

Kobe jabbered on. Sometimes, if I thought the advice was good, I'd slip it into a conversation with the GM or head coach.

During the summers, I made it a point to go train for a couple of weeks wherever Kobe was. Kobe's work ethic was legendary among his peers. He had an insane drive for perfection and would lock himself away in a gym all summer to master one skill, if that's what it took. Meeting and working out with Kobe that first time made up for some of the Draft's bite.

The next week, I flew up to Cleveland to meet my new team and coach, John Lucas. We would train together for a couple of weeks, then join about thirty other NBA teams in the annual Summer League. Coach Lucas was the reason I got drafted and the longer I spent with him, the less I held on to the fact that eleven teams had passed on me.

Coach Lucas had been the first pick in the 1976 Draft. Under stratospheric expectations, he'd shown brilliance as a lightning-fast point guard who could score as fluently as he could lead an offense. His career had also been riddled with failed drug tests due to a recurring cocaine addiction. It would lead him to launch a substance-abuse recovery program for athletes later in life. During his fourteen-year career, Lucas played for six NBA franchises, then coached in the league for nearly a decade before I landed on his doorstep. This man understood struggles and I knew immediately he was the kind of guy I could play for.

For a twenty-year-old kid entering the NBA, I couldn't have asked for a more patient and attentive teacher than Coach Lucas. He had an immediate faith in me when so many skeptical coaches doubted me. Our team traveled to Utah for the Summer League, a less publicized series of games where the NBA teams tweaked and cemented their lineups, mostly away from the public eye.

"I see that chip on your shoulder and I like it," Coach Lucas told me before our first game. "Go out there and remind everyone how they overlooked you."

*Overlooked* was the same word my father had used the night of the Draft; that word was a trigger. I was a bull seeing red.

"Don't worry," I told him. "I'm going to ball out, Coach." And that's exactly what I did. I averaged 25 points and 12 rebounds per game, multiple games a day over the entire week. I kicked ass in that Summer League so thoroughly that I swear I saw a few coaches look Lucas's way with jealous longing.

I flew back home to North Carolina energized for the wedding CeCe and I'd been planning since I'd proposed to her a year earlier. The plan had been to get married as soon as I secured my NBA contract. Buoyed by my strong Summer League showing, Rob negotiated me a rarer two-year deal with an option for a third year, when most rookies only got one and one. My starting salary was $425,000, an astronomical sum for something I loved to do, but also a relief because it meant I could finally help improve my family's quality of life.

CeCe and I were married that August at her family's church in the town of Hamer, about an hour north of Durham. I was half an hour late to the ceremony because I'd booked a hotel too far from the church. CeCe gave me a mildly perturbed glance when I joined her at the altar, which I chased away with an apologetic smile.

Otherwise, it was a beautiful affair set against the lush Carolina scenery. I was flanked by my Duke brothers, J-Will, Chris Duhon, and Dahntay Jones. My assistant coach, Wojo, also attended; Coach K wasn't able to make it. My best man and brother, Charles, who was forging his own high school basketball career right behind me, raised his sparkling apple juice for a touching toast. He told me how proud he was of me, and the feeling was mutual. Charles would go on to play for Iowa State University and overcome a torn ACL injury his junior year to play for the NBA's minor "G" League and the National Basketball League of Canada. It wasn't easy following in his big brother's footsteps, but Charles did it well.

CeCe and I finished packing our belongings into her Jeep Cherokee and a Lincoln Navigator I'd bought with part of a $100,000 advance, and we drove the 545 miles north to Cleveland. The Cavs paid for movers for our bigger items and we settled into an apartment downtown by the arena. I loved being close to my job, and I was dead serious about being good at it. I spent five to six hours a day with Coach Lucas and the team, running our plays and reviewing film on the teams we'd be facing. Coach also had me at the gym an hour before practice, working one-on-one. And I'd stay an hour after practice working with him some more.

Money wasn't one of the first things that initially drew me to the NBA, but after the years of financial sacrifice my family had made for me, I was glad I could finally start repaying them. I used some of my initial salary for a down payment on a home for my family back in North Carolina. My parents, who never once complained about their surroundings, picked out a five-bedroom house with a basement and a big backyard. My parents and siblings had lived in apartments going back twenty years to DC. They'd only moved into their first rental house the previous year. This would be the first house my family would own, a culmination of the effort everyone put in to help me get to the NBA. My parents' contributions were too many to list, while Natasha babysat countless weekends so they could attend my many tournaments and camps. When my parents decided to move the clan to North Carolina for my second year at Duke, Charles and my two younger sisters didn't moan, though it meant they were leaving dear friends in high school and middle school behind. Not all athletes are born into families that support their careers the way mine had. They put all of their eggs in one basket with me. The least I could do was buy them a house.

As my family gushed over their new castle, CeCe and I set out to make a home of our own in Cleveland and soon my first NBA season opener was upon us, an away game against the Sacramento Kings. In the ARCO Arena locker room, that feeling of nerves and excitement rose in me like a familiar friend. The last time I'd felt this way was three years earlier, standing behind the curtain before I'd entered the arena for my first Duke game. The same feeling I got when my mind and body went into autopilot, prepared to level up. By now, this extra rush of adrenaline let me know that I was ready.

That's not to say I didn't think about Chris Webber, the first NBA player I'd be facing off against in my professional career. Basketball is a team sport until your stats are held up to the player you're defending, and my first draw was one of the best in the league. One of the University of Michigan's legendary Fab Five squad, Chris was nearly a decade into his NBA career and on his way to his fifth All-Star appearance. I'd watched him on TV for years with my father. He was one of the best power forwards in the world and I knew he was better than me. That was a simple fact. Still, there was only one way to improve in the NBA. I had to go out there and meet him.

*Ready to level up, Chris?* I thought. Chris gave me the affirmative. I could feel it in my bones.

I played eleven minutes and forty-one seconds in my first game, an away loss to the Sacramento Kings on October 29, 2002. I scored two baskets, but Coach Lucas said I'd done a great job, regardless. He was very supportive like that and sometimes I wished I could see myself through his eyes.

I didn't have to wait long to figure out what Coach had seen in me. Thirteen games into the season, I became a starter and jumped to over thirty minutes of game play, racking up a very decent 16 points. I started for the majority of the season.

A couple of weeks later, I was on the court, standing just feet away from my idol, Michael Jordan, when we took on the Wizards in a 107–100 loss. I'm not sure the word *surreal* could do those few minutes justice. My mind truly struggled to comprehend I was sharing the same court with the man who had inspired my entire basketball journey. I was so enamored with Jordan that I approached him in the Bulls' locker room afterward, my own Air Jordans in hand for him to sign. I wasn't going to take the chance of not meeting him again, embarrassment be damned.

"I don't like a lot of new guys," Jordan said, his eyes on scribbling his name with a black pen, "but the NBA needs more players like you. You play hard. You play passionately. You're very enthusiastic about the game."

I think I thanked Jordan, but I'll never know for sure if I actually got the words out. Our team played Jordan and the Wizards two more times during my first season, both losses, before he officially retired.

In truth, my childhood idols were coming at me left and right. In January 2003, I was paired against Shaquille O'Neal in a 115–99 loss to the Lakers. The big guy racked up 26 points in thirty-one minutes and I know he got a couple highlight-reel dunks in over me, leaving me befuddled under the net. I scored 6 points.

At seven foot one and 330 pounds, Shaq defied the laws of physics. Maybe gravity, too. You can be seven foot and a clumsy clown, but Shaq was so athletic and far more coordinated than a man his size should be. When you added in his power, everyone knew to have his feet firmly underneath him if Shaq came barreling his way. The man had brute force that made your teeth rattle upon impact. He was like nobody else I'd ever seen before, a puzzle on the court I wasn't sure I could solve.

In February, six-foot-eleven Kevin Garnett—already a seven-time NBA All-Star and the MVP of its 2003 All-Star game— gave me all I could handle when we faced off against Minnesota twice. The combination of the Big Ticket's size, athleticism, touch, footwork, defense work, and determination made him one of the greatest challenges I'd face. Anytime I was able to push 25 or even 30 points past him—which happened only twice in seventeen games—it was because I'd worked my tail off to get it. I considered that a major accomplishment, even in defeat.

In March, I started to hit my stride with my teammates. Many of us were NBA newcomers, so we called ourselves the "Young Gunners." It was us against the world. Ricky Davis, a swingman who could play shooting guard and small forward, remained our best scorer. He was very capable, averaging 20 points a game. Seven-foot Zydrunas Ilgauskas was one of the best players to come out of Lithuania. "Big Z" was a six-season veteran, a real workhorse who averaged about 17 points and 7 rebounds per game. He took me under his wing, meeting me every morning to get our first workout done. I brought him coffee.

As the season rolled on, my teammates tallied good stats, and mine were improving, but we always seemed to lose. It eventually dawned on me during a midseason game, sitting on the bench, watching another defeat play out in front of me. Coach Lucas hadn't played our two best players, Ricky and Big Z, in the fourth quarter.

"What's the deal?" I asked a teammate, who smirked that I'd finally connected the dots.

He mouthed two syllables.

"Le-Bron."

LeBron James. Everyone had heard of the unreal high school senior playing out of St. Vincent-St. Mary's, who was heading straight into the next Draft. A game-changing athlete like LeBron—heralded as the next Jordan—came through the NBA once in a generation, and every franchise wanted to be the one to catch lightning in a bottle. But what made LeBron especially tantalizing to Cleveland was that he'd been born in Akron, forty miles outside of their city. He was a homegrown superstar and the Cavs wanted him badly—badly enough to lose. The NBA rules stated that the league's worst team had the best statistical chance of winning the first Draft pick the next year. It seemed to me that the franchise was throwing an entire season to get the best possible odds for LeBron in the Draft—from whose orders I had no idea. I was never told to play poorly or throw a game. We just weren't playing the right players and the results were obvious.

"It doesn't feel right to lose like this, Pops," I told my father in frustration. Winning was in my DNA and going against it, sitting around and doing nothing as the seconds ticked away, was difficult for me.

"Los, don't forget that the NBA is a business first, and a game second. The ownership can do anything they like because LeBron is a unicorn. He has the potential to transform any franchise into something big and highly profitable for many years to come. If he comes to Cleveland and plays with you, all the better.

"Just concentrate on your game," he added. "Cram those minutes they give you with as many attempts and rebounds as you can. Support your teammates. The rest is out of your control."

I wondered where Coach Lucas stood on all of this, but when our record hit 8–34, he was unceremoniously fired. He privately told a few of us he'd had a hard time treating professional athletes this way and was no longer willing to toe the line. I had a lot of respect for Coach Lucas. He was honorable to the core.

Keith Smart was brought in to replace Coach Lucas and we went 9–31 under his leadership, finishing 17–64 for the season. The Cavs franchise seemed pleased. Our dismal record gave it the highest 22.5 percent chance of winning the Draft's first pick. Now it would come down to a bunch of Ping-Pong balls tumbling around a lottery machine cage.

A local TV station jumped on the news the night of our last game, running a what-if segment on LeBron coming to Cleveland. It included locker room interviews shot months earlier, right in the heat of our grueling season.

The reporter asked many of us what we thought about LeBron

coming to Cleveland, but they asked me while the guy who played the same position sat behind me within earshot.

"He's good, but we have other guys in the same position that are better," I answered, "but the sky's the limit for him." I was hoping to spare my teammate's feelings because I didn't want to discount his growth and progression throughout the season. Instead, it came off like I didn't think LeBron was as talented as everyone else did. That couldn't have been further from the truth. I was excited at the prospect of finally winning and we all knew he brought a skillset that could help get us there. That July, the Cavs signed LeBron James to a four-year contract for $18.8 million, changing the Cleveland franchise forever.

As for me, I had a great first season, averaging 10 points and 7.5 rebounds per game. I had 54 starts and 21 double-doubles, where my scoring and rebounds counted into the double digits. I'd performed well above what was expected of a second-round draftee, so much that I was named to the All-Rookie second team, an honorary role voted on by the coaches. The media was calling me the biggest steal of the entire 2002 draft and that felt good. Really good. This was more like it.

# CHAPTER 9

## LEBRON

"Did you hear what happened to Jay Williams?"

My eyelids opened suddenly, my neck snapped up from my dazing in the hot tub, as another teammate slipped down into the round pool to join us. Big Z and I had finished our morning workout at the arena and the steaming water eased our muscles.

"He was in a bad motorcycle accident."

"You're lying," I said. The words fell out of my mouth before I could stop them. I'd just spoken to Jay a week earlier. He was getting ready to go on vacation with his family to Aruba. There was no way something happened to him. Still, I pulled myself out of the tub and walked briskly into the locker room. A TV mounted in the corner, set to ESPN 24/7, confirmed the unbelievable news. And it was bad. As bad as it gets.

It was mid-June, and Jay had wanted to take advantage of the sunny weather by riding the motorcycle he'd purchased a week earlier to a business meeting. He hadn't been wearing a helmet when he and his bike collided with a utility pole in Chicago. Luckily, Jay wasn't riding alone when he crashed and help got to him quickly, possibly a saving grace for what the *SportsCenter* commentators were calling a "horrific" accident. My heart sank down to the pit of my stomach.

I grabbed my cell phone from my locker and frantically dialed Jay's number, convinced he'd pick up and tell me he was fine. However, a dozen attempts went straight to his voice mail. His mother's and girlfriend's phones were the same. I wanted to get to his side, but I couldn't reach anybody for the next few days, as details from the collision trickled through the media outlets. Even Jay's agent was having difficulty getting information about his whereabouts. I knew he was likely still in Chicago, but I didn't know which hospital.

"It's very bad, Carlos," Jay's mother said, when she called me back, four days after the crash. I could hear the exhaustion in her voice. *Bad* seemed to be the word everyone used to describe Jay's current state. "He was going too fast."

I'd figured that already. I knew my best friend had a penchant for speed and an adventurous, boundary-pushing spirit. I hopped on the first plane I could to Chicago, but couldn't get in to see him. He was heavily sedated in the intensive care unit and had already undergone at least one major operation to mend a severed artery in his left leg.

"He jerked his bike enough to avoid a head-on collision, but he almost lost his leg," I was told. "The doctors weren't even sure he was going to survive the surgery."

Though we spoke sooner over the phone, I didn't see Jay for another two months, as he remained in the hospital undergoing a series of additional surgeries to repair his left side. He dislocated his knee, tearing every ligament in the process and needed over a hundred staples to bring his muscle and skin back together. Jay had a lengthy recovery period ahead of him if he hoped to walk again. Professional basketball was out of the question, though. About a week after the crash, the Chicago Bulls released Jay from his contract and drafted a replacement. Jay never played in the NBA again.

Jay's family brought him back to Durham for his rehabilitation through Duke University Health, which boasted some of the best facilities and staff in the country. As soon as he was settled, I flew in to meet my former teammate at his parent's house. He was sitting in a wheelchair, left leg elevated, his face thin. His loose sweatpants bulged over the leg, covering whatever gruesomeness lay beneath. It was a shocking visual. In the blink of an eye, the No. 2 pick from the Draft the year before was in a wheelchair in his parent's living room. A bird with clipped wings, and my thoughts drifted to Chris. So much potential cut too short. Jay looked over to me.

"The stuff they have me on makes me so loopy," he said, wincing hard as he jostled his body the tiniest bit in his chair.

"I bet," I answered, taking a seat on the couch across from him. We sat in silence for a while, both of us not ready yet to face that our basketball journey together was ending. We'd made plans to play at All-Star games and the Olympics together. We were going to play in the NBA Finals together, but all of those plans were over.

I watched Jay's eyes drift shut and rose to leave him, but he jerked awake at my movement. "Stay," he said. So, we sat some more in silence, the radio on low in the background.

I stayed with Jay, his parents, and their two Rottweiler dogs for a couple of days, trying to keep our time together lighthearted. There was no talk about the accident nor the NBA. It was a confusing time for Jay and his family and I wanted to be the calming presence that my best friend said I'd always been for him. When I went to leave, he wished me a good season, and I had to swallow down the bitterness I felt for such a talented athlete to be cheated so early in life. In the coming months, Jay and I would speak a few times a week, as he battled through recovery, depression, and a suicide attempt. He lost his identity without basketball.

Jay's untimely NBA exit was quickly overshadowed by LeBron's arrival, and the Cavs franchise went all out in their preparations. They hired a new coach, Paul Silas, and we got new uniforms with a different color scheme and a revamped logo—all not-so-subtle ways of conveying that a new era was upon us. For a town like Cleveland, that had been cursed in all three major sports for decades, LeBron was the second coming.

The hype surrounding LeBron had been building for years, accelerated by the introduction of internet videos that gave everyone a glimpse of his talents to dissect and discuss—something Jordan hadn't had the benefit of for the majority of his career. It's no small feat for a high school player to make the cover of *Sports Illustrated*, but LeBron did it as a junior in 2002, beside the words "The Chosen One." Kevin Garnett was the only other high school player I'd seen on the magazine's cover, and his 1995 title was more subdued with the phrase "Ready or Not..."

Teammate Darius Miles was also criticized for what he'd said about LeBron in that locker room video prior to his joining the team. Still, Darius had made a good point. "You really think just bringing in a high school player will turn things around like that?" he'd asked the interviewer, not out of maliciousness, but with the knowledge that a direct leap from high school to the NBA had been a tough one for every single player who tried it.

Even Kobe hadn't made an immediate impact in the NBA when he'd been drafted out of high school by the Lakers in 1996. There was always a period of adjustment over a few seasons before a player's career started to cook. How long would it take LeBron to adjust? At our first summer practice, we started to find out.

LeBron took it to the hoop on a drive and leaped from outside the paint, sailing clean over six-foot-three Belizean point guard Milt Palacio and finishing with a crisp dunk. I'd heard stories about Jordan or Julius "Dr. J" Irving pulling amazing aerial moves in practice that were sadly never captured on camera. Watching LeBron at that first practice gave me the feeling that this should have been recorded. By the end of that first practice there was no doubt that LeBron was the best player on our team. LeBron had the same skills as the rest of us, though he moved faster and jumped higher—pretty amazing for a teenager when the rest of us were in our twenties.

The league got to know LeBron alongside us during our summer session. The NBA Summer League was typically a pedestrian affair, with press and public alike paying it little notice. Its function wasn't to publicize the league or build anticipation for the season, but to give green players a chance to get valuable game experience, and teams a good look at budding talent that might otherwise not be initially seen.

LeBron changed all that because everyone couldn't wait to see him play against NBA-level competition. Over a month that summer, in four different locations, the media and fans followed LeBron on the circuit. Summer League games were usually held in smaller practice gyms with anywhere from a few hundred to a couple thousand spectators on hand to watch. LeBron's debut happened at the Orlando Magic's sold-out 17,000-seat arena. When we made our way onto the floor, the crowd erupted for LeBron, as if we were already deep into the regular season.

The eighteen-year-old didn't disappoint. He defended on every possession, made steals, was a disrupter, and snatched rebounds with authority. He drew fouls and baited people into traps, then slammed them shut with crossovers, feints, and magnificent body control. He even pulled off a 180-degree dunk. LeBron was a Swiss Army knife—he had everything, and man, was he handy. And he wasn't finished. LeBron was still growing into his body, but he was already on another level than the veterans surrounding him.

The moment of truth, however, was our season opener against the Kings at Sacramento's ARCO Arena. There were seventeen thousand hardcore fans there, all rooting for LeBron to fall flat on his face, plus the rest of the world, watching from home.

A typical NBA game might attract one hundred to one hundred fifty camera people on the sidelines; LeBron's debut must have drawn a thousand media members, who spilled out from the sidelines onto the court during warm-ups.

"Yo, back up, bro," I heard a teammate yell at a cameraman who'd almost gotten plowed over by him.

If LeBron was affected by the crushing attention, he didn't show it. He dished out his first assist, an alley-oop dunk that wowed the crowd. Then, he hit a fade-away twenty-footer from the corner over six-foot-eleven All-Star Brad Miller.

Near the end of the first quarter, LeBron connected with me for a two-handed dunk on a fast break. Then, on a break-away moments later, he kicked the rock to Ricky Davis and let him crush the ball in. This was quintessential LeBron. We all had chemistry with him right away because he was an unselfish superstar, who had no qualms passing the ball away to score. Top scorers usually kept that title by shooting the ball themselves. LeBron kept the ball, baited in two or three defenders, then passed it to the free man. He wasn't greedy. This was a player who could score whenever he wanted to, but chose to pass to his teammates—an underrated trait reminiscent of Magic Johnson. Even sharing the ball as he did, LeBron still walked away with 25 points, 9 assists, 6 rebounds and 4 steals in that first game. Losing seemed secondary to how promising our team's future suddenly looked.

As our season progressed, LeBron continued to impress us. He could think on his feet like a computer, observing and inputting data that could help us in real time. I called him the "Human Rolodex" for his ability to pull up info on an opponent he'd stored away in his mind that helped us in some way.

"Booz, your guy's eying me," he said during a three-man play designed to feed "Big Z."

"When we run this again, just duck inside." I got his understanding immediately, moved inside when we ran the play again, received the ball from LeBron and scored. LeBron's on-court acuity matched, if not exceeded, every top player I'd interacted with.

Throughout the season, the entire team was continuously impressed with what was thrown the star rookie's way and how poised he was handling it. Before the season started, Nike flew a few team members out to Sacramento on a private jet to shoot LeBron's first television commercial with the sneaker giant. Shot in one of those narrow old-school gyms to give it the feeling of a church, comedian Bernie Mac gave a rousing sermon about LeBron's arrival to an enthusiastic basketball "congregation." The gym's double doors then parted to reveal LeBron, who completed a series of scorching slam dunks. The rest of the team, myself included, cheered from a second-floor balcony. It took two days to shoot the footage, with a lot of stops, starts, and general waiting around; while Bernie provided comic relief between takes. LeBron was the focus of this circus most of the time, but I didn't hear him complain once. I never saw his face sour, not when he was swarmed by strangers patting him with makeup, straightening his jersey, and water-misting him to give him a sweaty gleam. Even as we shot late into the night, when the thrill was gone, LeBron was courteous and kind. The commercial was a tongue-in-cheek commentary on the crazy expectations being placed on him before he'd even played a game. And with everyone fawning over him, LeBron still walked away from that experience grounded.

That's the thing about LeBron. He was a grounded person heading into the NBA and he stayed that way during a demanding rookie year. When we weren't on the road, he still lived at home with his mother. He dated his high school sweetheart through superstardom and married her a decade later. LeBron had integrity.

Everyone wanted to see LeBron play. For the first time in the Cav's history, all eighty-two games were broadcasted that season, whether by ESPN or a local network. Our games were always packed, but the hot ticket would be when LeBron and the Cavs hit LA. The Lakers always drew a colorful cast of famous actors, musicians, directors, and other Hollywood types to the front rows. Among the crowd, I noticed the Pump Brothers, David and Dana, at a few games and finally got enough courage to go speak to them.

"I know this might sound corny, but I just have to thank you guys," I said. "I was discovered at the Double Pump Camp. You let me bust up one of your boards. I wouldn't be here without it."

That brought identical smiles of recognition to the twins' faces. The Pump Brothers had such a passion for the game and their camp was synonymous with success. If you wanted to take your game to the next level, you attended the Double Pump Camp and you got offers.

For the first half of our season, I don't think the Pump Brothers, nor any other spectators, were disappointed with LeBron's performances. We didn't win often, but we put together some top-shelf plays that ignited the crowd.

Behind the scenes, LeBron reminded me of a prince who'd been molded from birth to do nothing else but be crowned king. No aspect of his basketball career—from the way he dribbled to the way he spoke to the media—seemed to have been left to chance. LeBron wasn't conceited or elitist or even the slightest bit withdrawn.

"Kremes have arrived," he'd announce enthusiastically, delivering a box of the decadent Krispy Kreme donuts to the locker room at every home game.

"Roookieee," a few of the players always yelled, as the team would converge on LeBron holding the box open, a wide smile on his face. LeBron was the best player on the team, but he still had his rookie duties to complete like the rest of us had. LeBron was the eager new kid in school—engaged with everyone and willing to pay his dues to earn his place among us.

Being from the area, he organized pickup games for us at Cleveland State. He went out of his way to be a team player.

LeBron handled everything he did with gusto, and without complaint or a bad attitude. He wasn't cocky or conceited, though he probably had room for a smidgeon of it—that's how good he was. He didn't complain or slack during practice or at games, which goes the longest way on any team. We all liked him. How could we not?

LeBron was humble, almost too humble for what we needed. I noticed that he deferred a lot to our lead scorer, Ricky Davis. It was a sign of respect for the veteran, but as the season wore on, it wasn't winning us games. By midseason, we'd lost more than half the games we played.

After another blistering loss, I boldly approached LeBron in the locker room, finally voicing what all of us were thinking.

"When are you going to step up and take over?" I asked. The locker room hushed around us. The franchise had sacrificed an entire season to draft LeBron. We'd lost sixty-seven of our eighty-two games my rookie season to get him, and we all knew we could be doing better. LeBron was holding back.

Surprise washed over LeBron's face and I saw a flash of the eighteen-year-old kid we'd all forgotten was him. LeBron was the best player on our team, but he needed to hear it said and it needed to be said in front of our entire group. The rest of the locker room chimed in with encouragement after me, making it clear to LeBron that he had all of our permission to tear loose. LeBron then did something that all NBA players do well: he kept it short and sweet.

"I got you, Booz," LeBron said, with an uncharacteristically stern expression that told me we'd gotten through. He turned to the rest of the team. "I've got all of you."

That's when LeBron took off like a rocket. Against Atlanta,

he busted out for 34 points with 7 assists and 6 boards. In early April, we hosted the Nets, and he torched them for 41 points and 13 assists.

Amazingly, during this stretch of stepped-up scoring, LeBron maintained his assists and rebounding. He knew what he had to do and did it. But it was just a little too late. We finished 35–37, just a couple games short of the playoffs behind eighth-seeded Milwaukee. I truly believe that if we'd had that pivotal conversation in January, the Cavs would have made the postseason.

LeBron averaged 21 points a game in his rookie season, though I bet he could have been closer to 25, if not for his generous passing. With LeBron at the helm, playing was a lot more fun. We all felt utilized and became better players. My stats rose from 10 to 15.5 points scored per game, while my rebound average jumped from 7.5 to 11.4 grabs.

I'd also given my agent, Rob, another strong season to tout to the Cleveland owners when we'd sit down to negotiate that third-year option. I'd made $695,000 in my second year with Cleveland. I was a starting forward, who pulled solid digits in scoring and rebounds. I was only twenty-two. No nagging injuries. Plenty of room for growth. I had major upside.

I sat down with Rob, Cavs owner Gordan Gund, and general manager Jim Paxson in his office at the arena. My wife, CeCe, came along at my request, to silently support me. My decision was really ours to make together and I wanted to discuss the details with her afterward.

The franchise had the right to pick up my option for another $695,000, but we discussed an alternative where they'd allow me to become a free agent, so the franchise could offer me a clean-slate contract with a much larger salary to reflect my stats, but for a longer period of time.

"Once you become a free agent, we'd like to offer you a six-year deal for $39 million," Paxson said. I tried to stay cool when Rob exchanged glances with me.

Rob calmly thanked them for the offer, knowing we couldn't commit to anything official until June. We left the room in good spirits, though I couldn't process much after Pax said, "$39 million." It was such an outrageous amount for a kid who'd once been homeless sleeping in a cold, dirty stairwell. I held it together just long enough to make it to the elevator bank.

"Rob, this changes my life. No one from my family has ever made close to this," I said. "I'll be able to pay my parents back."

In June, news of my free agency hit the ESPN ticker. The Cavs had released me from my option, as they told us they would. I waited for Rob to call me with the new offer the Cavs had proposed. $39 million. Playing alongside LeBron all the way to four or five NBA championship titles. I was set.

I was coaching at a kids' basketball camp in New York when Rob called a few days later.

"Hey, Rob, you're going to have to speak up," I said, plugging my free ear to drown out the blare of fifty basketballs slamming into the floor.

"Los, the Cavs have made the offer," he said.

"Great," I answered. "Let's do it."

"But I wouldn't be a good agent if I didn't tell you we have another offer," he interjected before I could hang up.

"From another team?"

"Actually, from a few," he corrected. "Denver and Utah want to make offers, as well as the Atlanta Hawks and the Charlotte Bobcats. Denver and Utah are willing to sign you for $70-$75 million."

Now I knew I'd heard that wrong. The pitter-patter of balls was like a stampede of elephants across the hardwood floor.

"Seventy-five million," he said, overenunciating each syllable.

*That couldn't be right*, I thought. That was nearly twice as much as what the Cavs were willing to pay. *Was I really worth $75 million?* Apparently, there was at least one other franchise that thought so.

"Call the Cavs and see what they can do," I suggested. I wanted to stay in Cleveland, but Pax got back to Rob a few days later to say they couldn't squeeze any more money out of their budget for me.

As soon as the other offers hit the newswire, the media jumped all over it, claiming that I'd broken a verbal "gentleman's agreement" with the Cavs by not signing with them immediately. However, neither Rob nor I had solicited these new teams. There was a process the players and the franchises had to follow, and though our discussions had been promising, I wasn't allowed to commit to a deal in that room, per NBA guidelines. That didn't stop the media from branding me an opportunist, at best.

What no one ever knew was that the NBA office contacted me, highly concerned that I might have made a "gentleman's agreement" with the Cavs prior to my free-agency period. Gentleman's agreements were prohibited by the NBA, they said, and if I took the deal with Cleveland, they'd launch an investigation into me and the Cavs.

I didn't have to look far back in the NBA's history to know they were dead serious about this. In 1995, Joe Smith was the No. 1 Draft pick who went to Golden State Warriors. Joe cruised in his first few years, but after the 1999 NBA lockout, he was re-signed as a free agent by the Minnesota Timberwolves for one year for $1.75 million—well below his market value. It made no sense, as Joe turned down an $80 million extension with the Warriors to take a chance in free agency. The move raised red flags and an NBA investigation revealed Joe had an under-the-table deal for three measly one-year contracts up front for an $86 million contract promised later. But Smith never reached the end of that rainbow before he and Minnesota were caught. The punishment for this illicit agreement was harsh. All three of Smith's one-year contracts were canceled, and Minnesota lost Smith's Bird rights, an exception clause named after Larry Bird that would have allowed Smith to re-sign with that cushy

*Top:* Big sister Natasha, my first and longest-ever best friend. (West Germany, November/December 1981)

Photo Credit: Provided by Boozer family

*Bottom:* Our family lived on an army base in West Germany during my father's service.

Photo Credit: Provided by Boozer family

*Right:* Hitting the water at an early age with my Pops, I'd grow to love boating, and share it later with my own children.
Photo Credit: Provided by Boozer family

*Far Right:* Have a Coke and a smile: Tash and me.
Photo Credit: Provided by Boozer family

*Right:* I scaled my siblings Nakeisha and Charles during a slam dunk contest.
Photo Credit: Photo by Brian Wallace

*Opposite Top:* The Boozer family complete (L to R): Charles, Natasha, Natanya, Booz, Nakeisha, Renee, and Carlos Sr.
Photo Credit: Provided by the Boozer family

*Opposite Bottom:* I'm forever connected to nature, all due to my time in Juneau (Mendenhall River and Glacier).
Photo Credit: Photo by Brian Wallace

*Top:* The warm reception I received at my high school games, from fans young and old, helped feed my drive to make it to the NBA.

*Right:* I finished 95–12 with the Crimson Bears, scoring over 2,500 points during my high school career. (Juneau-Douglas High School, 1999)

*Opposite:* The Brotherhood in action (L to R): Booz, Shane Battier, Jayson Williams, Nate James, and Chris Carrawell.

*Right:* I returned from injury to contribute 19 and 12 points in our final games versus Maryland and Arizona. (2001 NCAA Finals)

Photo Credit: Photo by Duke Men's Basketball

*Opposite Top:* At nine, I'd watched this moment on television, and then got to experience it a decade later when we won the 2001 NCAA Tournament. Priceless.

Photo Credit: Photo by Brian Bahr/ALLSPORT

*Opposite Bottom Left:* The Beast Unleashed 2.0—NBA version. (December 3, 2003)

Photo Credit: Photo by Robert Laberge/Getty Images

*Opposite Bottom Right:* My Pops's foresight (and his pants belt) made me basketball-ambidextrous.

Photo Credit: Melissa Majchrzak/NBAE via Getty Images

*Opposite:* The births of our boys—Carmani, Cameron, and Cayden—beat out any NBA moment I could have ever had. (July 2007).
Photo Credit: © Vanessa M. Lam/ LAM Studios

*Top:* I didn't get to compete with the All-Star West team due to injury, but Kobe and I still had fun getting ready. (February 17, 2007)
Photo Credit: Photo by Joe Murphy/NBAE via Getty Images

*Bottom:* I was lucky enough to experience Olympic gold with two key NBA teammates, LeBron James and Deron Williams. (Beijing, August 24, 2008)
Photo Credit: Photo by David Eulitt/Kansas City Star/Tribune News Service via Getty Images

*Top:* You better believe my Pops was there to watch us win Olympic gold! (Beijing, August 24, 2008)

Photo Credit: Provided by Boozer family

*Bottom:* Cayden takes an urgent call after we beat the Denver Nuggets 112–104 in Game Six of the Western Conference Quarterfinals. (April 30, 2010).

Photo Credit: Photo by Melissa Majchrzak/NBAE via Getty Images

*Top:* The Boozer boys take no prisoners on the court—sporting my jersey numbers: #1 (Cleveland Cavaliers), #4 (Duke), #5 (Utah Jazz, Chicago Bulls, LA Lakers)

Photo Credit: Provided by Boozer family

*Bottom:* My man Nate left this bad boy in my locker after a hair-dye mishap brought me more attention during a prime-time game than I'd ever wanted. Ruthless.

Photo Credit: Courtesy of Nate Robinson

*Opposite:* My Pops
and I mutually love this
shot—scaling Mt. Shaq.
(December 3, 2010)

Photo Credit: Photo by
Brian Babineau/NBAE
via Getty Images

*Top:* Playing my last
NBA season with Kobe
and the Lakers was
the cherry on top of
my career.
(November 12, 2014)

Photo Credit: Photo by
Layne Murdoch/NBAE
via Getty Images

*Bottom:* Coach Houston
and I still talk regularly
to this day.

Photo Credit: Photo by
Brian Wallace

*Top:* "The most important thing in the world is family and love." —John Wooden (Cameron, Booz, Carmani, CeCe, and Cayden, 2023).
Photo Credit: Provided by Boozer family

*Bottom:* From a poor kid eyeing snowboards through the store window to hitting the slopes every winter in Park City, Utah, with my younger brother, Charles.
Photo Credit: Photo by Greg Nelson

*Top:* "When roots are deep, there is no need to fear the wind."
—African Proverb (Neeka, Bloom, and Booz 2023).
Photo Credit: Provided by Boozer family

*Bottom:*
The "Nothing but Net" Posse—Kelsey Riggs, Luke Hancock, Booz, and Joel Berry II— with a Cameron Stadium cameo in the background. (2022 NCAA Tournament)
Photo Credit: Photo by Phil Ellsworth/ESPN

*Top:* "A flower does not use words to announce its arrival to the world; it just blooms." —Matshona Dhliwayo (Bloom Boheme Boozer, 2023).

**Photo Credit:** Provided by Boozer family

*Bottom:* Eighteen years delayed but never denied. I earned my sociology degree in 2022.

**Photo Credit:** Provided by Boozer family

contract they'd spent three years building toward. Minnesota was fined $3.5 million and forfeited their first-round picks for the next five years, handicapping team growth for numerous seasons to follow.

I got off the phone with the NBA office panicked, thinking I'd screwed up my life in royal fashion. I thought I was going to lose all the contract offers, get dumped by the NBA, and have to crawl back to my parents in North Carolina with my tail between my legs.

"Pops," I said when I called my father for advice. "I don't know what to do."

At this point, I couldn't take the Cavs deal without bringing grief down upon myself and the franchise. No player in their right mind would turn down an extra $36 million without suspicion of something nefarious at play. When I spoke to Rob, we made the decision to have the league's Players Association step in to represent the rest of my negotiations so there would be no question of my dealings from that point on.

I was counseled not to speak with anyone. Unable to follow the advice Coach Houston had given me in high school, the story took on a life of its own. The media called me dishonorable, not knowing that my back was against the wall. One media outlet falsely reported that Coach K was trying to contact me to honor the Cavs deal—quite a detail that was made up out of thin air. None of the players seemed to care. Even LeBron told me to take the bigger deal. For my peers, my worth would be decided on the court.

By mid-July, the Players Association had negotiated me a six-year, $75 million contract with the Utah Jazz. Cleveland owner Gordon Gund probably had the harshest words for me as the dust settled.

"I decided to trust Carlos and show him the respect he asked for," he wrote about that May meeting. "He did not show that trust and respect in return." To this day, I don't know if Gund or the rest of the Cleveland franchise knew that the NBA office had called me. Gund's comments make me suspect they didn't. Regardless, I will always be grateful for the opportunity Coach Lucas and the Cavs gave me—sight mostly unseen.

Before I could think more on my Cavs departure, LeBron and I were both called up to the U.S. Olympic Men's Basketball team to represent our country at the 2004 Summer Olympics in Athens, Greece. Competing at the Olympics was something I'd never set my sights on because it went beyond my goal of making it to the NBA. When I called my father to tell him the news, it felt like a pretty sweet consolation prize for not making the playoffs.

Larry Brown, who'd just coached the Detroit Pistons to the NBA championship a few weeks earlier, was brought in fresh to lead us. He'd been coaching big-time college and NBA teams since 1965, so the chance to play under him, even if only for five weeks, got me excited.

However, when I reported for training in Jacksonville, I was surprised by who *wasn't* there. Where was Jason Kidd, who led on assists in 2000? Or that team's scoring leader, Vince Carter? Surely, Kevin Garnett, the 2000 squad's rebound leader, would come bursting through the gym doors any second. It turned out that a lot of elite players just didn't want to make the trip to Greece that year. It was the first Olympics to be held after 9/11 and seventeen months following the United States' invasion of Iraq, a move that made Americans unpopular throughout the Middle East and the rest of the world. Images of irate foreign crowds burning US flags became common on the nightly news. We'd had numerous anthrax scares, as well, so as crazy as it sounds, chemical terrorism was a possibility that the team would be alerted to. Without strong security precautions in place, I could see some of the veterans passing, especially if they'd already won gold in 2000. And that's just what they did. None of the 2000 Olympians returned to the squad.

I looked around our Jacksonville gym and counted twelve guys with an average age of twenty-three. None of us had competed at the Olympics before. Most of us had no experience with Coach Brown at all. That's not to say we didn't have the goods with the team amassed by him. On paper, our squad had impressive credentials. Four-time All-Star and scoring leader Allen Iverson. Two-time NBA Finals MVP Tim Duncan. All-Rookie selection Carmelo Anthony. Two-time All-Star point guard Stephon Marbury. And LeBron, of course, who'd just been crowned Rookie of the Year. We were all competent, score-generating players, though balancing in some Olympic veterans would have certainly given us a steadier hand. Maybe the older players would have taken to the perennial Coach Brown's hard-nosed style, but the young squad he had in front of him bristled at it within the first hour.

Huddled in a circle, Coach Brown asked each of us to state out loud what our goals were for this thirty-eight-day journey. Many of us said "Gold," or gave some other pledge to play our best, but Stephon Marbury had other thoughts.

"What about fun, Coach?" he asked. "Don't forget about having fun." Stephon's remark drew a few laughs, but not from Coach Brown. He looked at Stephon for a moment before he addressed us all.

"You hear this guy?" he asked, his voice dripping with condemnation. "This guy is talking about having fun."

The rest of us went dead silent, what little trust we had for our new coach dissipated into nothing in an instant. It set a pensive tone for everyone, which wasn't the best way to begin our campaign.

As we trained, a clear division emerged between the NBA vets and rookies, only widened by Coach Brown leaning on the former and underutilizing the latter. Even the veterans struggled with Coach's unbending style. It was his way and nothing else. We left Jacksonville for Athens a disconnected group of NBA stars who didn't have their plays down, but who also lacked a general feel for one another and a way to communicate on the fly. We were simply underprepared, but we were NBA players, so we should be able to wing it. Right?

You could argue that the US wasn't sending its strongest-possible team to the 2004 Olympics, but there was still massive pressure for us to come home with the gold. The 1996 and 2000 teams had both won gold, decimating the world competition in ruthless fashion.

Basketball has always been viewed as a uniquely American sport and the NBA its pinnacle. You could be the best player from your country, but if your country wasn't America, your odds of breaking into the NBA were pretty slim. In the US, you could have a basketball placed in your hands at age four and make it to the NBA sixteen years later. Our country has the infrastructure to support every year of that player's growth. The same couldn't be said for most other places in the world. Our squad, though green as could be by American standards, was still expected to trounce the rest of the world.

Our elite image was perpetuated—at least when we arrived—when word spread that we wouldn't be staying in the Olympic Village with the rest of the athletes, but on the *Queen Mary 2*, a luxury ocean liner docked in Paraeus, about thirty minutes away.

That July, our team, coaches and immediate families boarded the *Queen Mary 2*, which had been commissioned to dock for the Games' duration. For two weeks, the *QM2* served as a floating hotel for a few of the US Olympic teams and their supporting staff, and world leaders like President George Bush and Prince Charles.

At the dock, my parents, CeCe, and I were led to a perimeter fence manned by armed US military. The team had been prepped on how tight security would be for us to get on and off the ship. Weapons would be in plain sight and Navy SEALs patrolling the waters around us. The US government was sending a clear message not to mess with this ship and its occupants. Once IDs were checked, our group moved through the fence, all our necks craning up simultaneously for our first unobstructed view of the ship. I think I heard our collective jaws drop into the dock and someone let out a wolfish whistle, as if Halle Berry was standing there to greet us. Two weeks on a vacation cruise liner only royalty and millionaires could afford had us all buzzing. It was good our families were around, for despite being docked, we had some choppy seas ahead.

The *QM2* had made its maiden voyage six months earlier; our select group of 2004 Olympians was only the second tranche to board the ship. It had over 150,000 feet of deck space wrapping around the liner's circumference, plus five swimming pools— two on the outer deck alone, as well as a state-of-the-art gym and a full-service spa.

Inside, the interiors were all rich reds, blues, and gold. Tapestries, portraits, Oriental rugs, and other fine artwork adorned the walls and floors. My and CeCe's state room was as nice as any high-end hotel we'd stayed in. There were multiple restaurants to eat at, including a twenty-four-hour food court. The largest restaurant sat at the center of the ship, where the glass-paneled ceiling allowed sun rays in at breakfast and lunch and gave us a great place to stargaze during dinner.

In terms of decadent extras, the *QM2* had it all. I'd like to say that we took advantage of the *QM2*'s 8,000-book library with its ample reading rooms or its first-ever ship planetarium, but it was the casino's bells, whistles, and blinking lights that lured many of us in during our downtime. If you wanted to go watch a stand-up comedian or take in a film, you could do that, as well. If you needed a trim, the barber had his clippers at the ready.

Besides our team, the women's US basketball team and members of the women's volleyball team also stayed on the ship. But altogether, we couldn't have totaled more than a few hundred people. I don't know if the ship was fully staffed for us, but it sure felt like it. We wanted for nothing.

We attended the opening ceremonies, but wouldn't get to see much else for the next two weeks. Other than practices and games, we didn't go anywhere but back to the ship. We weren't encouraged to attend the other events, as nobody could guarantee that Tim Duncan wouldn't get kidnapped from the stands watching Venus and Serena Williams playing tennis. There were too many civilians to account for in those settings to ensure our protection. We couldn't even walk around the Olympic Village. We didn't eat and socialize with the other players in the cafeteria where hundreds of athletes congregated every day. I know I would have loved that part.

My parents, CeCe, and I ventured out a couple of times for lunch, but it was always with a security team, which drew extra attention to us anyway. We saw the disappointed fans' faces when the security kept them at bay. So many had traveled hundreds and thousands of miles to see us. It just wasn't an ideal situation.

Our first game was on a Sunday against Puerto Rico, a team that had one NBA player on its squad. Puerto Rico shouldn't have beaten us, but they did it by 19 points. Coach Brown didn't play me, LeBron, Melo, or D-Wade. We just didn't play, which is a weird feeling when you've been a starter for fifteen years straight. The news of our defeat reverberated through the entire Olympic Village like a church bell. The Americans lost? Hope sprang eternal for every other team that day.

When we reboarded after that first game, I'm sure there were a few of us who were upset with how we'd played. We didn't sulk, though. This wasn't March Madness, where one loss knocked you out of the competition. We had a lot more basketball to play and there was still a pathway for us to win the gold medal.

We steadied ourselves by winning our next two games, but we dropped our fourth to Lithuania. It was like chum had been thrown in the water. The sharks circled us. A semifinals loss to Argentina sealed our fate. We settled for the bronze medal in the consolation match with Lithuania. We lost three of our eight games in Athens, the poorest showing for an US Olympic squad since the '80s.

At the medals ceremony, a camera shot panned across our disappointed faces as we stood together on the medalists' podium. During my senior year of high school, our team lost a crucial tournament and didn't advance to the state championship because of it, when we'd previously won back-to-back titles. I was named an All-Tournament selection and had been called in front of the crowd to accept my award. Yet, I was so upset and angry with myself for not finding a way to win, that I couldn't face the crowd afterward. I sent my ten-year-old brother, Charles, out to collect my award. It wasn't my finest moment as an athlete, and I'm certainly not proud of it. Still, if I could've sent Charles out onto the Olympic podium to accept my bronze medal, I would've seriously considered it. I think the entire US squad might've sent Charles up there for us. We were disheartened not to have won gold, but for those of us who didn't get a real chance to contribute, it was especially hard to accept. There was no slick play or crazy dunk I could point to during my Olympic experience. LeBron, Melo, D-Wade, and I—we could have made a difference, if given the chance.

At the same time, I don't want to disrespect the athletes who qualified from all over the world. It was a huge honor to have the bronze medal placed around my neck. The two teams sharing the podium with us had worked incredibly hard to get there and had every reason to be proud. They'd bested us, fair and square. We were the third best men's basketball team at the 2004 Olympics. If we wanted to change that in four years, a different approach would be crucial. Still, Olympic redemption was four years away. There was a new home, a new franchise, and a new head coach to meet as CeCe and I returned to the States. My mind turned to Utah, and what awaited us.

# CHAPTER 10

## PRINCE

I nearly sued Prince.

Yes, *that* Prince. The seven-time Grammy winner. Musical icon. Nearly fifty top 50 songs. Nineteen top 10 songs. Five No. 1 hits. Over one hundred million albums sold the world over. Recognized the world over.

I met Prince during my first season with the Utah Jazz, though my path to the musical legend began two years before that, when Cleveland played the LA Clippers.

"Hey!" a blond, clean-cut man yelled from the front row during warm-ups. "I know the Brotherhood." Like he'd uttered a secret password, I tossed away my ball and walked over to him. His name was Gunnar Peterson, and he was one of the most famous personal trainers in the world, though I didn't know that from our first encounter.

"Class of '85," he said. "If you're ever out in LA, I'd love to train you."

Gunnar hadn't played sports at Duke, but he'd befriended a lot of the athletes who valued physical fitness as much as he did. We exchanged numbers, and when I next hit up LA, I called him, curious to see why so many celebrities and professional athletes worked with him. Gunnar's personal gym was built inside a massive guesthouse next to his even more massive home. It was a secluded Bel Air property one couldn't see from the road. The first time I drove up and parked outside the gym, another car pulled in alongside me. I glanced over to see it was Jennifer Lopez. I looked away quickly, not wanting to be accused of staring.

"You train JLo?" I asked Gunnar, who met me at the entrance after Jennifer walked inside.

"Oh yeah," he said. "I trained Ben before he even met JLo. Pre Bennifer. You'll probably recognize a few people I train."

Indeed. I'd come to learn that Gunnar was considered a fitness guru among celebrities that included Denzel Washington, Hugh Jackman, and the Kardashian/Jenner family. However, what piqued me enough to take up his offer was Gunnar's pro-athlete clientele, which included NFL legend Tom Brady and tennis ace Pete Sampras. Gunnar's training was functional and adaptable across the sports spectrum. I began booking sessions with him anytime I was in the area.

In the summer of 2004, fresh off our mixed Olympics experience, CeCe and I made a pit stop in LA on our way to Utah. The only neighborhood I knew well enough was Bel Air, thanks to my visits with Gunnar, so we rented a place in the extremely affluent area. The warm weather was enticing and with each passing day CeCe and I talked dreamily about buying a house there. We hadn't even purchased a house in Salt Lake City yet, but my next NBA check was going to be a big one. CeCe and I thought it might be nice to have a house here for our eventual family. She enlisted an agent and suddenly, we were touring Bel Air mansions. We ended up at a gated property at the cusp of nearby West Hollywood, perched on the same Santa Monica Mountains as the famous Hollywood sign, overlooking the city itself.

"This gorgeous place was owned by the president of Interscope Records," our Realtor, Roxanne, told us, a morsel that meant nothing to us at the time.

It was an extravagant 18,000-foot Mediterranean-style palatial estate house sitting on a little over two acres. Built in 1953, the six-story concrete structure had 10 bedrooms, 13 baths, plus all the bells and whistles you could imagine. The multiple "living areas" were so vast and spacious, it would take a couple sets of living room furniture to fill them.

"This room could hold hundreds of people," I said, envisioning the get-togethers we'd have with the new friends we'd make. Sunlight poured in from the floor-to-ceiling windows. The parquet floor was flawless and buffed to a shine; a 15-foot-wide glass light fixture hung dramatically from the ceiling.

"Three hundred—give or take," Roxanne smiled. "This was originally the Ballroom."

Another living area revealed an intricate marble floor, while the backside of the house boasted a greenhouse conservatory with a wall of glass that looked out onto the property. Elaborate marble fireplaces adorned many rooms, while two stone staircases connected floors. Black, wrought-iron guard-railing was utilized throughout the interior and exterior.

"The styles kind of straddle art deco with the more modern styles," Roxanne said of the eclectic design. We weren't quite sure what she meant, but these details alone made the house breathtaking. However, it was all the outrageous extras that really took CeCe and I aback and had me planning how I'd enjoy the place. In multiple rooms, French doors opened onto large terraces with ocean and city views. The terraces, which took up thousands of square feet, were decorated with stone fountains of Grecian statues. This place was designed to entertain hundreds of guests at every turn. It had that distinctive "Old Hollywood" vibe. I pictured some famous 1950s actress stepping out onto one of the terraces in a flowing silk gown, sipping a martini while gazing toward the sea. I could see my parents sitting here, sipping their morning coffee on a visit.

The complex also boasted a rooftop tennis court with an elevated clubhouse to oversee the matches. This could be easily converted to a basketball court, I thought. Then, my younger brother, Charles, and possibly a son or daughter, could shoot with me.

The pool moved through a stone grotto, which hid a hot tub and wine room. I envisioned my kids skimming down the built-in slide jutting out of the rocks and splashing into the water. A private parking area, lined with the same rose cobblestone that paved every road on the property, could hold a dozen luxury cars. We'd need these spots when my family came to visit.

The property also included a Tudor-style four-bedroom guest-house, where our relatives could stay. The dense landscaping enveloped the entire property by design, ensuring no one could look in on this fantastical property from street level. Whoever designed it thought of everything.

As we moved from room to room, I justified a purchase more and more. I was smitten. CeCe favored a newer house, for about the same price, on the other side of town. Still, this place just felt right to me. Was it a flex buy? One-hundred percent. I was in the grocery checkout aisle grabbing copies of all the tabloid magazines with the juicy covers. "Impulse buy" pretty much covers it.

CeCe decorated the house in gentle earth tones. She ordered lush cream carpeting from Italy to match the off-white furniture. Flowy, beige draperies silhouetted the windows. By the time CeCe was done with the house, it was sleek and chic.

My biggest contribution to the project was transforming the rooftop tennis court into a basketball court. Now that we had the money, I always wanted somewhere to put up shots at any hour, somewhere only a few steps away and warm. I always wanted to be able to practice somewhere warm. Buying this particular property was an extravagant move, but I saw our families enjoying it with us.

CeCe and I traveled on to Salt Lake City that fall, leaving our newly furnished home behind. I knew there would be times when we'd be in LA to enjoy it, but as the season got underway, my focus fixed on Salt Lake City.

That September, I got a call from our real estate agent, Roxanne. It turns out the house had some serious history of its own. It was a well-known destination for entertaining in elite circles, designed by an eccentric architect who'd invited celebrities and starlets to mingle about and enjoy it. Elizabeth Taylor had been among the rumored visitors of that time, and in later years, the house was said to still attract the Hollywood set. She said a few parties had independently inquired about renting it, but I didn't want someone moving into our newly decorated house for a couple months, when CeCe and I hadn't lived in it yet. A few weeks later, Roxanne called back a second time, this time with a substantial offer. The dozen-plus offers had fallen away, leaving one.

"They want to rent it for the eight months," Roxanne said, "but wait to hear what they're offering a month. Seventy thousand dollars. A month."

That was a chunk of change enough to give this twenty-three-year-old pause. This would-be mystery renter, who kept their identity hidden when they made the offer, was persistent. Curiosity consumed us enough to where CeCe and I finally relented. It was a decent-enough sum to put toward our mortgage and we'd rent another place in LA, if need be. Plans were set for me to fly out to meet our new tenant on the property to sign the contracts.

A standard black limousine pulled in through the gates. I was curious to see who wanted my house badly enough to drop over half a million dollars for it. The person who climbed out of the car was a five-foot-two waif of a man who nearly knocked me over with his presence, alone. I looked at my real estate agent, who was as stunned as I was.

"Wow," my mouth leaked, before I regained my wits. "Ah, nice to meet you," I said, stepping forward and extending my hand to Prince, who shook it lightly. He wore oversized, Audrey Hepburn–style sunglasses, but there was no doubt it was him. He had that pencil-thin mustache and goatee, and precisely coifed hair. Prince introduced his entourage, while I stared at his outfit. His svelte form wore tight-fitting black leather pants and platform boots, my guess to give him a couple of extra inches. He finished the outfit with a billowy purple blouse. It was very fashion forward, very cutting-edge. I was immediately taken with how comfortable he was in his own skin. This man was a fashion plate; his frilly blouses and long purple coats are iconic. My mother had gone to one of his concerts during the '80s, and when Prince gyrated away from the crowd, he revealed his other set of cheeks hanging out of his pants. Now, that's confidence.

"I think I was conceived to 'Purple Rain,'" I said, thinking I was clever. He nodded, as if he'd heard that one before.

"I watched you come out of Duke," he shared, returning the compliment much better than I could. "Aggressive."

We proceeded inside, Prince leading the way with his hands clasped behind his back.

I began the tour, trying to remember anything of value I could scrape up from memory. Prince moved silently from room to room, as if he'd been there before. He had. Many times. When that president of Interscope Records owned the joint.

"There's something about this place, Carlos," he said in a soft-spoken voice that didn't match his wild on-stage persona in the slightest. "It's the place I need to be to write my next album. This place will fuel my inspiration."

Up on the rooftop court, Prince picked up a stray ball and sunk a solid jump shot. Prince was a well-known NBA fan.

"How do you think the Lakers will do this year?" he asked. I grabbed a ball and shot, myself, launching into my predictions for the Kobe Bryant–Shaquille O'Neal super squad.

"How about Garnett?" he asked, lobbing in another shot. Prince had skills. No doubt about it. And everyone knew Prince was from Minnesota, thus his love for Kevin "Big Ticket" Garnett and the Timberwolves.

"He's one of the toughest guys I've defended," I said. "I haven't been able to go off on scoring with him yet. Shuts me down every time."

That brought a grin to Prince's face. I'd passed a test, apparently. My real estate agent presented the contracts, which we signed that night. Prince's father was coming into town in a few weeks, and he seemed anxious to get his homebase set up before that. I stayed in LA a few more days, and we met up for dinner one night to talk more basketball. He was an expert on the sport.

I went back to Utah and Prince got to work on his album. I didn't return to the house for a couple months, when business brought me back to town. I dialed the number Prince had left me on my way from the airport. It went straight to voice mail, so I left a message.

"Yo, P," I said. "I'm heading over to you now from LAX and I wanted to see if you needed anything." He hadn't called me back before I pulled up to our gates nearly two hours later. I went to punch my passcode into the keypad when I saw a large purple symbol adorning the gate where golden lions used to be. I had the wrong house. I backed out and retraced my steps, keeping a closer eye on my surroundings. Again, I ended up at the gate with the purple symbol. I couldn't even tell what the contorted symbol meant. I cautiously dialed in my code and the gate swung open.

It was hard not to miss the purple carpeting cascading down the off-white stone steps leading up to the house's main entrance. Purple flowers gushed out of the planters. The symbol from the gate was embroidered on the entry-way carpet in black. And were those purple stripes painted on that exterior wall?

Inside, the neutral wall-to-wall carpeting had been replaced with black. Every piece of furniture CeCe selected was replaced with puffy couches and chairs that looked like violet and amethyst clouds. Where had he stored everything?

A spare bedroom had been transformed into a hair salon with chairs and overhead heaters. Mirrors covered every wall. I turned the handle of one of the sinks used for washing hair and water came out.

"How did he get running water into this room?" I asked out loud. He must have hired a plumber to install piping through these old walls.

My weight room, one of the few areas I'd had any input on, was now a dimly lit dance club with a glittering disco ball and a DJ booth. A purple heart-shaped bed occupied our master bedroom with matching monogrammed carpeting.

However, the most egregious alteration was the doorway Prince created by pulling up the baseboards and cutting a hole between two previously unconnected rooms.

"What happened to our house?" I asked out loud, but even the Hollywood ghosts that roamed its halls had been stunned into silence. I immediately left a message for Prince, trying to hide my displeasure. Then, I left another. Days went by and my messages to Prince gained urgency. A month passed with no word from him. And then another. My lawyers urged me to file a lawsuit to protect my very big asset, but I stalled.

"Are we really going to have to sue Prince?" I asked CeCe in bed one night. "It seems, well, wrong. I really don't want to do it. My mom would never forgive me."

"Maybe it's just to get his attention, to get him to answer your calls," she reasoned. "We can always settle things once he answers you."

The next day, I fumbled through a final voice mail message for Prince.

"P, I've been trying to reach you," I said. "I've been trying to get a hold of you for two months. I don't know where you are, and I hope everything is okay with you and your family. It's just I'm about to sue you because you changed my whole house around and that's a breach of contract."

Not knowing how to sign off, I left it at that. Three days later, a foreign phone number with extra digits flashed over my phone's screen. It was Prince. He'd been out of town for months, overseas in Asia. He'd finished the album, entitled *3121*, and left to go on world tour.

"I'm so sorry, Booz," he said in his calming, voodoo voice. "When the lease is up, it will be like I was never there. Trust me."

There was something in his voice that told me it was going to be alright. I've only met a few people in my lifetime that had that kind of pull over the phone the way he did. He also sent me an additional $500,000 to further ease my mind, doubling what he'd agreed to pay us. I contacted the Realtor and lawyers and told them to put any legal action on hold. All told, Prince paid $95,000 a month for an entire year, and that didn't include the half a million bonus he tossed our way faster than a John Stockton pass.

In his final months at the house, Prince called me to ask for one additional alteration. He asked to raise the dense shrubbery surrounding the compound to obstruct the view of the paparazzi helicopters swirling over it.

"I don't know how they figured out I was here, Booz," he lamented.

Once Prince's lease was up, CeCe and I flew to LA to survey the damage, like parents coming home from a weekend to find their kid has thrown an absolute rager. Pulling up, the gate symbol and the purple exterior carpeting were gone. Inside, harsh purple and black had faded back to the neutral palette CeCe had selected. The furniture and other decor were where we had left it. The discotheque was gone, as was the hair salon. My weights were where they were supposed to be. Everything was back in its place, down to the silverware. Prince kept his word. He and

I kept in touch, too, catching lunch or dinner when we were in town at the same time.

When *3121* released, CeCe and I couldn't believe what graced the CD's front and back cover and inside jacket. It was stills of our house, albeit with Prince's modifications. That house was truly his muse.

In 2015, I ran into Prince at the NBA All-Star weekend festivities in New York City. He performed at Michael Jordan's annual party, the last time I saw him alive, clutching one of his fancy purple guitars. We exchanged quick greetings backstage. He was standing next to Jay-Z and Beyoncé. Ten months later, he was gone.

We'd sold the LA house a year after we purchased it, but there was another property I'd had my eyes on for a few years.

I'd never forgotten about the middle school teacher who'd told the entire class that I'd never make it to the NBA, that working at a Kmart or a gas station was more in the cards for me. It was an awful thing for an adult to say to a kid. Ironically, it was a memory I drew upon in key moments when I needed to get things in gear. It was such a visceral memory that it helped me get to the NBA. Juneau had four gas stations, so I purchased one. Nobody knew I'd bought it, and I didn't hold on to it for long, but I think it gave me a sense of closure.

In Utah, CeCe and I purchased a home on the edge of the Wasatch Mountains, overlooking Salt Lake City. It had a home theater in the basement, and I envisioned watching sports down there with my children someday. Every morning, I drove to the Delta Center for practice and at night we looked down on the city, a grid of glittering lights.

I didn't know much about the Miller family, who'd purchased a 50 percent stake of the Utah Jazz in May 1985 for $8 million to keep the franchise from heading to Miami. I learned quickly that Larry and Gail Miller were a beloved Utah institution, especially when they bought the remaining 50 percent the following year for $14 million, again to keep the franchise on Utah soil. The Millers nurtured and grew the franchise for decades. In 1991, the Utah Jazz debuted at a brand-new 19,000-seat arena. In 1997 and 1998, they made the NBA Finals, led by one of the greatest power forwards ever, Karl Malone, and legendary guard John Stockton. They did all of this in the NBA's smallest media market, a testament to everyone involved.

Larry, the outgoing Miller patriarch, made his presence known from his courtside seat or around the arena, where he greeted everyone that passed him by name, from the executives down to the janitors. I liked Larry right away.

"Wait until I pull out my algorithm for you," he said when we met. He was wearing a blue polo shirt, khaki shorts, and white sneakers—the same casual outfit he'd wear everywhere. I asked someone about the algorithm, and they said it was better that I wait for Larry. "The man has an incredible mind," the other player said. "He's like a mathematician or something."

Larry's beginnings were humble. He'd started as a teenage mechanic at an auto parts shop and built that into a car dealership, then a dealership empire in Utah. Talk about a self-made man. If Larry had an opinion about the team, we'd all hear about it, whether he was losing his stack from the sidelines or popping champagne with us in the locker room. I don't know of many NBA owners who'd break the employer-employee wall and join their players to celebrate like that. Larry was loveably unique.

As synonymous as the Millers were with Utah, legendary Jazz power forward, Karl Malone, reached out to me when I got to Salt Lake City, offering his knowledge from eighteen seasons with the franchise. Malone, who trailed only Kareem Abdul-Jabbar as the NBA's career scoring leader, was a two-time league MVP. The only thing he hadn't accomplished was a ring, but that was during the Jordan era. He invited me to his log cabin-style ranch, situated on the same mountain as mine.

In 2002, I'd played Karl just once. He dominated me for

thirty minutes, scoring 38 points and securing 15 rebounds. His jump shot was wet from anywhere on the court—playing off that Stockton pick-and-roll.

I didn't share Karl's affinity for hunting, which rivaled any Alaskan native I'd known, by the looks of the dozens of mounted animals hovering, lurking on all fours, and even towering over us in his Alfred Hitchcock–style home. The centerpiece was a twelve-foot bear, displayed behind the couch where he sat. He had a gun range and an artillery room on the property.

Karl also owned a cabin in Kenai, a fishing city on Alaska's western coast where he'd escape for a week or two for hunting expeditions. Karl was a private guy who valued solitude. Still, he was gracious enough to lend me his time and made some suggestions to add to my game, which started our years' long mentor-student relationship. Everything I was about to go through, Karl had already experienced in Salt Lake City. I was being asked to take the mantel, so his tailor-made advice was welcome at a time when I needed direction.

I'd been brought to Utah in the great power forward tradition of Malone and it was easy for the media to push the narrative that I was somehow replacing him. We were in the midst of a power forward–driven era dominated by big men like Jermaine O'Neal, Rasheed Wallace, Ben Wallace, Amar'e Stoudemire, Dirk Nowitzki, Kevin Garnett, and the great Tim Duncan. It was this very market that got me four unsolicited offers. Still, I appreciated that Larry, Coach Jerry Sloan, and the other franchise execs never expected nor asked me to fill Malone's shoes. The man had a statue outside the arena, for God's sake. It would have been like asking a player to attempt to fill Jordan's void, a disservice to the new player and the legend he was meant to emulate. Coach Sloan only asked me to be the best player I could be, then asked me how he could help me get there.

Coach Sloan was a big reason I signed with the Utah Jazz. In Chicago, four retired jerseys hang from the rafters. Everybody knows Jordan and Scottie Pippen, who played masterfully next to him. Then, there's Bob Love, who averaged 30 points a game in the '60s and '70s. The fourth retired jersey belongs to Jerry Sloan.

I'd never forgotten an interview I watched with NBA champion and fourteen-time All-Star Jerry West years earlier. When asked who the toughest opponent he faced was, he answered Sloan without hesitation. "I always leave the game with some welts and bruises, sometimes a cracked rib," he said.

Jerry Sloan the player was a tough motherfucker. He was the rare player who competed for a Division II college, but still found his way to the NBA. He was the fourth player picked in the 1965 Draft, going to a new expansion team called the Chicago Bulls. Jerry Sloan was called the "Original Mr. Bull" for a reason. He was literally there from the ground floor up, helping build the franchise over a decade with his aggressive defensive style. The two-time All-Star led a fledging franchise into nine playoff seasons, an incredible feat in the '60s and '70s.

With Coach Sloan, I knew he'd be hard-nosed—and I welcomed it. At our first practice, he told us we'd meet just two hours a day, yet maximum effort would be required.

"Win or lose, we're going be in the best shape," he said, a green John Deere hat adorning his head. Coach Sloan had grown up on a farm, the youngest of ten children, where chores started before the sun rose. "We're going to play hard together and we're going to give it everything we've got."

Coach Sloan was a big believer in playing all out, all of the time, and he had no interest in the athletes unwilling to do that. If you slacked during practice, you wouldn't play the next game. He was very serious about that. I think Coach Sloan could live with any game's outcome, as long as his players left everything they had on the court.

We kicked off our season with a win against the Lakers, where I scored 27 and had 11 rebounds. In fact, I had double-doubles in nine of our first ten games. I was off to a solid start by any-one's standards.

My stats stayed strong into the winter, though we struggled to string wins together. We hit a nine-game slide that took us into the new year. Something wasn't working, but I couldn't put my finger on it.

We were 17-34 when I strained my right foot with 44 sec-onds left in the second half during a loss to the Phoenix Suns on February 14, 2005. We were all initially relieved when X-rays didn't indicate a fracture of any kind or the need for surgery, so the hope was I'd return to the lineup, posthaste. I was about to learn that sometimes these "minor" injuries are the most mis-leading and can take the longest to recover from.

I followed my rehab protocol and continued to travel with the team, but we had a rough month. We lost four times dur-ing the first week of March, part of a nine-game losing streak that had Larry Miller spewing vinegar to the Utah press. Appar-ently, he'd said I didn't "play hard" enough at times on a local radio program. I took that to mean I hadn't put enough effort into my performances before the injury.

When I heard what Larry had said about me, I completely understood. The man spent $75 million out of his own pocket on me—he had every right to critique me. Larry was very com-petitive and didn't shy away from his emotions toward the team, whether he was ranting about something that displeased him or gushing over something that made him happy. It wasn't as if I was singled out, either. Andrei Kirilenko caught Larry's ire, as did Deron Williams, who'd be drafted the next season. Larry's public spats with a vocal Karl Malone were well-documented. Larry threatened to trade Karl on many occasions, while the superstar dangled a free agency exit in response.

Larry's tough love motivated me. I was in the gym within hours of hearing what he'd said, putting up shots. I wanted to prove him wrong, but I also didn't want to let him and my teammates down. Luckily, I could kill two birds with one stone by steering our team to the playoffs. I couldn't control how Larry had perceived me, but I could control my work ethic.

I also took a page out of Karl's book and confronted Larry when I saw him next. I didn't want him disappointed in me, and I'd much rather have heard his criticisms from his mouth, then from the press. Larry, the upstanding human he was, apologized to me, endearing me even more to him. I vowed to him to do better because I suddenly wanted to do it for him.

Though Larry and I smoothed tensions over, it didn't heal my foot and I was never cleared to play again that season. I missed thirty-one games and we finished a dismal 26–56, dead last in our division. This was only the second time in twenty-two seasons that the franchise hadn't made the playoffs and the media hitched itself to that angle. Back on my feet, I headed to LA to train with Kobe that summer, keeping up a schedule that had me in the weight room at 7:00 a.m., then on the court for three hours a day for our pickup games. I also enlisted Gunnar, who helped me get my body fat percentage down. I was shrinking, and if I'd been paying more attention, I'd have seen that CeCe was growing. She had some surprising news once we returned to Salt Lake City.

"Remember that great weekend we had in Vegas?" she asked coyly.

"You mean our getaway two months ago?" I asked. "Do you want to go back? I could go for some Nobu. How about we stay at the Mandalay Bay this time?"

We were preparing to fly to Miami for the summer, where we'd purchased a house we hoped to make our primary residence.

"I do want to go back," she said, a smile spreading across her face. "But maybe in another seven months or so."

"What's in seven months?" I asked before it dawned on me. I took CeCe into my arms. We'd planned to have our first child in another two or three years, but there was no reason we couldn't start a family now. When I told my parents, they were elated. My father's eyes brimmed with the prospect of adding more athletes to the Boozer brood, but in general, we were ecstatic. Boy. Girl. Athlete. Nerd. None of us cared. CeCe and I had the financial means to care for a baby and we were still in our twenties. We felt ready.

# CHAPTER 11

## CARMANI, CAMERON, AND CAYDEN

"We have an issue."

CeCe gripped my hand even tighter. I can only think of one or two things worse your doctor can say to you when your wife is four months pregnant.

"It's called sickle cell disease," he said, "and it affects the blood's ability to circulate through the body and do its job. His immune system will not be able to fend off illnesses, even a common cold. It's rare for one parent to carry the gene and it's even rarer for both to carry it."

The doctor paused just slightly, but it was ample time for my mind to take off like a race car driving perilously fast toward a brick wall without my seat belt fastened. All I could do was brace for impact.

"You are both carriers," he finished. "There's a 25 percent chance your child will have the full-blown disease."

I stared at the checkerboard of diplomas hanging on the wall behind him, trying to piece together what was just told to me. CeCe was twenty-eight; I was twenty-four. We were still newly-weds. This was supposed to be a happy time, but there was a good chance our baby would be born, only to suffer all his life. As our doctor began to rattle off the awful complications that children endure with the disease, our terror only grew.

"This is all my fault," CeCe told me between sobs on our drive home. "I should have known. I should have known about my background."

We pulled up to a red light and stopped. I turned to CeCe, who was puffy-faced and clutching a balled-up tissue.

"CeCe, if that's the case, then I'm just as equal in the blame," I answered. "My father never knew who his own father was. We know nothing about my grandfather's past. Nothing. Please don't blame yourself for this."

The internet only confirmed what the doctor had told us. As I hunched over CeCe's shoulder, we watched videos of kids having seizures in a variety of settings. At home. At school. At the supermarket. This disease was unpredictable. Our child could be born paralyzed or lose the use of his legs at any time. He could lose control of the left side of his body sitting in class. As those sickle-shaped cells flow through the bloodstream, they can cause artery blockages, kidney failure, or even total organ system failure. People die from sickle disease. Kids die from it. Grown men die from it—many of them in their late forties.

And then there was the pain he'd experience day in and day out. His bones would ache. Joints would throb. His hands and feet would swell. Strokes were also another possibility, even in young children. It seemed like the list of symptoms was endless. How could we bring a child into this world when they had such a bleak future ahead of them? We prayed for an answer and we prayed hard.

CeCe must have called every specialist in the country, from Los Angeles to Chicago to Boston to New York City. The responses were all the same. We were told repeatedly to concentrate on soothing our baby once he was born. Nothing could be done before that. I think most expectant mothers would've taken multiple doctors, all in consensus, at their word. CeCe was not most mothers. There were about three thousand hospitals operating in the US in 2007—CeCe would've called every single one if she had to. Luckily, she made progress before that.

CeCe connected with an Atlanta hospital performing bone marrow transplants on sickle cell patients with great success. In fact, it appeared to be the only facility in the country to offer the operation. However, the medical team felt the risk was too high that something could go wrong with a baby. When they wouldn't give Carmani a slot in their program, CeCe pivoted like a pro and asked more questions until she gleaned the information she needed. This facility had a blueprint CeCe could try to piece together on her own. And that's just what she did.

The first step was to find the best possible human leukocyte antigen (HLA) match. As Detroit geneticist Dr. Mark Hughes explained to us, there could be a viable donor candidate.

"There is a chance we cure him to a degree," Dr. Hughes said cautiously over speakerphone. "We've had a lot of success in trials with mice, but it's never been performed on a toddler before. And there would be a lot of, uh, preparation."

"What kind of preparation?" I asked eagerly. I'd spent years repeating basketball drills in temperatures so frigid I didn't stop at times for fear I'd freeze solid. I could do anything the doctor asked. I would do anything. Anything.

"It's a new type of transplant," he continued. "The best blood match for your child would be a sibling. A parent isn't compatible. The sibling's umbilical cord would be used and that blood could, in a way, flush out the affected sibling's blood."

Had he just told us to have another kid? We hadn't even had our first yet. I looked at CeCe, with her swelling belly beginning to show. I lightly placed my palm on her stomach. Without saying a word, I could see the answer in her eyes.

"Now, there are always concerns and dangers," tempered the doctor. "If the baby's body doesn't accept their sibling's blood transplant—well, there is the chance your first child could die. Please, take what time you need to weigh all of the potential outcomes."

Silence hung in the air for a few seconds after he said the word. *Die.* Our baby could die. But if we left things as they were, there was a good chance our baby would live a terrible life and die early anyway.

"We're doing this," CeCe said after we got off the call. There was no argument from me. She was as determined as I was to save our child's life.

Finding Dr. Hughes was only the first step. After CeCe gave birth, he'd test her embryos for the disease and for their compatibility with our first child, and another doctor would fertilize and inseminate the embryo. Still another would perform the blood-cord transplant after the second child was born. CeCe found Miami-based Dr. Mark Jacobs, an in vitro specialist for the second step. Dr. John Fort, of the Miami Children's Hospital, would perform the blood-cord transplant. CeCe and I quietly made preparations through the summer, too scared to share our plans outside our immediate family.

That fall, I reported to camp fully healed, but felt a distinctive pop in my left hamstring during a full-court layup drill, which pulled me out of the lineup before our early November season opener in Dallas. I'd busted my butt over the summer to come back in better shape, but nobody would get to see it if I didn't rehab and get back out there.

I started the rehab protocol, but a hamstring injury is tricky because you stop feeling pain after a few weeks, even when the muscle hasn't completely healed. By mid-November, an MRI showed my hamstring was getting worse, not better. I'd get cleared to practice, only to overexert the muscle and have to start the rehab program from the beginning. I was frustrated that I'd followed the doctors' instructions to a T, but still pulled my hamstring three times in about ten weeks. This wasn't working. I called my agent, Rob, and asked him to find me a top-notch physical therapist.

I traveled to LA to work with Miss Judy Seto, a Stanford alum and specialist. She wrapped me up in kinesiology tape and took me through drills I'd never seen before. The Jazz staff wasn't pleased when I told them I'd be returning to see her on a regular basis, but the proof was in the pudding. As soon as I started with Miss Judy, I made it successfully through my rehab protocol and finally got back onto the court in February. I returned for our forty-ninth game that season and got to work. My stats started to pick up again that March, especially as I became accustomed to the new players I hadn't interacted with before. The Jazz had scooped up the 2005 Draft's No. 3 pick, guard Deron Williams, and as we became accustomed to one another, we seemed to be able to connect and make baskets quite well together.

Meanwhile, CeCe prepared for our son's arrival in Miami. We kept our plans close to our chest, only telling our family and superclose friends. Years later, I'd be asked if CeCe and I got criticism for having another child just to save another? CeCe and I never thought of it that way. If you could save someone in your family, why wouldn't you do it? At the end of the day, our whole goal was to have three, four, or five kids. We'd just be speeding up the process a bit.

I told Larry and Coach Sloan what was happening. We were setting up a homebase in Miami not only for the medical care, but to give our son an environment more conducive with his disease once he was born. Larry was generous enough to commit to trading me to a different team and locale, if need be, as Utah's high altitude would cause additional health issues after our son's birth.

The last few months of CeCe's pregnancy were tense. Your mind plays tricks on you. *Is my kid going to come out deformed? Without a lung? A leg? An arm?* All of these were possibilities, and the internet does nothing to quell the worries that keep you up into the early hours of the morning. It only feeds the monster. What made it even tougher was being separated. I wasn't much for hanging out with the rest of the team. I felt guilty going out and socializing when CeCe was home alone. I spent a lot of nights alone in my hotel room, either on the phone with CeCe or worrying in private.

In the thirty-three games I played, I hit 10 double-doubles, including three games over 30 points. We didn't make the play-offs again and Larry was unhappy, but there were glimmers of the team we could become when I returned to the lineup.

On May 31, 2006, Carmani came into the world with a room full of doctors and nurses at the ready. I'd always liked the name "Armani," and added the *C* rather than name him after me. Carmani was positive for sickle cell disease, but the doctors agreed he seemed well otherwise. He was perfect in CeCe's and my eyes. The first hurdle had been scaled.

I can only tell you that once I held Carmani in my arms for the first time, everything I wanted to accomplish in life for myself I now wanted to suddenly achieve for him, whether it was in basketball, business, or some other future pursuit. We're all narcissists until we hold our first child; then everything becomes about them in an instant. You are now a provider, teacher, and protector to someone whose very life depends on it.

The Jazz franchise gave me as much extra time off with our little prince as they could spare that first summer. Of course, I utilized that time wisely to introduce him to the game.

"See there, little man?" I said, dividing my attention between him and our television. "See that big guy? That's Tim Duncan and he's two inches taller than Daddy. Yes, he is."

It was impossible not to devolve into baby talk with that cherub face looking up at me.

"Now, Tim's a slick player, but Daddy's gonna have his number," I continued. "He's going to spin out when I cut him off in the paint, but you know what Daddy's going to do?

"That's right," I answered my own question. "Daddy will be ready to stop him. If he tries to hook left or right, if he pops off his jumper in the elbow, Daddy will be there."

As I spoke it aloud, I realized I wasn't just talking about Tim. I was referring to my son, as well.

Within weeks of his birth, Carmani began showing symptoms. Two months in, CeCe woke up one morning to find Carmani's hands and feet swollen and tender. His temperature spiked to 105 degrees and he was admitted to the hospital with a low hemoglobin count. The doctors pumped antibiotics into his little veins for four days. This became the pace of our lives, as Carmani was in and out of the hospital every few months for the next year and a half.

When Carmani reached four months, I had to return to camp with the Utah Jazz, but I couldn't take CeCe and him with me due to Salt Lake City's high elevation. The thought of leaving CeCe alone in this situation made me feel guilty, again. The symptoms were harshly unpredictable; I could talk to CeCe that morning with Carmani seeming fine, only to check in that evening to hear his tormented cries in the background. He could need serious medical care at any time—and I wouldn't be there to drive him to the hospital, to hold his hand, to give him a reassuring smile. It's something that should have rattled me—and it did at times off the court—but on it, these swirling emotions gave me a great deal of focus.

I knew one thing backward and forward, and that was basketball. The court is always ninety-four feet long; the basket always ten feet off the ground. I could count on that never changing. I couldn't control Carmani's future, but I could slam that ball into that hoop. The path to the net wouldn't always look the same, but the target was always there at the end.

Before each game, while the national anthem blared through packed arenas, I'd picture CeCe and Carmani in my mind, smiling, happy, and healthy. I couldn't be by their side, but I could be strong for them on the court. Besides, slam-dunking away my frustrations proved therapeutic. Coach Sloan picked up on that angst and helped me channel it. He added me to more drills and patterns, increasing my playing time.

I had my bad days. There were rushed trips to the hospital I wasn't there for, when all I wanted to do was drop basketball, hop on a plane and get to my son's side as fast as I could. Instead, I went to practice, but the guilt consumed me like Alaskan quicksand. Seeing me struggle to land easy baskets, Coach Sloan pulled me aside. The team had a general idea what was happening with Carmani, but Coach Sloan wanted to know more. I explained my predicament and Coach listened, nodding his head as I took him through the steps to try and save my family.

"Carlos, I'm a firm believer that family comes first," Coach said after I finished. "You can walk out that door and get on a plane—but tell me. Will it make any difference how the doctors and nurses treat him?

"I have another way you can look at this," he added. "Carmani's job is to fight sickle cell disease until he can get that procedure. Your wife's job is to help him get there. Your job is to make an income to pay for all of it. You're a team. Everybody's got a job. Now, go do it."

Coach Sloan's words hit home. I couldn't be in two places at once and my family really needed me to stay and play well. "I can do this, Coach," I said, feeling a whole lot better.

Coach Sloan eased my mind, but he also showed immense faith in me at a crucial point in my professional life. He gave me the chance to become a star. I took that opportunity and ran with it. I became a key player in many of our drills, and my stats rose even higher.

"If he's on the left side anywhere, pass it to Boozer," Sloan told my teammates, his white locks flopping around for emphasis.

I formed a bond of telepathic proportions with guard Deron Williams. "Williams to Boozer!" was a regular call from the broadcasters' booth. "Time to take a Booozzzeee Cruise!" By season's end, Deron trailed only Steve Nash in league assists, a good portion of those passes connecting with me. I skyrocketed to ninth overall in effective field-goal percentages (another hat tip, Pops) and was No. 18 in scoring—in the entire NBA.

Every chance I got, I hopped on a plane back to Miami, even if it was only for twenty-four hours. I was there when the doctor harvested twenty-six of CeCe's eggs for in vitro fertilization. The doctors braced us for the possibility that the eggs might not take. Some couples tried in vitro for five or six years without any results. We were told to be patient. The doctors tested each egg to see which one would match Carmani's immune system. Ten were found compatible, and among those, two eggs were sickle cell–free. It was recommended that we implant both eggs to increase our odds that one would take.

"Sometimes one will boost the other," the doctor told us.

When Carmani reached four months, CeCe was inseminated. We prayed just one fertilized egg would take. Six weeks later, we were told to expect twins, which was double the blessing. We hadn't been told twins could be an option, but things were moving so fast, we didn't have time to react. We were up against the clock with Carmani's illness and there was no time to spare.

If we ever doubted our plans—and that happened often—we needed only listen to Carmani's whimpers. Babies cry when they're hungry or need to be changed, but for Carmani, crying could mean agonizing pain stemming from any part of his small body. It wasn't always as obvious as swollen hands and feet. Staring down into his soulful brown eyes as I held him, there were times I couldn't tell where he was hurting, or what I could do to make him feel better.

The threat of a seizure became a time bomb ticking over us, ready to blow up our lives. In 2006, about 87 percent of sickle cell patients suffered seizures. It seemed inevitable, but as the months went on and CeCe's belly grew with the twins, we started to wonder if we should just leave Carmani alone. There was no guarantee his body would accept his sibling's blood. The procedure could kill him. We lost sleep over this, crying at night holding each other, second-guessing if we were making the right decision. We talked ourselves in circles, yet we always came back to the same conclusion. If we could take Carmani's pain away, and it would never go away on its own, why would we make him suffer at all?

I hated each time I had to leave CeCe and Carmani. Every ringtone sparked uncertainty and anxiety. Carmani made seven emergency hospital visits before he was six months old. CeCe called me upset and sobbing many times, and I did my best to calm her. I was frustrated I couldn't be there to support her, even though she is one of the toughest women I know. The NBA schedule was tight, too, especially around the holidays. Right before Christmas, we had a series of five away games over eight days spanning the entire country. I considered dropping everything to fly back to Miami on more than one occasion.

Leave it to Larry to find a way to lift my spirits at the start of the new year.

"This is it," he told me at practice, as we stood together on the sidelines. "The algorithm doesn't lie. You're going to be an All-Star this year."

I'd forgotten about the magical algorithm Larry had mentioned in passing when we met.

"Are you sure, Larry?" I asked. My stats were strong, but you never knew how strong they had to be. Starters for the All-Star teams were voted on by the fans, players, and the media. Then, a slate of reserve members was selected by the team coaches. How Larry's algorithm could account for all that I had no idea, but I wanted to believe.

"You're playing phenomenally, and my algorithm has never failed me," he said. "I'll just congratulate you right now and save myself some time."

Larry's prediction gave me a little boost and a couple weeks later, I was notified that I'd been selected as a reserve player to the All-Star game on February 18 in Las Vegas. I was ecstatic at the nomination, but more impressed by Larry. He had a beautiful mind for numbers. I was playing my best ever and the only thing that could stop my momentum would be another injury. Three weeks before the All-Star game, I bruised my knee in a collision with New Orleans' Tyson Chandler in our forty-fifth game of the season. At that moment, I was second in the NBA with 33 double-doubles, ranked fifteenth in scoring (22.6) and fourth in rebounding (12.0). The bruise was upgraded to a hairline fracture just below my knee joint. I jumped into rehab, not wanting to miss my first All-Star game, but I didn't heal completely in time. I returned to the lineup on February 23, only missing eight games over three weeks.

It took a few weeks for me to get back to where I was before the injury, but when I did, I came on roaring like a grizzly bear. In March, I scored a career-high 41 points, and would tie that record a month later. We finished our season at 51–31, a ten-game improvement from the year before. We led our division and qualified for the playoffs. I know Larry was pleased because he joined us in the locker room to celebrate. He was a unique NBA owner.

We faced the Houston Rockets in the first round of playoffs, with all of our cylinders rolling. The additions of Ronnie Brewer, Paul Millsap and Dee Brown from the Draft had fleshed out our team. Deron was finding me more with a pick-and-roll play that would pay us dividends for seasons to come. Still, my nerves got the best of me and I played horribly in the first game, sinking only 11 points. I was panicked. I'd been brought on to lead the team into the playoffs, and I was floundering. I called Karl Malone and Charles Barkley, who'd both been in similar playoff situations like this before, as well as Coach K for advice. They all suggested the same thing.

"Everybody has bad games from time to time," Karl told me. "What would happen if you went out there all aggressive? Lay it all on the table."

With Karl's words repeating in my head, I tore loose from the tip-off, notching another career-high 41 points in the second game. In the seventh deciding game, I exploded for 35 points, 14 rebounds and five assists, which was heralded as one of the best series-closing games for the Jazz franchise ever.

"Whatever you ate before yesterday's game, whenever you took a shower—I want you to copy that routine for the rest of the playoffs," Coach Sloan told me the next day. I nodded in affirmation, knowing Karl and the others had given me extra fuel to burn.

In the second round, we met the Golden State Warriors—the Cinderella team that had surprisingly dispatched the No. 1 seed Dallas Mavericks before meeting us. I collected a crushing 20 rebounds in game one and scored 17 points. I made double-doubles for the rest of the series, including the game-high 34 points and 12 rebounds I earned in game four. We only faltered in game three, clinching the series 4–1. For the first time since 1998, Utah advanced to the Western Conference Finals.

The San Antonio Spurs, led by power forward Tim Duncan, were a championship team. Tim had already led the squad to three NBA championships in their previous six seasons and they'd eventually win their fourth championship once they got past us and the Heat in this one. I'd never played against a championship-level team before this, nor had my teammates. Boy, did we get a lesson in poise and composure. After each game, win or lose, I always had the same thought: *Damn, I want to be like that when I grow up.*

I knew we were in trouble early in the series, when I scored 10 points in a row and we took the lead. I looked to Tim's face, expecting it to betray emotion, but he was a placid Alaskan lake at dawn. I'd thought I'd been pretty good at reading on-court faces, but this lack of any reaction at all was unsettling to me.

I was such an emotional player by comparison; our entire team was. With every run we made against the mighty Spurs, we were overjoyed. We'd go through the roof. But this is where experience came in. It's a game of runs with the young players, and the Spurs turned that strength against us. Every time we got the upper hand, we'd search our opponents' faces, but get nothing. They weren't rattled. They weren't nervous. Not even a flinch of fleeting frustration. They had an inner peace only bestowed upon those who have already been to the mountaintop and conquered the unknown.

When we realized we couldn't bend the Spurs mentally, our confidence slipped. Then, every time they took the lead, we became even more distraught. At the same time, the Spurs stayed even-keeled as they overtook us. We couldn't tell if we were winning or losing, despite the scoreboard. The Spurs were just masterful, schooling us over five games.

The Jazz franchise was ecstatic with our results. We'd exceeded expectations, especially in the playoffs. We'd started to find a winning synergy we could build on for the next season. I played seventy-four games out of the eighty-two-game regular season—my first full season with the franchise. My first two seasons with Utah had been so fractured because of my injuries. It felt good to know I was finally delivering on the job I'd been hired for.

My season ended on May 30, in just enough time to make final preparations for the twins' arrival at our home in Miami. CeCe gave birth to fraternal twins by C-section on July 18, 2007. I pulled Cameron, then Cayden out myself, both a healthy seven pounds and six ounces and sickle cell–free. I watched as Cayden's umbilical cord was carefully placed in a metal dish and promptly taken away to be frozen.

The most difficult part of the plan to save Carmani was that he'd have to endure getting very sick from chemotherapy before he could get better. Seven weeks after the twins' births, our fifteen-month-old Carmani was admitted to Miami Children's Hospital in Coconut Grove for forty days to begin chemotherapy treatment, which would attack and destroy both the sickle-infected and healthy cells. Before the transplant could be done, the sickle cells would have to be destroyed. There was no way around it. I was in the off-season, so I tended to the twins during the day, while CeCe stayed at Carmani's side. We took shifts with Carmani; I usually arrived at 7:00 p.m. to be with him overnight, while CeCe went home to catch as much sleep as she could with infant twins. That became our routine for the next forty days.

On the first day, the doctors implanted a port on top of Carmani's left pec muscle that would stay in place until the day he left the hospital. It was incredibly uncomfortable for him, and he repeated the only two words he knew, *Ma* and *Da*, to try and tell us. He cried and reached for us as the nurses steadied his wiggling body. Intravenous tubes were attached to the port to administer the drugs and draw blood multiple times a day for testing. Carmani touched the port often, his face always distraught. Like anyone else, he just wanted it out of him.

During his two-week chemo treatment, Carmani's immune system was virtually wiped out. He was placed in a white sterile room at the end of a white sterile hallway. You had to scrub your hands like a surgeon and don a cumbersome paper apron to enter his room. Germs couldn't be introduced; Carmani wouldn't be able to fend them off. It was a scary environment for a little kid. They'd already put an uncomfortable metal box in his chest and plugged it full of tubes. Now his parents were mostly unrecognizable, covered from head to toe in barriers. As the days wore on, Carmani got sick from the drugs and his hair fell out. Both were expected, but Carmani's hair loss still upset me deeply. He became lethargic. We tried to make him as comfortable as possible, bringing his favorite toys and pictures from home. Carmani's nanny, Margarita, made rice and beans every day and brought it to the hospital. It was all he would eat. My teammates took turns visiting Carmani when the team was in town, so he'd never be short of someone to play with.

With careful timing, Cayden's cord blood was flushed into Carmani's body. Each day, the doctors drew Carmani's blood, checked his cell count and usually had the results for us when I got to the hospital in the evening.

In the second week, Carmani's doctor came into his room smiling.

"We're very early on, but it appears Carmani's blood is starting to take on the characteristics of his younger brother, Cayden's," he told us. It was working.

During our final week at the hospital, I came in one night to find CeCe sitting in the corner reading. Carmani was asleep. I looked down at my poor son, snuggling with a stuffed Spider-Man doll. My little superhero. I stared at him for another moment. Something looked different, but I couldn't quite place it.

"Is he—?"

"Darker?" CeCe finished my sentence. "Yes, you're not seeing things." CeCe and I were light-skinned. The twins were light-skinned. The doctors couldn't say why, but Carmani's complexion had darkened—closer to my father's coloring than my own. It was a subtle change that didn't affect Carmani's health and one I don't think anyone outside of my family noticed.

Carmani perked up a little more each day. The doctors were very encouraged. We were all encouraged. It was as if he was getting a fresh slate. The morning they took out his port, I saw something I hadn't seen in a while. Carmani was smiling.

When our family was finally reunited under one roof, the reality of having three kids under the age of two truly sunk in for us. Three times the feedings. Three times the diapers. Three times the spit-up. Zero sleep. And a full NBA schedule.

Three kids in eighteen months, but we were finally smiling, happy, healthy, and together—exactly how I'd pictured it in my head.

I'd like to say it was happily-ever-after for us after that, but that's not how life works. We had two infants, but also a toddler whose entire immune system had been wiped out. We were sent home with a list of instructions to keep our house immaculately clean. Counter surfaces and door handles were Clorox-wiped throughout the day. Curtains were taken down and carpets removed. CeCe and I watched Carmani diligently, pulling his curious hands away from anything with germs, which was everything. It was imperative that Carmani not get sick while his body's immune system rebuilt itself. A runny nose or a cough was cause for panic. Fevers, no matter how low-grade, meant all-hands-on-deck. We also had to watch for signs of Carmani's body rejecting the transplant, which could come on at any time and give us little time to react.

Carmani had a checkup every month to make sure his immune system was building back up after the chemotherapy and that no new sickle cells appeared. It was the only time CeCe and Carmani left the house. CeCe also had to keep our relatives at bay; nobody visited our house that first year—not my parents nor CeCe's mother. Everyone wanted to dote on the boys, but it was too great a risk to Carmani's life. After a few months, we all wanted to relax the rules, but CeCe stood firm. I went back to Utah and she had to continue to protect Carmani without me, sometimes from well-meaning relatives who showed up at our door.

CeCe and I had never argued once before the twins were born, but the strain of taking care of three babies under such extreme conditions gave us things to bicker about. My relatives wanted to see the boys, which put continued pressure on CeCe and me to relent. I probably didn't feel this way at the time, but I'm grateful she didn't fold. We have three healthy boys because of it.

For the next two years, CeCe and I separated and reunited a few times, trying to make our marriage work. I turned to my bishop and father for guidance, but there were times when I walked away because it was easier than staying. I made the mistake of getting caught up in the NBA player's lifestyle and I took CeCe for granted—something I regret to this day.

# CHAPTER 12

## PICK-AND-ROLL

You know you've made it when the *New York Times* pens an article about you and a teammate titled "A Twosome Reminiscent of the Stockton-Malone Era." I can't say there was any secret ingredient that made my connection with guard Deron Williams so strong, but we were young and hungry. When he joined Utah in my second year, the franchise was smart enough to see I needed someone who could feed me the ball often, yet accurately. Deron fit the bill perfectly, while becoming one of our top scorers at the same time. By the end of two seasons together, we could sense where the other was on the court without looking. And the more we ran our pick-and-roll, the smoother we became at it.

I kicked off my fourth season in Utah with 19 double-doubles in twenty-four games. In December 2007, I was named the Western Conference Player of the Month, having scored at least 30 points six times and posted 12 double-doubles the prior month. I was on fire, and I torched the Atlanta Hawks with 39 points and 12 rebounds right before Christmas.

I didn't need Larry's algorithm to tell me I'd make back-to-back All-Star teams. My stats were that good. I was named to the squad again in late January, then erupted with my only career triple-double against Seattle four days before the East-West showdown. I had 22 points, 11 rebounds, and 10 assists. To this day, I am the only Utah Jazz player to record a triple-double in a regular season.

On February 17, 2008, I was the sixth man off the bench at the annual All-Star game in New Orleans. Having sat out the year before from an injury, it felt like a major accomplishment just to participate alongside Shaq, Kobe, Melo, Tim Duncan, Allen Iverson, Yao Ming, and others. Of course, my parents flew into town to see their son play with the greatest players of his era. The All-Star weekend was more than just the one game, though. It was a weekend-long experience in celebration of the best in basketball—and I was there in the middle of it all. Crowds flocked to the three-point contest, slam dunk contest, and the celebrity game before we hit the court for the big Sunday showdown. My teammates and I received enthusiastic welcomes as we walked the French Quarter's cobblestone streets. We were cheered and toasted when we entered restaurants. Meals were on the house. This town couldn't have been more inviting.

As for the game itself, I notched a respectable 14 points and 10 rebounds in nineteen minutes of play. My parents were thrilled to see my name flash across the jumbotron each time I scored. In five NBA seasons, I'd gone from an overlooked second-round Draft pick to an All-Star. LeBron, the All-Star MVP, led the East to victory, 134–128.

Charged up by our All-Star appearances, Deron and I anchored our squad to fifty-three wins and twenty-eight losses in the regular season. I played eighty-one games and had 51 double-doubles. We qualified for the playoffs for the third year in a row.

Shane Battier was a familiar face when we met the Houston Rockets in the first playoff round. The Rockets were an easy-enough team to manage and we took the first two games in Texas, though we faltered in our third game back in Salt Lake City. The series was decided in our favor in a sixth game, 113–91. We were on to the next round.

The bad news was we faced the Lakers, led by the unflappable Kobe and skilled power forward Lamar Odom, who was just as aggressive as when I'd first seen him on the circuit at age twelve. We had our hands full in every area. The Lakers' defense stunted every player's scoring by 5 points or more, which added up, while Kobe unloaded for 38 points. We were battered and tossed, unable to find our footing as each wave crashed into us. We finally won the third game, despite Kobe's 34 points, then took the fourth game, breaking through the stifling efforts to put a lid on our scoring. We kept things alive for a sixth game in Utah, but the more seasoned Lakers had our number. They took the series 4–2, and advanced to the finals.

With my seventh NBA season in the books, I hardly had a moment to catch my breath when Coach K's name popped up on my cell phone. "You ready to suit up again?" he asked me. Of course, I knew what he was talking about. Coach K had been asked to coach the 2008 Olympic men's team, and I hoped he'd give me the opportunity to avenge our unfulfilling 2004 performance. Even during the average three-year NBA career, you always get the chance to rematch a player or a team, usually many times over. Yet, the Olympics are a one-shot deal. Few NBA players make an Olympic squad. Even fewer make two.

"Yeah, Coach," I answered. "When do we leave?" The 2008 Olympics were a month away in Beijing. We'd leave in two weeks.

I'd been hoping for, though not expecting, Coach K's call. The lead-up to this Olympics had been much different than the 2004 experience. After our bronze medal performance in Beijing, the US Olympic Committee decided to revamp the entire program. Who did they bring in to do this? Coach K, of course.

I was in the mix for the 2008 Olympic squad, as was D-Wade, LeBron, and Melo. You better believe we all wanted to make the squad for a chance at redemption. For the next two summers, Coach K molded together a new team of NBA stars that included Chris Bosh and Chris Paul. Kobe joined the team in 2007, fresh off two NBA championships. Kobe's cool, sometimes aloof demeanor raised doubts he could be the team player needed here, but I knew Kobe. Once he got in front of the other players, his intensity would rub off on them. It had on me. No one took this game more seriously than Kobe. I missed the team's rebuilding summers, but I had a good excuse for sitting them out with the births of my three children. Cradling Cameron and Cayden in each of my arms, I received the news that Coach K and the team swept all eight games in Las Vegas in 2007, qualifying for the 2008 Olympics in Beijing. I aimed to go with them and Coach K had obviously agreed.

Our final team had about a month to prepare together. Kobe, LeBron, and Jason Kidd, who was returning from the 2000 squad, were named co-captains. Deron Williams, Chris Bosh, and Chris Paul returned from the 2007 squad. At our orientation, I got a kick out of watching the best of the best react to Coach K's enthusiasm.

"Hey, I don't want you to come without your egos," he explained. "The egos you have on your current teams—bring them to this team and put it under one ego umbrella."

Coach K knew how to talk to college players. It turns out, he knew how to appeal to NBA players, too. To players who already had fame and fortune, he spoke about legacy. Coach K spoke about selfless service and inspired us by inviting military heroes, soldiers that had lost their vision in combat, to share their stories with us. What a swell of national pride Coach K inspired in us. By the time we'd hopped onto our 17-hour flight to Beijing, we were a focused army marching into battle.

Again, it was decided that our team wouldn't stay in the

Olympic Village, but at the InterContinental Hotel, a luxury hotel in the city as grand as the Four Seasons. I'm not sure this move had to do so much with our security, but our comfort. The beds in the Olympic Village were only five feet eight inches long. Other than that, our Olympic experience was quite different this time around.

As a team, we attended as many of the other events as possible. I saw the fastest man on the planet, Usain Bolt, with my own eyes. After breakfast each morning, our routine included the aquatic center, where we'd watch Michael Phelps win another gold medal. We were loud, but friendly in the stands. We also visited the Olympic Village every day.

Like he'd done in Las Vegas, Kobe set the tone of our visit on the competition end.

We met every morning for breakfast at 7:00 a.m., collected our gear from our rooms, and would leave together on a bus for the stadium. None of us missed breakfast—except for Kobe. For the first few days, he'd join us at the bus, but one day he missed our transport altogether and no one could find him. Kobe was already at the gym. He'd been going there all along to get in some baskets before breakfast, then would make it back to the hotel. He gave us all a quick nod and went right back to his main focus.

As we all rode back after practice, I tried to work it all out in my head. There was one shuttle bus that swung past our hotel about five-thirty every morning and Kobe had somehow made sure he was on it. Thirty minutes to the stadium gave him about one hour to put up shots and then he'd catch another shuttle bus back to the dorms. We could have asked him why he was doing this. We were overwhelming favorites to take gold. Top-level players from other countries were rejected from the NBA all of the time and those were the guys we'd be playing against. Kobe didn't see that as an excuse not to keep his tools as sharpened as he could right up to game day. This was what he did in the

NBA. This is what he did in the off-season. Why should any of us expect different?

Kobe hadn't asked any of us to join him. We were already practicing together with Coach K two times a day. What Kobe was doing was extra. He was in the gym practicing for that moment the team got the ball into his hands and it was all up to him. Talk about making every shot count.

We must have all thought about discovering Kobe at the gym that morning. He hadn't opened his mouth to anybody about the extra sessions, which made it an effective rallying call. The next morning, a few of us stood with Kobe in the chilly air waiting for that little shuttle bus. By the next day, it was all twelve of us. And would you believe Kobe got us all to start putting up baskets after dinner? That was the Mamba Mentality. There was nothing that matched it in pro basketball.

Thanks to Coach K, we were relaxed and confident heading into Olympic play. Everyone knew their role, which was a vast difference already from the 2004 Games. In our downtime, we played cards, ribbed each other, and clowned around. We even got Kobe to crack an unexpected smile or laugh here and there. Still, on the bus rides back to the hotel each night, while the rest of us dozed off, I'd see the fluorescent light coming off Kobe's laptop. He was watching tape on our opponents. Repeatedly.

After The Dream Team's 1992 success and the two squads that followed it, our 2004 bronze medal had been regarded as a letdown to some, but with Coach K at the helm, we'd been dubbed "The Redeem Team" before we even stepped on Chinese soil. Coach K was the right man for the job with his ability to bring athletes from different walks of life, from different experiences and views, together as a collective team. I'm not sure there are many coaches who could take twelve NBA superstar studs and make them set aside their egos for one another. With Kobe, LeBron, and Dwight Howard at center, and the rest of our lineup so deep, D-Wade—probably among the top three NBA players *ever* at his position—came off the bench and ended up being our highest scorer. Our bench was so deep, that I didn't mind playing three minutes here and five minutes there. Not one bit. I trusted Coach K, as did the others, to play us as he thought best. I thought he did a great job of getting us all playing time.

Our first game was probably our most watched. We were told over one billion Chinese viewers tuned in to see us play against their home team, led by the seven-foot-six Yao Ming. We trounced them 101-70, sending an immediate message to the rest of the world that the Americans were back.

The rest of our slate were basically blowouts. We won all eight games we played in Beijing, including the gold medal match against Spain. We won that one 118-107. Being back on the podium, and knowing we'd performed up to our potential was deeply fulfilling. For returnees like me, LeBron, D-Wade, and Melo, coming back this second time was also a personal redemption, a chance to right a wrong. Athletes live for opportunities to do this. It's one of the few ways we can put the ghosts of our past performances to rest.

After the medal ceremony, I was anxious to get to my father and CeCe, who'd watched us play all eight games from the stands. Growing up practicing with my father, we'd never talked about the Olympics. We'd only dreamed of the NBA, and I hadn't thought there was anywhere to go beyond that. The past four years of my life had also been so hectic that I hadn't had much time to celebrate my professional success with my father and the rest of my family.

"Let me see this thing," my dad said, proudly touching the medal hanging around my neck. "Man, this is heavy," he added, dipping it up and down in his hand.

"It sure is, Pops," I said, turning from him to a grinning CeCe for a photo. "It sure is."

★ ★ ★

Once a franchise finds its sweet spot, everyone wants to keep it going for as long as possible. An NBA team's success has a lot to do with the ten athletes who trample the hard maple. But the people surrounding those ten can have just as much influence.

As I'd prepared to leave for Beijing, the Jazz front office called me with horrible news. Larry, our revered leader, had suffered a heart attack and been hospitalized. When I returned to the States, I was scared to learn Larry was still in the hospital, battling complications from diabetes. He stayed in the hospital for two months. The next time I saw Larry, he was in a wheelchair.

Greg, Larry's son, took over a lot of his father's Jazz responsibilities that summer, so when the team returned that fall for the 2008–2009 season, Larry's diminishing health seemed that much more serious. I'd seen Greg cheering for us at the games, but he hadn't been a component of the franchise's workings. We all missed Larry's larger-than-life personality bouncing off the arena's walls. The place wasn't the same without Larry, so I started calling him a couple of times a week to "update him on the team." Larry was like a family member to me.

I'd returned to Utah that season alone; CeCe and I had separated and we were contemplating divorce. That's an awful feeling to carry onto the court, but, again, I found refuge there. No matter what had ever ailed me, basketball had always been my medicine. From grief to heartache to resentment to self-doubt, basketball healed all. I was safe on the court and I always left it more relaxed than when I walked onto it.

In our first twelve games of the season, I broke 20 points eight times and had 7 double-doubles. I'd achieved a high level of consistency over multiple seasons, an elusive goal for any NBAer. But that came to a crashing halt, literally, on November 19, when I collided midair with Luc Mbah a Moute during a routine rebounding attempt against the Milwaukee Bucks. I'm a big guy, so bouncing into another behemoth, this one six foot eight and 230 pounds, sent me flying sideways, causing me to land awkwardly and crumple to the ground. It was a basic rebound I'd executed thousands of times, but when I rose and tried to put some weight on my left leg, a pain shot up it like an electrical current. Only twelve games in and my body was betraying me again.

I sustained a hyperextended strain of my left quadriceps tendon and pain radiated from just above the knee cap. The entire joint was inflamed. I underwent surgery soon afterward in Los Angeles to clean out the loose pieces of cartilage. Then I began a four-week rehabilitation program in LA, after which I was told my return to activity would be re-evaluated. As always, I was anxious to get back to my teammates, but this rehab was a lot more tolerable when I met another patient I'd be healing beside.

"Car-los Boo-zer," Queen Latifah sang when we saw each other. I was stunned she was sitting there on a leg machine, rehabilitating her knee after a skiing accident.

"Now what can we talk about?" she teased. Just like Prince, Queen Latifah adored basketball. Her roots were with the New York Knicks and her home state team, the New Jersey Nets. Her game knowledge was top-shelf. She understood who could play and who couldn't and why.

Given the chance, I wanted to hear what it was like to be a world-recognized rapper and acclaimed actress. After earning an Oscar nomination in 2002 for *Chicago*, Queen had churned out some crowd-favorite comedies, like *Bringing Down The House* with Steve Martin, and *Last Holiday* with L.L. Cool J. She had a slew of projects on the horizon, including a film she'd just wrapped, about, of all things, basketball.

"It's more a romance," she said, "about a physical therapist who falls for the basketball player she's treating." Ah, Hollywood.

Our conversations about our lives were lively and fun. She was like many of the characters she's portrayed: a strong woman who went after what she wanted. By the end of our time together, we'd made plans to meet up at a game. A few months later, we did just that when Queen came to Miami. About a year after we parted ways from rehab, *Just Wright*, starring Queen and rapper Common, was released.

While I was away in rehab, Larry's condition took a turn for the worse, and he was admitted again to the hospital. In the last six months, he told me he'd nearly died four times. In an attempt to save Larry's life, doctors amputated both legs, six inches below the knee.

Three days after the surgery, the team huddled on the court after practice. We were heading over to visit Larry together and wanted to collect our thoughts and present a united front. I'd spoken to Larry the night before, and he seemed tired, if not in good spirits. I don't think any of us knew what to expect when we arrived. We filtered into the room and there was a moment where I'm sure we all looked to where Larry's legs should have been, tucked under his blanket.

"Hey guys!" Larry said welcomingly, dispelling the silence. "Why the long faces?"

We all laughed. It was a surprise visit, full of hugs and reminiscing about all our Jazz glories. I had a nagging feeling that this was the last time I'd see Larry. I told him I loved him before we all shuffled out to give him some privacy with his wife, Gail, and his five children. Less than a month later, Larry died. He was sixty-four.

I returned to play on February 23, 2009, missing forty-four games over three months. The squad had done well in my absence, winning thirty-two games, so we were still in the playoff hunt. My return kicked off an eight-game winning streak, as we pushed through the remaining twenty-six regular season games.

In Miami, CeCe and I continued to work on our marriage. But somewhere between Salt Lake City and Miami, within the hundreds of hours we were away from one another, the chasm between CeCe and I became too far to cross. I was seventeen years old when I met CeCe, but I wasn't that kid on crutches in the school bookstore anymore. I was a twenty-eight-year-old man, a different person, who wanted different things from life. That March, I filed for divorce. Carmani was not quite three years old; the twins were nineteen months.

CeCe and I sat our boys down to ease them into our plans. It was a difficult conversation, and they began to cry when we explained that I would be living in a new house. The thought of it tore me apart.

I didn't want to be away from my boys any more than I had to, but I knew they were in great hands. CeCe was a wonderful mother. She'd singlehandedly orchestrated Carmani's lifesaving procedure, a three-baby-delivery process. She protected our cubs like a lioness, particularly Carmani, whose immune system was vulnerable for years. I knew they would be safe, protected, and cared for as they'd always been with her—I just wouldn't be around as much to see it.

I felt like a terrible failure because my only example of marriage had been my parents. They'd had their ups and downs, and were still married forty years and counting. Divorce with CeCe had never crossed my mind. I thought we'd be together forever, but now the best we could hope for was figuring out a way to work together as co-parents in our kids' lives.

We finished the season with a 48–34 record to make the play-offs. We faced Kobe and the Lakers in our opening series, and as usual, it was like driving full-speed into a familiar brick wall. We dropped the first two games in LA playing our best. We squeaked out the third game, 88–86, thanks to Deron hitting a nice fadeaway with 2.2 seconds left. However, we couldn't sustain it, not with Kobe putting in 38 and then 31 points the next two games to close out the series 4–1.

"Your man's a liability," Kobe told me, after the Boston Celtics beat the Lakers in the 2009 NBA finals and he was back home.

Kobe's critique was very pointed, explaining in detail why our team wasn't working, something he'd been able to observe up close and firsthand when the Lakers took us out in the first round. The scary thing about Kobe was he could pinpoint our weaknesses and use them in real time against us. His analysis made so much sense that I wondered why our franchise hadn't seen this glaring hole.

When I returned to training for the sixth and final year on my contract with the Jazz, I slipped this information, sans its origins, to Greg, with some suggestions on how to shore up our formidable, yet still leaking boat. When I'd brought ideas to Larry, he'd been receptive. He didn't necessarily act upon them, but he was open to a serious discussion. Sometimes he'd explain why he couldn't do it, which would send our conversation in a new direction. The goal was always to evolve the team. Greg's response was swift and telling.

"We're only going to pay for what we have out there now," he told me. It wasn't the approach Larry had taken with the franchise. All along, Larry had spent money out of his own pocket to grow the franchise. Greg had a different vision for how to run the family business, which is exactly what this was. I had no ownership claim nor was I footing the bill. Still, I realized that there were new limitations. Greg wasn't willing to pay beyond the two stars we had in Deron and myself. And with Kobe and the Lakers still out there, a championship would likely remain out of our grasp. My differences with Greg were only about the business. I had nothing personal against him. Likewise, when Greg critiqued the way I played, like his father had, I understood that was his prerogative.

Greg's decision-making didn't affect how I or the rest of the team played. We remained competitive throughout the entire season, finishing 53–29 in the regular season. I believe our consistent chemistry had a lot to do with the time we spent away from the sport.

Deron Williams, my quiet pick-and-roll accomplice, threw the most epic Halloween parties at his house every year. The players and our families congregated in Deron's backyard around the pool. Spiders in cobwebs hung from every corner. Costumed children sailed through the air on the trampoline while some of the adults splintered off to the garage to play with the golf simulator. DJ Juggy, a famous local artist, spun tunes all night, while the veteran players plied the new blood with Deron's "jungle juice" from the punch bowl. If any of them canceled their plans the next day, we knew we'd done our jobs.

We were a tight-knit team. We'd return from road trips so wired that we'd huddle together around the TV, playing video games together until morning. None of us could go home to sleep, so we'd wind down together, cracking on one another until our adrenaline levels stabilized. If you ever played an aggressive *Call of Duty* team out of Salt Lake City at two in the morning, there's a good chance you were playing the Utah Jazz squad.

In mid-April, we entered the playoffs as a fifth seed against the Denver Nuggets, led by forward Carmelo Anthony. In the first game, Melo scored 42 points to Deron's 26 and my 19, paving the Nugget's path to a 126–113 victory. We stepped it up—and slowed Melo down to a degree, to take games two and three. Back in Salt Lake City, Melo had another monster game with 39 points, but I evened things out a bit, firing back with 31 points and 13 rebounds of my own, extending us to a promising 3–1 series lead.

Game five took us back to Denver, where the top-heavy Nuggets suddenly had four standout scorers that night. Even Deron's 34 points and my 25 points couldn't stop their momentum. There would be a sixth game in Utah.

I asked CeCe and the boys to attend this game even with its

late 10:00 p.m. start. There was a chance I wouldn't return to the Jazz next season, and I wanted my family with me for what might be my final home game with the franchise.

We won the game, 112–104, to take the series. I had a big game with 22 points and 20 rebounds, but that's not what I remember about that night. After the game, I stayed on the court to tape a TV interview with Charles Barkley and Shaq for TNT. CeCe took the twins backstage to the press conference to wait, but Carmani wouldn't leave the court, not without me. He stood off to the side, looking dapper in his white button-down shirt and blue sweater vest. When I finished the interview, Carmani launched at me, jumping into my arms. I carried him out of the arena, as blue and white confetti drifted down from the rafters onto us like snow.

I wish Kobe wasn't always right, but he was dead-on about our weaknesses, which we didn't fix before we met the Lakers again in the second series. Kobe couldn't be contained; he scored 31 points or more over their four-game sweep.

At the end of my contract with Utah, my agent, Rob, started renegotiations with the franchise. The wheel wasn't broken there—far from it—but he felt there might be new offers. I wasn't set on leaving Utah, but I wasn't sure what other interest was out there. Yet, before I had time to dwell on it, my cell phone rang. I looked at the familiar name, realizing that question was about to be answered.

"What's crackin', LeBron?" I asked.

# CHAPTER 13

## CHICAGO

LeBron and I had something big in common that summer—our contracts were up. It was no secret that LeBron was looking for a new home. After seven years with the Cavs, my former teammate was free to sign with another franchise.

I'd kept in casual touch with LeBron since our Cav days and we'd seen each other around during our summers in Miami. LeBron's second son, Bryce, played against my twins, Cameron and Cayden, on the same local basketball circuit. Sometimes we sat together in the bleachers, shamelessly hooting and hollering for our kids like we were at the NBA Finals. LeBron was a good guy. Trustworthy and unpretentious, even though he was on a first-name basis with everyone else on the planet. It was good to hear from him with my own career at a crossroads.

We reminisced, then talked a bit of shop. I wouldn't have minded playing with LeBron again for any franchise, if that's the way the chips fell. We'd both come a long way since the Young Gunners, and we'd experienced the 2004 and 2008 Olympics together.

It was clear that LeBron had outgrown the Cleveland market

and needed to go somewhere bigger. Moving to a larger franchise like the Lakers or New York activated a crazy pay bump
in LeBron's Nike contract that he'd been waiting seven years
to cash in on. New York and three other franchises had the cap
space (or budget) to afford LeBron, along with one or two supporting players. LeBron was ready to move, but not without
some firepower to help him.

Needless to say, free agents that particular summer were of
extra interest to everyone: read the tea leaves correctly and one
might figure out where LeBron was going. Free agents that
summer included Joe Johnson and Dwyane Wade at guard, as
well as Chris Bosh, Amar'e Stoudemire, and myself at the big-
man, power forward spots.

I tried to temper my excitement. There were more puzzle
pieces in play than just me and LeBron. The other free agents'
destinations could either entice or discourage him in the end.
This was a high-stakes poker game, but only a few franchises
could buy a seat at the table.

Miami, Chicago, the Knicks, and the New Jersey Nets were
all in the running for LeBron. The other franchises didn't have
enough cap space to support his vision and he had no interest
in settling or compromising. He made that very clear from the
onset. After seven seasons with the Cavs, LeBron could pick who
he played for and who he'd play with. I had faith that a few NBA
trophies were in his future. I'd chosen to part with LeBron earlier on in my career. Was fate's wheel swinging around a second
time and beckoning me to jump on board?

My agent cautioned me to keep an open mind.

"Let's do what's best for you," Rob said one evening over
dinner. "LeBron will do whatever he's going to do. Let's explore his scenario, but there will be other offers, other options. I
don't think we can say Utah is completely off the table, either."

I nodded in agreement and tackled my ribeye steak. Utah still
had a strong team and Greg Miller had kept our negotiations

open. Was I willing to give up the good thing I had going with Deron and Coach Sloan?

There were other teams for me to consider. The New Jersey Nets reached out to me, but it wasn't a very exciting offer. Mikhail Prokhorov, a Russian-Israeli billionaire, had recently purchased the franchise and tapped former Dallas Mavericks coach Avery Johnson to breathe some life into a squad with a 12–70 record. Coach Johnson had worked wonders with the Mavs in his tenure, but this was too much of a rebuilding scenario for my tastes.

I was really thinking about going to the Knicks. Amar'e Stoudemire was a good friend of mine. We'd battled for a long time against one another and developed a mutual respect. Amar'e signed with the New York Knicks, and word quickly spread that LeBron didn't want to play with him. I don't know why and hadn't heard of any beef. I also didn't ask anyone about it. It was none of my business.

The dealer dropped the flop card on the table: Amar'e was going to the Knicks. The franchises looked at the cards they held, adjusted their bets and tossed their chips into the kitty— the cost to see the next card dealt in the LeBron World Poker Championships.

On my own front, I had other teams to consider. Bulls general manager John Paxson invited me to Chicago, a sensational town with gorgeous architecture and a rich cultural history. From its delicious deep-dish pizza to its museums and gangster landmarks, Chicago had a feel all its own that I tapped into right away.

The Bulls squad was loaded. It included No. 1 draftee Derrick Rose, Duke alum Luol Deng, and Joakim Noah, a defensively-gifted center. I could clearly see how the franchise was trying to build a championship roster, and where I'd fit into the equation to support the franchise star in Rose. I didn't care if I was the star at the top. I wanted a championship. Plain and simple. Newly hired coach Tom Thibodeau was a defensive guru, illustrated by the Celtics league-leading stalwart defense during their 2008 championship season. Really, all the Bulls were missing was a starting power forward.

The turn card was revealed—and it was me. I signed a five-year deal with the Bulls. With me off the market, everyone was waiting to see what LeBron would do, and the Bulls were still in the running. But I felt ready to commit to a new beginning in Chicago, whether LeBron followed or not.

Of course, I did everything I could to swing LeBron our way. I suggested bringing on Kyle Korver and Ronnie Brewer, who I'd played with for the Jazz, to make the squad look even more appetizing. Korver was a knockdown shooter, and Brewer excelled as a sixth man with terrific defense. GM Paxson listened, and the Bulls added both players to the roster, along with signing CJ Watson, a solid backup for D-Rose, our nickname for Derrick.

With Joakim at center, averaging double digits in points and rebounds, the squad looked solid—at least on paper—for the 2010-2011 season. Signing LeBron to the Bulls could produce multiple championships and we all knew it. We were as anxious as everyone else to hear his decision, though I thought the team Chicago had assembled would be a contender with or without LeBron.

The final card of this grand poker game, the river, was a twofer. Dwyane Wade and Chris Bosh were both represented by Hank Thomas, a phenomenal agent based out of Chicago. Wade and Bosh were shopped as a package deal and they landed together in Miami. This double acquisition happened on the eve of LeBron's announcement to the world of his plans.

On July 8, 2010, thirteen million people watched LeBron announce his choice on "The Decision," a special that aired on ESPN. Having not spoken with LeBron in a few days, I was just as in the dark as everyone else tuning in. It was down to Chicago and Miami, so we had a 50 percent shot. All the cards had been dealt and Miami stood up from the table, extended its hands and pulled the chips from the table's center. The Miami Heat had won the LeBron James jackpot.

I could see how LeBron made his choice. It's hard for stars to live in the shadows of those who've preceded them, which is why I think Chicago fell to his wayside. He'd have been living in the shadow of Michael Jordan, whose six championships in the 1990s will forever be the measuring stick when judging other basketball greats. Going to Chicago would have unfairly amplified that comparison.

I'm not saying LeBron couldn't have done that in Chicago, but I think he wanted a clean slate on which to build his own legacy from the ground floor up. In choosing Miami, he'd also team up with a close friend in Dwyane Wade. Miami had a capable coach in Erik Spoelstra, and Pat Riley in the front office, who would ultimately win nine championships in various capacities as a player, coach, and executive. Florida also had no state tax and for a guy like LeBron, making hundreds of millions of dollars off the court, he could save eight or nine million dollars in one year. That definitely wasn't chump change to live in a perpetually sunny city on the water.

While LeBron was reborn in Miami, I looked to my own reinvention of sorts in Chicago. Divorce proceedings between CeCe and me had begun that summer, so my life was changing on every front possible. I'd done a lot of self-reflection over that summer, trying to figure out the man I wanted to be and hoping I could get there. I wanted to be a good father and co-parent with CeCe, but I also had to forge ahead to find happiness on my own, whatever that looked like.

I'd never lived alone and not in need of a family home, I settled into an apartment in the upscale Elysian Hotel. The lobby was adorned with modern sculptures on pedestals. It was an extravagant choice, but it also afforded me a little more privacy, not being the type of hotel where the other guests would typically feel compelled to approach me, if I was noticed at all. Walking through the lobby without being stopped before you get to the elevator is an underrated experience. However, I think it was the private spa that probably sold me on the Elysian the most. Hot tubs are never underappreciated by NBA players.

Our preseason team practices hit the ground running, as Coach "Thibs" ran us through our new plays. Coach Thibs had been an assistant coach for six NBA franchises over two decades before taking the Bulls' helm. He was younger than Coach Sloan, but that worked to his benefit with our team's vibe. In those preseason practices, something was percolating.

Everything was clicking on the court. Our timing came together quicker than we'd anticipated. But off the court, things were more complicated for me. My fancy apartment was gorgeous, but without my sons there to live in it with me, it might as well have been a shack. Under our custody agreement, I'd get them all summer, but that was more than six months away. I was distracted, which is why when I heard my doorbell ring one night, I raced to it, tangled my foot in my unpacked gym bag, and tripped in the dimly lit hallway. Two hundred and fifty-five pounds came crashing down awkwardly onto my curled right hand. I felt initial pain, but it didn't register as anything of concern. Of course, no one was at the door.

The next morning, my swollen hand pulsated with pain. I reported to the Bulls' medical team, where X-rays showed a fracture of the fifth metatarsal, the pinkie finger of my right hand. It was two days before our first preseason game and I was angry with myself for not being more focused, as my team would suffer for it. On October 7, I underwent surgery on my hand and it was sealed in a cast for six weeks.

Another NBA season started without me, as I began rehab yet again and reported to the games in a suit. I was one of seven new players brought on that season, and I had a specific role on the championship team Chicago was trying to create. It takes time to build chemistry and I wasn't building it sitting on the bench, shackled by a cast. I stayed irate with myself for my clumsiness, for not putting my gym bag away that entire first month, as I watched fifteen games crawl by without me. Those fifteen games were particularly torturous because the team already knew we could play well together, except that I'd mucked it up. If I could have beat my cast over my head to heal faster, I would have gladly endured that punishment.

I made it back onto the court against the Orlando Magic on December 1. The Bulls had gone 9–6 in my absence. I had a slow start, played twenty-one minutes, picking up 5 points and 2 rebounds. Orlando smashed us under its boot, 107–78, but Rome wasn't built in a day.

If the Jazz organization had felt like a family to me, the Bulls felt more like five brothers that left the family and got an apartment together. I no longer had a wife and kids to get home to, so I had more time than ever before to bond with my teammates. We loved to dress up to go out to eat together, both around Chicago and on the road. Breaking bread as a team was a new experience. I'd eaten a lot of room service alone during the earlier years, making sure I connected with CeCe each evening. The team started going everywhere together outside our games, from nightclubs to movie theaters. It became easier to play together because we developed trust. We joked and made fun of each other in that way that only comes from shared history. It made communication on the court, in the heat of the moment, more efficient and effective.

I was all about communication. You couldn't shut me up on the court, but Chicago is where I perfected a couple of slogans I'd become known for. I borrowed one of my catchphrases from Joakim Noah, when I heard him utter it under his breath while taking a shot.

"What did you say?" I asked him.

"Holdat," my quiet teammate said. "It's a bit of a humble brag." That word made it so frequently into my shouts, that my borrowing from Joakim was more of a hijacking. Soon the whole team was shouting "Holdat" as we made baskets. "And One" was another tried and tested phrase I'd shout out during the game, referring to the single point you score from the free-throw line, though my use of that one became more liberal over time.

The nights we ate out together, learning about one another, translated into the language we used on the court. Once I was back in the lineup in early December 2010, we dove into a seven-game winning streak that garnered us mild media attention. At the end of December, we clocked in another five victories in a row. The media threw a little more love our way.

While our season revved up, I was eager to explore Chicago's hotspots, and had someone in mind to join me. I'd met Aneshka a few years earlier through a mutual friend's gathering at The Forge, an upscale Miami lounge that had chandeliers dripping from its ceilings. She hadn't recognized me as an NBA player at the time, which any NBA player will confirm is an appealing concept. Sometimes you feel like the NBA logo and your salary are tattooed across your forehead, the way peoples' behavior bends and distorts around you. It can be difficult to judge people's true motivations. I never sensed an ulterior motive with Neeka. She was down-to-earth, a bohemian artist with a shared appreciation of good food and culture, of which Chicago had plenty to offer. We discovered the city together, enjoying sushi at the Niu Fusion Lounge, biking on the path along Lake Michigan, and gazing at the exotic fish and dolphins at the Shedd Aquarium, one of the most visited attractions in the country. Experiencing new things together for the first time, we fell in love against the backdrop of Chicago. I was thrilled when Neeka moved to Chicago to be with me. I can't think of Chicago without my thoughts jumping fondly to her.

Hailing from the Pacific Northwest, Neeka was a kindred

spirit who loved nature as much as I did and wanted to explore the world with me. Together, we'd travel to Bali, Morocco, Egypt, Spain, and Italy, to name a few destinations. We went on a conscious journey together and connected spiritually discovering cultures so different than our own. I'd declared myself a sociology major at Duke because I had a general interest in learning how others lived.

Though not an athlete, Neeka was athletic and adventurous. When I ran off a sixty-foot cliff into Belizean water, Neeka was right behind me. If she was hiking up an Italian mountainside, I was following behind her. Neeka also introduced me to yoga, which she practiced every day. I welcomed the strength and flexibility yoga gave me, but also its centering and calming effects. Finding peace in difficult poses translated so well into real life.

Neeka came to a few games to watch me play. She hadn't been an NBA fan when we'd met back in 2008, but she was excited to see what I'd spent a lifetime investing in, which gave me good vibes about a future together.

That January, we played against Shaq, now a Boston Celtic, one last time. The game didn't make a particular impression on me, but what happened afterward did.

"Yo!" someone yelled as I exited the court toward the locker rooms. I could pick that low-register voice out of a lineup with my eyes closed.

"Hey, Booz. I want to talk to you for a minute," Shaq said, beckoning me over with one hand, the other dabbing his forehead with a white towel. The last time I'd spoken with Shaq off the court was at the 2008 All-Star game. I'd been in the locker room before tip-off, sweating like a snowball in a microwave, when he'd noticed my nerves. It was my first All-Star game. It was Shaq's twelfth.

"Hey, I like how you compete for your team," he'd said. "You bring it every night. You put your hard hat on and you bring your lunch pail and you go to work. I like that about you."

The most dominant player in the game was telling me that he liked my work ethic. Those words were precious to me as a young player trying to find my place in the league. They were an instant confidence booster. So, when Shaq flagged me down at our final game in January, I knew it was going to be good. Who didn't love this guy?

"Booz, I see you've been working hard here," he said as he nodded toward the court. "And out there," he said, tipping his head to the exit, while he placed his giant hand on my shoulder.

"Whoa!" he broke off into a howl. "Everyone! Look over here! Between the lines, this kid brings it," he said to anyone who might be listening. A few production guys looked up from their tangle of wires, smiled when they saw where the noise had come from, then crouched down again over their work. That was Shaq. He loved coaxing smiles from peoples' faces. He really enjoyed making people feel happy and comfortable. That's just genuinely who Shaq is. I knew immediately that I'd miss his court jester presence, the one that always found a way to make the most serious players lose their composure with an unexpected joke or hilarious observation.

The rest of our season sailed by; each week we got stronger, led by D-Rose. Chicago itself was getting excited. With sports bars on every corner, the city was salivating for another championship basketball team. *Was Rose the next Jordan? Was this the team that could once again go all the way?* When we finished the season, 62–20, clinching our Central Division in the Eastern Conference, our sports-obsessed town wanted to believe so.

In the playoffs, we took our opening series against Indiana 4–1, but it was closer than the final stats indicate; the first four games were settled by 6 points or less. We were just a little bit better than the Pacers. An extra pass here, an unexpected rebound there was what made the difference.

In our next bracket against Atlanta, I had my best postseason performance in game six, earning 23 points, 10 rebounds, and 5 assists in the series' clincher.

LeBron and the Miami Heat awaited us in the conference finals, but after taking the series opener on adrenaline alone, we dropped four straight games like a kid on a sugar crash. It was competitive and we'd been in the lead going into every fourth quarter. We just couldn't get over the hump once LeBron really took over scoring and playmaking in those last minutes. LeBron, supported by Chris Bosh and D-Wade, averaged 28 points over four games. This was one of the best teams that money could buy, after all. The Heat was a well-coached team, and their clever adjustments were just too much for us.

Still, we'd made it within eight games of winning the entire NBA championship, and many considered us serious title contenders for the next season. D-Rose, the twenty-two-year-old dynamo and the center jewel in our crown, won the Most Valuable Player award. He was the youngest-ever MVP at the time. And though I'd missed twenty-three games, I'd still managed to average 17.5 points and 9.6 rebounds; I also ranked twelfth in the NBA in defensive rebounding, nabbing 7.4 per game. I loved rebounding because it gave someone on the team the opportunity to score more points. I gave it as much attention as my scoring attempts.

I returned to Miami for my first summer with the boys since the divorce settlement. Carmani was four, the twins three and getting their hands into everything. I bought a house with a pool, perfect for a Miami summer. The boys and I were out by the pool one afternoon, when I heard Cayden ask his older brother a question.

"What's that on your chest, Mani?" he asked, pointing to the deep scar on Carmani's pec muscle. We hadn't spoken to the boys about their miraculous conceptions and Carmani's cured sickle cell anemia at length yet. I realized it was time. I motioned the trio to come closer, sitting Carmani down next to me on my lounge chair. The twins sat down on the chair opposite us. I started their origin story, explaining how their mother scoured the country for a team of three special doctors, who worked together to cure their older brother.

"This mark is special," I said pointing to the scar. "You didn't know it at the time, but you were all fighting for one another during different stages."

"Like a superhero?" Carmani asked. Even at four, Carmani had a seriousness to him, no doubt a product of his harrowing experience.

"Yes," I said. "You're all each other's superheroes."

I started pointing at all three kids, mixing my hands around like a dealer working his shell game on the street.

"You're his and you're his and you're his," I repeated, making them all giggle.

"Do we know any other heroes?" Carmani asked. It was a great question that I didn't have to think about.

"Grandpa and Grandma are my heroes," I answered. "They were Mr. and Mrs. Superman—but without the capes. They got me where I needed to go."

My parents had been and would always be my heroes for the time and effort they sacrificed from their own lives. They'd offered me the ultimate assist in my life, which I'd appreciate even more when it came time to help my own children in chasing their dreams. Staring at Carmani's scar, I was reminded of another parent who'd put her children first.

In our case, CeCe's efforts were both lifesaving and lifegiving. If CeCe hadn't rejected every "no" she heard from doctors along the way, all three of my strapping sons wouldn't be sitting there with me. I owed her more than I could ever express in words, which made we want to step it up as a co-parent. CeCe and I would always be bonded through Carmani, Cayden, and Cameron and I hoped to repair and strengthen that connection over time, no matter where each of us was in our own lives. In time, CeCe and I would explain more of our sons' unique origins to them. But dinner was in our immediate future.

"Let's get you three inside," I said, rising and shaking off my thoughts. "I bet your mom would love a call from you before bedtime."

# CHAPTER 14

## LOCKOUT

I cherished my first summer with the boys following the divorce after so many months apart, but I was anxious to get back to Chicago to play. Our team had exceeded all first-season expectations and wanted to keep the momentum going. No NBA team would get that chance, though, as we got word that the players and the franchises had failed to reach a new agreement and would enter a lockout beginning July 1. The lockout, as always, was about money. The franchise owners proposed to reduce the players' share of Basketball Related Income (BRI) from 57 percent to 47 percent. They also wanted to implement a hard salary cap and a harsher luxury tax, hoping to increase competition among teams.

I didn't have particularly strong feelings about the lockout. I understood that the team owners were trying to cut the players' revenues substantially. I also knew the fans paid to see LeBron James and Kobe Bryant, not the owners, and it was best to let the lawyers work it out. When both sides failed to reach an agreement, the NBA canceled the preseason and all games through December.

If you're a world-class athlete that gets extended downtime, for any reason, you still have to keep sharp. Formally, we couldn't practice at our arena, the United Center. Informally, a few of us local pros organized pickup games at the University of Miami.

We didn't know when the lockout would end, while overseas opportunities began to flood our agents' inboxes. NBA players were getting signed to contracts that would automatically terminate when the lockout ended, no strings attached. My agent fielded some incredible offers for me, including a team in Greece that offered about $10 million for me to play there for five months. I passed on those offers, but Deron Williams, my former Jazz teammate, took an overseas contract, then made his way back to the NBA afterward with zero issues.

The summer came to an end without resolution. September passed. Then October. Coach Thibs called periodically to check in on my status, but there was no movement until November 14, when the players dissolved our union, allowing them to file antitrust lawsuits against the league. After that, both sides moved quickly to reach a tentative agreement to end the lockout. Signed on November 26, the new Collective Bargaining Agreement called for a revenue split of 49 to 51.2 percent and a flexible salary cap structure with a harsher luxury tax. After the tentative deal was reached, owners allowed players to have voluntary workouts at team sites, beginning December 1. The deal was ratified on December 8, and we returned to training camp the next day. The season started two weeks later with no preseason.

Jumping into a season full swing, without our usual buffers, felt akin to getting shot out of a cannon. With sixty-six games compressed into four months, the schedule was taxing. The recovery days we had off in between games evaporated, with games scheduled three days in a row. That had never been done before in the NBA with good reason. Injuries were rampant across the league. Even guys with reputations as workhorses, the most durable players on the roster, were getting injured.

We kicked off our belated and chaotic season on Christmas Day against the Lakers in LA. Kobe put up 28 points, but we eked past them, 88–87. It was a good omen. By mid-January, we'd won sixteen of our first twenty, even with D-Rose out with a sprained toe and Joakim working through a bad ankle sprain. I felt we were the deepest team in the league because everybody kept finding a way to step up and get it done, regardless of the circumstances. We were very tough to beat.

I'd like to say that my excellent performances were all I was remembered for my second year with the Bulls, but that wasn't the case. On the eve of a major televised game against the Celtics in mid-February, and with no one around to counsel me better, I let my barber, Greg, talk me into getting a Bigen (pronounced "Beijing").

"The temporary dye will fill in your natural hairline, Los," Greg said.

I was turning thirty and had noticed a few bald spots of late, but my hair was only slightly thinning. No need for maintenance upstairs. I passed on the suggestion.

I flew Greg in for another haircut and again he brought up the Bigen. "I have it with me now," he said this time. Other players had used the technique with success, and I was in an adventurous mood.

"Why not?" I said. "Let's try it."

Bigens come in many shades. I'm light-skinned, so a dark shade would stick out even more against my skin tone. I thought Greg would accommodate for this. I thought wrong. Greg happily worked the dye into my scalp, massaging it in and telling me how great I was going to look. After thirty minutes, he was very pleased with the results.

"It looks awesome!" he said sincerely. What else would he say? I looked into the bathroom mirror.

"Bro, what is this?" I asked, my blood beginning to boil. "It literally looks like shoe polish. I've got a game tomorrow. It looks like you poured a bucket of tar over my head."

"You'll get to used it," were Greg's final words. He was *so* fired. I retreated to the bathroom and shampooed my head seven times in a row over the sink, each time checking my noggin for any sign of fading, but my scalp was stained like beets bleeding into a cutting board. This wasn't coming out. All I could hope for was for this monstrosity to somehow blend in overnight.

The stage for our next game couldn't have been bigger. We were the No. 1 team in the Eastern Conference. The Celtics were stacked with a murderer's row of All-Stars that included Kevin Garnett, Paul Pierce and Ray Allen. Two titan teams were clashing in primetime at a regular season game. This game was broadcasted on ESPN. The world was watching this game.

We tipped off and went to work, but I couldn't get my hair disaster out of my mind. Every time the action stopped, I could feel the other players' eyes on me.

"Booz, what the fuck happened?" Garnett finally asked in the second quarter. I'm sure he'd been staring at my head, perplexed the entire time.

"A mistake. A mistake happened," I grumbled.

With D-Rose on the sidelines, I rose to the occasion and had a monster performance—22 points and 7 rebounds—and when you're playing well, the camera is always on you. They zoomed in on my hair and the broadcasters tried to hold back their laughter. When I got back to the locker room, my phone was blowing up. I kid you not, I must have had a thousand text messages and about five hundred phone calls. It was one of those things that everyone wanted to comment on.

It took five days to wash it all out, and that was with me shampooing vigilantly five times a day. My family teased me. ESPN had a field day on their talk shows. Future teammate Nate Robinson bought my bobblehead figure, painted its plastic head with a black marker, and somehow left it in my locker.

"I should have asked you about the Bigen," I told CeCe over the phone. CeCe would've advised me against it. She'd always been my grounding influence. Despite the strain between us, we spoke daily about the boys. Divorce is difficult, no matter the circumstances, because it changes the family makeup. That included my parents, who hadn't seen their grandchildren in the divorce's aftermath for an entire year. No kids are happy when their parents divorce and I missed not being with my boys as much. We were all unhappy with the current arrangement. My mind churned with potential solutions, and it kept landing on one. In our family equation, I had been the catalyst for change. Maybe change wasn't always good. Maybe I was being selfish living my life in Chicago with Neeka. Maybe I was the one who needed to compromise to bring everything back into balance.

"I think we should get remarried," I blurted out to CeCe. There was a pause on her end. CeCe was surprised, but she'd caught me off guard asking me out after seeing me in Duke's bookstore. Now we were even.

CeCe and I privately discussed how it would work for us to get back together, though in the back of my mind, I knew I was throwing what I had with Neeka away. That made me uneasy. I shakily told Neeka my decision, my stomach pitting in revolt. It was one of the most dreaded moments of my life because I was in love with Neeka and I could see the heartbreak in her face. I wanted her to yell at me, to call me an asshole. Instead, she was gracious and understanding that I was choosing my children over her. The solution to my family's problems would benefit everyone but Neeka. She would be gone from my life. I certainly felt like I was letting something incredibly valuable slip through my fingertips, but I'd made my decision. That March, CeCe and I quietly remarried, reuniting our family again.

Our season built on our tremendous year before. We finished 50–16 and rolled into the playoffs as the first overall seed for the second straight year, which paired us against the 76ers, who had the worst record. We were well en route to winning game one, when D-Rose jump-passed to me, but I missed my shot with about a minute and twenty seconds left in the game. The 76ers rebounded and everyone—sans D-Rose—raced down the court to the other basket. I realized we'd left a man behind and he was on the ground, cradling his knee, wincing in tremendous pain. I felt the air go out of the arena in a collective gasp. I swiftly fouled myself to force a timeout and made it to D-Rose's side. Medical personnel enveloped him, stabilizing the knee enough to get him back to the examination room. Right away, we all knew it was bad. Really bad.

We finished out hard and won the game, 103–91. But it was a hollow victory. A few of us found D-Rose in one of the training rooms, being evaluated by our team doctors. Some of D-Rose's family, including his two brothers, were already at his side. Derek sat back motionless on the examining table with a stony face. There were no tears, no emotions bubbling to the surface, but I saw the slightest glint of fear. This is every professional basketball player's nightmare—to have the game they love suddenly cut off from them. I thought of J-Will, sitting in his wheelchair by the window at his parent's place, and I felt lucky in that moment that my own career injuries hadn't been more serious, when all it would have taken was something as minor as landing off-balance.

Before any scans or X-rays were done, we knew D-Rose wouldn't make it back on the court with us again that season. Only twenty-three years old, he'd torn the ACL in his knee, a common injury, but a lengthy recovery process.

"We're not going to be with Derrick for the rest of this journey," Coach Thibs said. "He'll be recovering and doing what he has to do to get his knee healthy. Which means everyone else is going to have to step up so we can win the series."

There wasn't time for us to mourn the loss of D-Rose. We all had to figure out how to win without him, which would be difficult. D-Rose was the key component of a lot of our plays and a consistent leader in scoring and assists. It was like trying to relaunch the Beatles without John. Coach Thibs reshuffled the team, but without any time to practice, we lost the next game. Joakim was also injured in our third loss in a row, which was a double blow. We lost the series in six games to a team we'd have likely quashed with D-Rose. We were the fifth No. 1–seeded playoff team in NBA history to lose to an eighth seed and that felt as embarrassing as it sounds.

I raced home to Miami for another summer with the boys. As part of our divorce agreement, the boys had stayed with CeCe during basketball season. I'd found small pockets where I could travel to them, but I'd barely seen them the entire season.

"Get it, Cay!" I yelled from the stands, watching my five-year-old pass the ball to his twin, Cameron, who planted his feet and took his shot. "That's right, Cam!" I encouraged him, more satisfied that he stayed focused and gave it his best effort than if he made the basket. In the moment, he made his shot count. Just like my father, Couch Houston, Coach K, and my other coaches had taught me, if Cayden gave every shot his best effort, it would become ingrained, and the baskets would eventually come. Watching my boys play gave me even more appreciation for the string of wise coaches I'd been blessed with throughout my career.

Even at their tender age, the twins were already confident ballers. Their competitiveness also gave me an idea. Over that summer, I asked my kids' coach, Devel King, to start working with me, too. After a decade in the NBA, my fundamental skills had dulled like an overused set of kitchen knives. I needed to take my blades to the stone and resharpen my basic skills—the ball handing, shooting, and rebounding. What better way to do that than with someone who taught the fundamentals from scratch? Individually, we had to find our own ways to handle the upcoming season without D-Rose, who handled the bulk of our offensive scoring. The supporting staff, myself included, would need to intensify our efforts to fill in the gaps.

As a rule of thumb, every NBA player goes into a season gunning for a championship, no matter what the team surrounding him looks like. Losing our star player to a devastating ACL injury was a major blow, but a regular season has eighty-two games over nearly five months. A lot could happen in that time, so Coach Thibs and the front office concentrated on hiring new players that could help us win without D-Rose, who the medical staff optimistically hoped would be reactivated by the April playoffs.

Refining my earlier statement, every NBA player goes into a season gunning for a championship, but a season's success isn't always defined by winning one. There was no replacing the league's MVP, D-Rose, but the addition of Nate Robinson and others fortified our team in other ways.

Nate had been the twenty-first pick in the 2005 Draft, but was well known for his height—five foot nine—and what he could do despite it. Nate was a three-time NBA Slam Dunk Champion, who could utilize his vertical gift so effectively. He blocked seven-foot-six Yao Ming's shot in his second season, a fitting example of his ability to achieve more than what was expected of him.

Nate had the tough mentality of a football player. His father, Jacque, had a short stint in the NFL and Nate was leaning in that direction, too. He nearly accepted a scholarship to play at the University of Washington, but switched sports at the last minute. I wonder how many people tried to talk Nate out of throwing away a sure deal like a football scholarship, when his height would clearly keep him out of the NBA?

After five seasons with the New York Knicks, Nate blew into Chicago like a chilly burst of wind that shot up our spines and woke us all up. From our first practice, he brought a positive energy to the squad that immediately helped offset the mental

strain of losing of D-Rose. He came into work every day as enthusiastic as any rookie I'd ever seen.

Nate's positivity followed him everywhere, even on our first
road trip.

"Chocolate or vanilla?" he asked, holding out a clear plastic
container. The cupcakes were iced accordingly, with little pink
flowers. I grabbed a chocolate one and bit into it. It was tastier
than I expected.

"You made these yourself?" I asked, chocolate crumbles cak-
ing at the corners my mouth. Nate nodded his head, proudly. We
all had our ways to relax away from the game. This was Nate's
thing—and that it was something that made others happy perfectly captured his nature. To everyone's delight, Nate baked
cupcakes to pass out for every away game on our schedule, cook-
ing up new flavors like a confectionary mad scientist.

Nate melded with our team immediately, which helped us
transition into the season without D-Rose. We all knew how
tricky ACL surgery and recovery could be, and didn't expect
D-Rose to return until the playoffs in April, if at all that season. But the media had a different narrative, raising hopes of an
earlier return by invoking Jordan's comeback in the 1985–1986
season. In his second season, Jordan broke his foot, which sidelined him for sixty-four games. But near the season's end, against
the advice of doctors and his coaches, he rejoined the Bulls and
ignited the team, helping them make the playoffs. Jordan's performance in game two against the Celtics, where he scored 62
points, is a classic playoff highlight.

The truth was that D-Rose's rehab was private and intensive,
and he was away from the team for much of it. A blown ACL
isn't the same type of injury as a broken foot. The timetables,
including the rate of recovery, weren't comparable, no matter
how hard the media and fans pushed the idea.

Our season started slowly, as we worked Nate and others
into the lineup. We won twenty-four of our first forty games,

which wasn't disastrous. In a January 4 battle against LeBron and Miami, we surprised everyone with a seven-point win. I scored 27 points with 12 rebounds, diving headfirst for loose balls in one of my better defensive performances. This is where my time with my kids' coach paid off.

When we played the Heat again in March, they were on a twenty-seven-game winning streak, which had lasted fifty-three days. That's an unreal statistic for the NBA, considering the level of competition and consistency required to sustain it. Everybody was following the Heat because of it, and everybody thought we'd gotten lucky besting them in January.

It was a physical affair, with plenty of bumping and pushing and nasty glares. With four minutes left in the game, LeBron and I collided, causing a tense, highlight-reel face-off between us and a foul for LeBron.

Fighting off two Heat players to grab an offensive rebound, I scored to make it 96–89 with fifty-seven seconds left. Nate put the game out of reach with a drive down the lane, LeBron and the rest of the Heat chasing after him, for a floater with thirty seconds on the clock. LeBron made a last-ditch effort to block the shot, but was left hanging from the rim. Even with a prime LeBron shooting 64 percent from the floor for 32 points, we took the game, 101–97. And we did it without D-Rose and our center, Joakim Noah, who also was out with an injury. It wasn't the NBA championship, but snapping Miami's winning streak like a twig, six games short of the Lakers' legendary thirty-three-game run in the 1971–1972 season, was a big accomplishment. It told our team that we had some fight still left in us.

My enthusiasm at besting the Heat had an unintended target a few days later; I celebrated a foul call with a haymaker that landed square in referee Danny Crawford's chicken nuggets. My eternal apologies to him will never be enough, though no one can ever doubt my commitment and follow-through.

We finished the season 44–37, placing us second in the Central Division. D-Rose hadn't returned to full practices, so he was out of the playoffs. The Bulls entered as the fifth seed in the Eastern Conference, which pitted us against the Brooklyn Nets. We were up 3–1 in the series, and I thought we were going to finish them off, but the young Nets team was scrappy, scratching back from the brink to take the next two games to tie it 3–3 apiece. We took the seventh and final deciding game, advancing to the conference semifinals against—who else?—LeBron and the Heat.

We'd made a season of being shorthanded and adapting, so it seemed our team, patched together at times with Scotch tape, might have Miami's number. Could we possibly beat them again, when it counted the most? In our series opener, it seemed like we would. From the tip-off, we hit that game full-force. Nate was on fire, dropping 27 points, while Jimmy Butler added 21 and snatched 14 rebounds.

Sadly, we wouldn't remain the Heat's kryptonite forever. They figured us out quick, and plowed through us over four embarrassing games. We got smashed 115–78 in game two, then put up a paltry effort in game four, losing 88–65. We suddenly looked like a ragtag team, as if the clock had struck midnight, turning our carriage back into a pumpkin. You're just not going to win in the NBA with that kind of offensive output, especially against a team like the Heat. Miami put us to bed, 94–91, ending our season there.

I was disappointed when Nate called to tell me he wouldn't be returning to the Bulls. He'd been a star of our 2013 playoffs, eating up a 109–95 deficit in the pivotal game four of our opening series against the Nets with 12 unanswered points that took us into a triple-overtime victory. Nate also banked 27 points and 9 assists in our surprising game one victory over Miami. He was truly a clutch player and the greatest teammate I'd ever had in the NBA. He would be missed in Chicago, but

Nate wouldn't be out of my life. He was my little brother. We continued to speak three or four times a week, as Nate and I had a lot in common. Our families grew in tandem, until Nate and I both had three sons and a daughter. We weathered each other through pregnancies, breakups, and other big life events. Our families vacationed together in the Bahamas. I lost the best teammate I'd ever had, but gained a best friend in the process. That will never change.

Nate was gone, but a familiar face came through the Bulls' revolving door that July: Mike Dunleavy, my former Duke teammate. "Dun-Dun" had been drafted third by Golden State in 2002 and had since built a solid career playing for Indiana and Milwaukee. Dun-Dun was also fluent in Boozer lingo, which proved valuable when injuries had us reshuffling plays on the fly once again.

"Yo, Dun-Dun! I'm the new Joe!" I'd yell to him when Joakim was out of the game and I'd moved to cover his position. My staccato outbursts made Mike laugh, and possibly rattled our opponents.

"What did you just say?" the player defending me asked.

"Don't worry about it, homie," I chuckled.

With D-Rose healed and back in the lineup, we charged into our season opener against defending champions, the Miami Heat. Our start was tepid, as was D-Rose's return to form, but that was to be expected having lost him for an entire year. Ten games into the season, we were still finding our groove, when D-Rose lost his footing trying to change direction during a November 22 loss against Portland. He left the arena on crutches. I felt bad for him, to push through an entire year of grueling recovery and rehab, only to get taken out again ten games into the season. D-Rose had the potential to become one of the all-time greatest players, but with another season gone dark for him, it would be that much harder for him to work his way back. His scans revealed a meniscus tear in his right knee, not as serious as the ACL tear, though it would require immediate surgery.

D-Rose was out again, his return uncertain. Coach Thibs gave us the news before our next game and it was déjà vu all over again. He tried to rally the troops.

"Derrick's out again," Coach Thibs said, "but we're not out of this. You guys played beautifully without him last season. I'm going to ask you to do that again. You *can* do that again."

Man, am I sucker for motivational speeches. That night, I put up 26 points and 16 rebounds in a tough overtime loss to the Jazz. Luol Deng also came through that night with big stats, which was why I was surprised when the Bulls traded him to Cleveland that January. Deng had been with the Bulls since entering the league in 2004 as a teenager. Even after twelve seasons in the NBA, I could never get used to showing up for practice, only for the coach to announce that a teammate had been traded. Luckily, I'd get to see former teammates like Nate and LeBron again on the court. When we donned our jerseys, we dropped our friendships and it became all about bragging rights. A dunk or a blocked shot could lead to some serious razzing that would extend into the summer. This also extended to our parents, partners and kids—all watching the games, ready to join the pile-on.

Back in Miami, the boys were splashing around in the pool, and I was lying out on a chaise lounge, enjoying our time together. I could see my boys anytime I wanted. It was a beautiful day. I should have been content. Yet, I wasn't.

You don't realize you've fallen into depression until someone tells you. At least that's how it happened with me. I became sluggish and began to sleep in late, taking long naps during the day. I'll always be grateful that my longtime housekeeper, Miss Lily, cared enough to grab me by my proverbial collar and shake me hard.

"Mr. Boozer, you need to get out of bed," she said, pulling back the window curtains to let the light in. "Your kids are worried."

CeCe would always be in my life. She was one of my best friends, and I hoped to preserve that bond when we filed for divorce again.

D-Rose never returned to the lineup, and we finished, 48–34, claiming the fourth-seed slot in the playoffs. Washington sliced through us in five games.

Looking back, we were never going to fully realize our potential as a team. D-Rose's injuries had been consistent, and though he was slated to return in the fall, everyone wondered how long he'd last before another injury sidelined him. Change was in the air. Budgets were being scrutinized; new game plans formulated. Toward the end of the season, I was called into the GM's office to talk about the Bulls cutting me with a year left on my contract, through a rarely used Amnesty Clause. The clause allowed franchises to release a player anywhere during his contract for another team to pick the player up in free agency. Both teams then foot that player's salary and the releasing team could put the money saved toward its salary cap. Amnesty could only be applied during a seven-day window in July, when Rob called me with the final decision.

"Pax said that they want to keep you, but this was an option for the owner, and he's decided to use it," Rob told me. "With D-Rose up in the air, they felt like they needed to make a move."

I understood that this was a business and there was a heavy financial burden for owner Jerry Reinsdorf. D-Rose was making about $20 million a year, and I wasn't far behind that at $17 million. A couple additional players were pulling in $10 million, so this was a fat payroll, and it was time to trim it. I hadn't been drafted by the Bulls, like D-Rose, Deng, and Joakim and I was the oldest of that group with more mileage and wear and tear. It made sense for them to let me go. I appreciate the way Pax and the others didn't spring their plans on me without notice. It never feels good to get fired—and I cringe to use that word—but the franchise did right by me and I have no complaints.

I loved Chicago and its ardent sports fans. The Bulls have a unique synergy with their city and I'm humbled to have been accepted into that tradition during my tenure. Each time our team scored over 100 points during a home game, the franchise handed out a McDonald's Big Mac voucher to every spectator who walked out the door. It was a fierce competition among us players to score the basket that counted, to become a local hero until the next home game. There was no feeling that matched strutting down the street, knowing you earned twenty thousand fans a free burger.

"Booz," passersby would say. "Thanks for the Big Mac. You're good people."

No Chicago, you are.

# CHAPTER 15

## THE LAKERS

That July, the Amnesty Clause entered me into the waiver pool, where any franchise could bid on me, then split the salary for the final year of my Bulls' contract. I didn't know if any franchise would be interested, but Rob's calls signaled that there were options. We had a short one-week window to make a deal, and it looked like I was going to Phoenix, after they posted a waiver fee just under $3 million. However, the Lakers came in just above that, and agreed to pay $3.25 million of my $16.8 million salary, while the Bulls paid the remaining $13.55 million.

"Did you know?" I asked Kobe when I spoke to him next.

"What do you think?" he shot back, his smirk almost perceptible over the phone.

I'd always wanted to play with Kobe. He'd been a big brother to me since the summer I met him in 2002, after I'd been drafted to the Cavs. Our annual, end-of-season conversations over the subsequent twelve years had been prolific; Kobe could and would talk for hours about basketball—I'd have to end the call with him to recharge my phone. I'd trained with Kobe nearly every summer, as well, and watched his stone-cold veneer melt a bit when he and LeBron led our 2008 squad to Olympic gold. I'd gotten to know Kobe's family and he mine. I'd always had aspirations of wearing the purple and gold, but to do it alongside Kobe was two dreams rolled into one.

However, I wasn't stepping into a replay of the Lakers' salad days, rubbing shoulders with modern-day equivalents of Wilt Chamberlain, Jerry West, Elgin Baylor, Kareem, and Magic. The franchise was coming off a shockingly bad season. Kobe had been injured for most of it and played only six games; the team had gone a dismal 27–55—the worst record in the history of the franchise since 1949.

Former guard Byron Scott, who'd excelled in the Lakers' "Showtime Era" of the 1990s, was hired as head coach to revitalize the team, but some things were out of his hands. Steve Nash was still recouping from a back injury from the previous season, so his return date was still up in the air, but Kobe was expected back at the start. He had eighteen seasons under his belt, but still approached the game with the balance of a young player's hunger and the gristle and experience of a seasoned veteran. Kobe's cerebral approach had been culled and perfected over the years. Nothing happened overnight for him. Fans forget that Kobe put up four air balls during game five of the 1997 playoffs, his first year in the league. Nobody remembers that Kobe didn't average 20 points a game until his fourth season and there'd been serious doubts that the Lakers had bet on the right horse. These forgotten years are where Kobe gained an edge, one that he never let go dull as he led the Lakers to five NBA championships. I couldn't think of anyone in the league I wanted to play with more. Not a one.

I'd spent my career in and out of LA, rehabbing with world-class doctors, working out with celebrity trainers, and even traversing into its wacky real estate market with my Prince home. I thought I had an understanding of Los Angeles, until our plane landed, and Neeka and I walked into the baggage area. A group of paparazzi were parked next to our conveyor belt, cameras around their necks and TV cameras hoisted onto their shoulders.

"And we wondered how long it would take to spot a celebrity," I teased into her ear. "Somebody famous must be here right now."

I scanned the area, expecting to see Robert DeNiro or Ozzy Osborne. Instead, a video camera was hoisted into my face.

"Carlos, how do you feel about joining the Lakers?" the cameraman asked. A few other paparazzi propped their microphones and video cameras into recording range. I'd had my fair share of paparazzi attention in Cleveland, Utah, and Chicago, but LA—where a salacious picture or racy video could sell for thousands or even tens of thousands of dollars—was instantly more intrusive. Most of my media interaction had occurred at games and practices. But in LA, a photo of me eating out at Crustacean with family and friends was somehow a commodity.

The paparazzi were everywhere. They were waiting by my car in Malibu. They were at the Beverly Hills mall where I shopped for clothes on my day off. I never felt threatened, and I had good conversations with all of them, but it was jarring to have so many people crowd your personal space within seconds, as if you were a human magnet. It gave me a better understanding of why Kobe was so reserved with fans and the media and kept his personal life incredibly private.

In addition to me, the Lakers drafted No. 7 pick Julius Randle, who'd played his freshman season at Kentucky and made the All-American third team in an impressive season. Julius, a power forward and center, was just the kind of young player that the Lakers needed to complement the three veterans in Kobe, Nash, and myself. Unfortunately, we lost Julius in our season opener, only fourteen minutes into the game—a bad omen if ever there was one. We lost our first game, as well as the next four—but that was a drop in the bucket compared with what was to come.

That December, a grand jury decided not to indict a white police officer who'd used excessive force and killed Eric Garner, a forty-three-year-old Black man accused of selling "loosies" from cigarette packs. A viral video, shot in Staten Island that July, captured Garner resisting arrest. A New York City police officer cinched a prohibited chokehold around Garner's neck, while additional officers tackled Garner to the sidewalk, face-down on his stomach.

"I can't breathe," Garner had told the officer eleven times over the seven minutes he was held down, but the officer kept his arms tightly squeezed against Garner's neck. Garner was pronounced dead at a local hospital an hour later, his death classified an intentional homicide. The decision not to indict the officer led to widespread protests that reverberated through every industry, including sports. LeBron and Carmelo Anthony spoke out, as did D-Rose and NBA commissioner David Stern. Jeannie Buss, who owned the Lakers with her husband, made it a point to address the team, making it clear that the franchise would support whatever message we wanted to convey to the public, if any at all.

A few days after the grand jury's announcement, Kobe walked into our locker room carrying a cardboard box. He plopped it down on the bench.

"Hey, guys," he said, signaling us to gather around. "I know we've all heard of Eric Garner." Kobe paused, allowing us all to fill in the gaps of his story on our own.

"I had enough of these made up for everyone, but there's no obligation to wear them," he continued.

Kobe held up a black T-shirt with the quote "I can't breathe" in white letters. I don't think anyone on the team passed on wearing the shirt during warm-ups and on the sidelines for our next five games. As a unit, we took a strong stance against police brutality at the time by wearing the shirts. There was a portion of our nation that didn't like racial injustice mixed into their sports, but Kobe understood that we had a responsibility to use our platform to do the right, and not necessarily safe, thing. He was that kind of leader, and we agreed that it was important for us to show a united front. We had a platform that most of our community didn't have.

Neeka and I spent Christmas in Los Angeles, where the weather was still warm enough for T-shirts and shorts and the snow was as fake as pro wrestling. We enjoyed that day with an outdoor barbecue of chicken, steak, collard greens, and mashed potatoes.

I loved being back in LA for an extended period of time, because I was closer to family living on the West Coast. About once a week, I shot up the Pacific Coast Highway to Malibu to meet my baby sister, Nakeisha, who was attending Pepperdine University. Nakeisha also had a passion for Asian culture and we'd meet up at a Korean barbeque joint. Nakeisha was nine years younger than me, and only eight years old when I left home for Duke, so these shared meals were a way for us to get to know each other more. Of course, we were never alone, as Nakeisha was as social as I was.

"How many have we got this week?" I'd ask her, counting the growing number of college friends following her through the entrance. She'd bring thirty, sometimes forty classmates along to the restaurant with her. It didn't matter to me. It made her happy and I wouldn't care if she'd brought along a hundred friends. Big brother could always foot the bill, which inexplicably never seemed more than $125, no matter how many hungry classmates packed into the place. Celebrity discount?

Neeka and I were having a blast in LA, though the team continued struggling to find its footing. At the season's midway mark that January, our team was forced to take stock. We'd only won twelve of our forty-three games, but our biggest loss, the one that would alter our season the most, happened during this unlucky game against the New Orleans Pelicans. In the third quarter, Kobe launched vertically for a dunk and seemed to throw out his right shoulder. He left the game, but with the toughness of a UFC fighter had returned to play the fourth, switching to his left hand to score. I'd like to see another elite thirty-seven-year-old, halfway deep into his nineteenth NBA season, do that.

A week later, Kobe underwent season-ending surgery for a torn rotator cuff. Having only played six games during the previous season, it was clear that Kobe's career was coming to an end. He announced his retirement not long after. Mentally, Kobe was as sharp as ever, but every athlete's body eventually betrays them, especially the ones who have stellar careers that spill over two decades. I'm glad I got the games with Kobe that I had.

The Laker's longtime leader and beating heart was gone. I looked around the squad and realized I was the old-time vet, surrounded by a bunch of young guns. They included Jordan Clarkson, another rookie, in addition to Julius, and Jeremy Lin, who was entering his fourth NBA season. We still had thirty-nine games left to play, so I took on more court time and mentored my younger teammates, some of them still learning who they were and what their capabilities might be. It wasn't how I imagined what playing for the legendary Lakers might be, but I found purpose in passing on what I'd learned in twelve NBA seasons. I didn't know it at the time, but this would be the final role I'd take in the NBA. I'd been an underestimated rookie, an All-Star, a supporting player, and now a mentor.

We tried as we might, but we were just too green a team to catch any momentum. Following Kobe's injury, we went 9–30 and finished the season a dismal 21–61, placing fifth in the Pacific Division. We completely missed the playoffs. No longer a consistent starter, my output that season dwindled from my previous heydays, but I managed 10 double-doubles. My agent, Rob, started renegotiations with the Lakers for another year.

Not a week later, I was back in Miami, picking up breakfast with Carmani when my cell phone rang. It was my father and mother, who I spoke to nearly every day together. I didn't have time to plant my feet under me before the blow hit.

"Los, we have some news," my father said, his voice shaking slightly. I knew instantly that something was wrong. "Your mother found a lump."

Cancer. My mother had breast cancer.

I'd stepped out of the car to spare Carmani such a heavy conversation, as my father continued speaking, filling in details, but my mind couldn't connect to their meaning. Fear took hold. *Was I going to lose my mom?* I immediately told myself to shut that thinking down.

"What are the next steps?" I asked. I needed to get out to Las Vegas, where my parents had moved a few years earlier, and I needed to hug my mother. After climbing back into the car, I dropped Carmani off with his mother, picked up some clothes at home, and headed to the airport. As I bought my ticket at the counter, I called Rob, asking him to tell the Lakers that I wouldn't be playing next season. I would spend that time with my mother.

I didn't think it was possible for me to respect my father, or anyone for that matter, more than I already did. Then, I watched him take care of my mother that year. There were doctor's visits, procedures, an eventual operation, then chemotherapy and radiation therapy afterward. He hardly slept, comforting my mother as she wretched over the toilet and ached with pain.

I split my time between Las Vegas and Miami, leaving the boys with CeCe, so I could spend a week at a time with my parents. I kept my siblings updated on her health and instructed them to keep phone conversations light and positive. When we all congregated at the hospital after her surgery, Natasha and I prepped everyone outside her room. I'd already seen how sickly she'd gotten, how pale her skin was, but they were seeing it for the first time.

"Wipe your tears away," I said. "We can cry, but not in front of mom. We cry on our own time. She needs positivity and laughter and our love. She needs us now, more than ever."

I was adamant that we all surround our mother in a protective cocoon. I policed my siblings about it, as my mother fought against that brutal illness. Occasionally, I'd get down watching her suffer, so I'd call one of my siblings and they would lift me back up. I had some meaningful conversations with my youngest sister, Natanya. Eleven years my junior, Natanya gave me a fresh perspective when I needed it. My mother never complained, not from getting her blood drawn so many times that they ran out of veins to tap, nor from the hair loss and nausea from her treatments and medications.

My father was there for my mother, slowly nursing her back to health, getting her to take a few more spoonfuls of apple sauce or getting her outside for a walk around the block. It took a tense year with some tense nights, but my mother was eventually deemed cancer-free.

In the blink of an eye, another NBA season approached, and I was itching to play again. Rob put out feelers with a few organizations and I gave a quick sigh of relief when we got a few bites. The San Antonio Spurs invited me in for a couple of workouts; while Coach Jason Kidd, a 2008 Olympic teammate, inquired for the Milwaukee Bucks. The Sacramento Kings also voiced interest.

"There's another offer," Rob said, the irony escaping him. "It's from a team in China. Five million for five months."

"China?" I asked. I immediately thought of Stephon Marbury, who'd made himself a second career there after the NBA. After joining the Chinese Basketball Association in 2010, Stephon averaged more than 20 points a game, leading the Beijing Ducks to CBA championships in 2012 and 2014.

"Man, Booz, you're going to love it over here," my 2004 Olympic teammate said when I called him for advice. "They have a huge passion for the sport and the NBA, and they'll treat you like a king. Oh, and the money is tax-free."

I thought about my mother, who looked cancer in the eyes and whipped its ass. Life was short and could end in an instant. You could pull back on the throttle or lean into it. I chose the latter, accepting an offer from the Guangdong Southern team to play the 2016-2017 CBA season.

Neeka and I headed to Shanghai, where we were put up in the poshest of hotels, with our own private chef and a spacious suite that overlooked the city.

We used our trip to China as a launching pad to explore other parts of Asia. Neeka and I went to Thailand and Bali, and other places that we probably wouldn't have seen if I hadn't taken the opportunity to go play abroad. I would suggest that every basketball player—no, every pro athlete—if they have the opportunity, go play outside of the United States. Neeka and I immersed ourselves in the culture, trying new foods and visiting the many temples and shrines that reflected the country's ancient religious beliefs. I really enjoyed getting to travel and expand my world view a bit in the process. *Can you believe all this, Chris?* I thought to my constant companion. Certainly not those two kids back in DC, sharing turkey heroes after school. This was another added perk I hadn't seen coming.

We had a strong squad, made up mostly of Chinese players, with two foreign additions allowed to the roster. Donald Sloan, who played point and shooting guard, hailed from Texas. The head coach spoke only Chinese, but there were also a couple of English-speaking assistant coaches, like Chris Hines, on staff to help with the language barrier. Chris had been in Shanghai for a couple of years already, and had a lay of the land, making him an exceptional tour guide for me and Donald.

I was surprised when some fans recognized me from the USA's showdown with China at the 2008 Olympics, though we'd been told that a billion viewers had watched the game.

Like my father, I had a great appreciation for Asian culture, but I especially loved the noodle joints, which were on every corner like a Starbucks. One of my teammates, Dong, owned about twenty hot pot restaurants and the team would always hit them up after games. The entire waitstaff would carry out trays of raw beef, vegetables, and noodles for us to drown in the boiling pot in the center of the table. We couldn't identify everything put in front of us, but most of us had never met an entrée we didn't like. At one point, I motioned the waiter over to ask what this stringy pink meat was that I'd been sampling the entire meal.

"You like it?" he asked, not realizing that he was drawing out the drama.

"Yeah, I like it," I said. "I wouldn't be asking if I didn't."

"Pig brains," he said with a grin, making me realize that sometimes I just shouldn't ask.

Another reason I chose to play in the CBA was to get the opportunity for my boys to join me in China during their winter break. I wanted them to experience a new country, to introduce them to the notion that not everyone lives the way Americans do, that there are other ways of building community. We toured Buddhist temples together and spent hours in the ample video game arcades, our heads buried in the machines. I watched my boys wrestle with chopsticks and new cuisine, but we usually resorted to Kobe beef steaks and grilled chicken from the hotel kitchen.

One night at a hot pot restaurant, I got down on one knee and proposed to Neeka. We'd known each other for eight years and had built an easygoing friendship that had blossomed into love. It had taken time, but Neeka had forgiven me for breaking her heart. She nodded "yes," as I slipped the engagement ring I'd purchased beforehand on her finger.

My game was on the winning swing, too. I led the Tigers in scoring and rebounding, averaging 22.8 points and 10.7 rebounds per game. Stephon was right, too. The Chinese fans fawned over the NBA star in their midst, and the games were always packed. We went 33–8 during the regular season, placing second in the Southern Division. We made it past two playoff series and into the finals, where we were swept in four by the Xinjiang Flying Tigers.

Neeka and I arrived back in Miami in early April, where we got to work on wedding plans. We decided to get married that June, and somehow Neeka coordinated a lavish affair at the famous Fontainebleau Hotel in Miami Beach.

The morning of our nuptials, I chatted with my father as he sipped his coffee, looking out on the water together from the hotel patio. My wedding party included Taj Gibson and some personal friends; nobody challenged us to a pickup game in our downtime. Neeka looked like an ethereal angel in a white lace corset dress that billowed out at her waist, her hair curled in soft tendrils, held back on one side by a white blossom.

We began looking for a home to call our own in Miami, knowing my competitive time was winding down. Neeka and I hoped to have a child and my body was telling me to slow down. I felt ready to retire on the high note that was China. I was eager to spend more time with my boys.

Watching my father shepherd my mother through cancer treatment reminded me of the care and patience he'd shown me as a child. Now that the boys were old enough to start planning their lives, I wanted to be there for them like my father had been for me. I would catch pop flies and put up shots with them, but I also wanted to get them thinking about some of the tricks that worked for me.

A lot of kids are physically capable of making it to the NBA, but only about 1 percent of them actually do. A handful of very minute characteristics separate those who make it from those who don't. For me, it was always a question of what I could mentally handle. I hit walls, but I always found a way to knock them down. There were times that I accepted failure, begrudgingly, so I could learn and grow from it. My three sons were all physical athletes; it's literally in their blood. The difference for them would be how well they handled the inevitable barriers coming their way, if they chose to become professional athletes.

This very topic came up while I watched Carmani hover on the mound at one of his games. I recognized the mother of one of his teammates from the season before, though one of her sons hadn't returned to the team that year. Though not a starter, her son had been a decent player. I was curious to know what had happened to him.

"I let him quit baseball," she said. "He hardly played last year and gave up."

I knew the kid had likely quit out of embarrassment, but I couldn't help but think that if he'd had someone like my father to toss the ball around with, even a day or two a week, just maybe he'd be on the field with Carmani right now.

"The next time he needs someone to catch with, you call me," I said. "I'll come over, myself."

Honestly, I wasn't sure I'd get that call, but I hoped my passion encouraged her to find someone in her son's life who could. I went home and called my own son.

"Hey, Boomz," I said, using the name we gave Carmani as a baby, when he'd push his tushy up in the air, like a diver bent over a springboard. "You up for a game of catch?"

# CHAPTER 16

## BLOOM

"Dad, I want to play baseball," my oldest son, Carmani, said, launching another scorcher to my mitt one balmy afternoon in our Miami backyard.

Carmani had just turned twelve years old, the same age I was when I swore off baseball and committed myself fully to basketball. They say life comes full circle, but they don't tell you how fast it comes whipping back at you.

CeCe and I had known that Carmani was a superior athlete as early as age three. Once his immune system was strong enough, we'd signed him up for gymnastics classes, then soccer, basketball, baseball, and even ice hockey. By age six, Carmani already had a great touch and could fire off from anywhere on the court. His footwork and on-court acuity only grew with each passing day.

Still, I'd suspected that Carmani's heart belonged to baseball. I'd taken him to his first New York Yankees game when he was two years old; he'd been so absorbed in what was happening on the field that he hardly moved, other than to get a better look. Most toddlers can't sit still that long. As Carmani grew older, he continued to play basketball and became a standout like his younger brothers, both at school and on the local circuit. But Carmani's bedroom posters, which included David "Big Papi" Ortiz, Ken Griffey Jr., and Barry Bonds, told a different story.

"Do you remember when the Minnesota Twins dropped Big Papi?" I asked. "What did he do next?"

Big Papi had always been Carmani's favorite baseball player. The Dominican-born first baseman was a home run machine. Ortiz was also darker skinned, and had a heftier frame, perfect for power hitting, much like Carmani, who was already six-foot-two and nearly two hundred pounds. I knew this example would resonate with him.

Carmani thought on his idol for a moment. "He didn't give up," he finally answered.

"That's right," I said. "Nobody wanted to sign him. Nobody. He packed his bags and went home. But he didn't give up. He got himself another contract with a different team and he made sure he never got cut from any team again."

Getting cut by the Twins was Ortiz's "Jordan getting cut from JV" moment. He went back to the Dominican Republic and happened to run into Pedro Martinez in a restaurant. Martinez campaigned for the Boston Red Sox to offer Ortiz the most basic of contracts. Ortiz extended that nonguarantee contract into ten All-Star game appearances and three World Series championships.

"Boomz, if this is your passion, you're only going to know how far you can go if you give it your all," I said. "If you commit, your mom and I will, too. Baseball. Let's do this."

Back from China, I'd officially notified the NBA of my retirement, and was looking forward to simply putting up shots in the backyard, but helping Carmani pursue his MLB dream seemed so much better. CeCe and I got to work on a new kind of research for Carmani, this time for summer baseball camps, of which Florida was plentiful.

That fall, Carmani became the only sixth grader to make the freshman baseball team for Westminster Christian Academy, the alma mater of New York Yankees legend Alex Rodriguez. Carmani's coaches had all played pro ball, while the school had graduated over two hundred eventual MLB players.

Cameron and Cayden, thirteen months and a school year behind their big brother, also excelled in baseball and basketball, though they seemed just along for the ride, at first. CeCe enrolled them in as many sports programs as they showed interest in. However, by the time the twins entered middle school, Cameron had shot up to six-foot-three, while Cayden reached just under six-foot. They both gravitated toward basketball, playing alongside each other on their school and summer circuit teams.

All three of my boys were excelling at the sports they loved with the hopes of going pro, and I put up shots or caught pitches whenever I was home. As for myself, my own career path was about to branch out in a couple new directions. What did I want to do with my life next? I had a slew of business ideas, but before I got anything in motion, Ice Cube offered me a contract with the Big 3, a 3-on-3 basketball league for veterans, which aired on CBS. It wasn't a full-time gig, so I was able to juggle it for a season or two.

My competitive days were numbered when we learned Neeka was pregnant, something we'd also planned through artificial insemination to ensure the sickle cell gene wasn't passed on. Retirement play and a fourth kid? This would have been enough for me. However, another opportunity came smack-dab during this time which seemed too hard to pass up.

A new avenue opened for me when an ESPN producer invited me to their Connecticut headquarters to do its "car wash"—an all-day interview marathon through the sports media conglomerate's TV shows, radio stations, and streaming platforms. I went on SportsCenter for a segment, then did a radio interview before heading back to the set for another show and so on. The perfect day for an athlete—outside of playing their beloved sport—is being able to talk about their love for their sport, to stay connected in some meaningful way. My media day at ESPN gave me a taste of what it would be like on the other side of the mic, and I liked it.

A Turner Sports producer watched me on ESPN and contacted my agent about doing some work for NBA TV, its studio in Atlanta. I worked unrestricted for both ESPN and NBA TV in-studio and on remote shoots around the country for over a year, learning how to prepare notes before games, read a teleprompter, toss my mic to an interviewee and back without notice, and pace my speech at the sports desk. I also found out that a lot of retired players wanted to be right where I was. It was an in-demand gig and I could see why. I figured if I was ready as needed, got in my reps, and built up some positive buzz, something could open up for me more permanently.

A little over a year into my burgeoning broadcasting career, I was flown into Charlotte to have lunch with Aaron Katzman, the president of the soon-to-be launched Atlantic Coast Conference Network (ACCN), a college sports channel owned and run by ESPN.

"What can you tell me about the Atlantic Coast Conference?" Aaron asked me over steak and mashed potatoes. What else?

It was as if the flood gates opened.

"I was fortunate to play in that conference," I said. "It was the stepping stone I needed to get me to the NBA." I then dove into my journey from Alaska to Duke, explaining how the Atlantic Conference's collective excellence forced all of us to address weaknesses that would have exposed us in the NBA.

"At that time in my life, with the skillset I had, I needed the

ACC. I needed Duke," I said. "That's the level of competition I needed to make it to the NBA."

Aaron seemed pleased with my answer; I signed my first contract with Disney, which owned ESPN. One of my first big assignments, and still one of my toughest, was reporting to ESPN's Stamford headquarters to discuss the death of Kobe and his daughter, Gianna, in a helicopter accident the day prior.

On a lazy Sunday morning in late January, my cell phone's consistent pinging woke me from a nap. Text messages were flying in fast and there were too many saying the same thing for it to be wrong. I turned on ESPN and there it was. Kobe and his thirteen-year-old daughter, Gianna, were dead.

Kobe, Gianna, and seven others had been traveling north from Orange County to a basketball tournament at her father's Mamba Sports Academy in Thousand Oaks. It was routine transit for Kobe, the twenty-minute ride was happenstance—until it wasn't. We'd find out later, through communications, that the heavy fog enveloping California's foothills played the biggest factor; the pilot flew dangerously low, but realized it too late to correct the helicopter in time. I try not to think about the crash itself that much. I don't like to think about what Kobe, Gianna, and the others must have gone through in the final seconds—if they understood what was happening.

That Monday morning, I sat at ESPN's SportsCenter desk with host John Anderson, to discuss the biggest sports story I could remember, but also my dear friend's death. There was little concrete information about the crash, so we spoke about my mentor, teammate, and brother. I described Kobe's legendary work ethic, how I'd sought him out during the summer before my NBA debut, our 2008 Olympic experience, and our brief time together with the Lakers.

Privately, our family checked in with Kobe's. Vanessa had her three girls to think of and we offered what support we could. Though we'd both retired from the NBA, which meant no summer meet-ups or marathon phone calls, we'd kept in touch via text and an occasional call. Kobe had always been a private person and he'd always given his time in controlled measure. I recognized that early on, so I always considered our interaction—however they came—to be pure gold.

Just a few weeks before his death, I remembered seeing pictures online of Kobe, Vanessa, and the kids at Disneyland. Kobe loved Disneyland; he took Vanessa there many times while dating and having kids didn't slow that down any. Remember how closed off Kobe could be as a player? He didn't engage readily with the media, and he was a tough interview. He didn't often sign autographs, but not because he had an ego or he wasn't a nice guy. Kobe became immensely famous, and he had to put up boundaries, both physical and mental, for his own self-preservation. That was his choice, what he needed to do to be the best player he could be and keep his sanity. "The Mamba Mentality" was a persona Kobe could step into to get the job done. After the game and media interviews, Kobe took that armor off and went home to his family.

At Disneyland, Kobe felt safe, even as people took more pictures of him than Mickey Mouse. This Kobe, the one with his three-year-old daughter on his shoulders, a Cheshire cat grin across his face, maybe on their way to the Mad Teacups ride—that was Kobe without the armor on. I had seen those pictures and smiled. It made me happy to think he was opening himself up to the world a little more. Kobe hadn't gotten the opportunity to be a "regular" guy very often.

ESPN also allowed me to continue appearing with NBA TV, which brought me to Atlanta every weekend during the season. NBA TV and the TNT Network, home to the very popular *Inside the NBA* series, had adjacent studios that shared a green room, where I'd regularly sit down with Kenny Smith, Ernie Johnson, Charles Barkley, and Shaq. We learned a lot about each other over pizza or takeout, while we waited to be called to set.

"You like Burger King?" Shaq leaned over to me one night, ripping off a chunk of his dangling pizza slice. We were sitting together on the lounge's L-shaped black leather couch, planted in front of a seventy-two-inch TV screen. Basketball was blaring, as usual.

"Yeah. Who doesn't?" I answered.

"Exactly," he said, content with my answer. He rested back into the couch. A few seconds later, he was leaning forward again.

"Five Guys makes better burgers. I own about one hundred and fifty Five Guys joints," he said proudly.

"Damn, you must really love burgers," I chuckled.

"It's not about what I like," he answered, some seriousness seeping into his tone. "I also own a bunch of Papa John's. People gotta eat, you know?"

I was thoroughly impressed as Shaq described his robust portfolio of quick service restaurants (QSRs), which included multiple Auntie Anne's, and (yes!) Krispy Kremes. I hung on every word, encouraging him to continue.

"I'll throw you another one," he said. "Do you hate washing your car?"

"Maybe it's a time thing for me, but let's just say I pay others do it," I said.

"Fair enough. I own a chain of car washes in the Southeast," he stated.

I suddenly realized I'd stumbled into a financial lesson.

"Passive income," he continued. "When you retire, those seven-figure checks stop coming, but you can invest in proven commodities to keep a flow of income. People love fast food and hate washing their cars."

I was a sponge. Since his own NBA retirement six years earlier, Shaq had been out in the big, bad world thriving. I didn't have his wealth, but I could recognize that he was making the money he'd earned from basketball go a long way for his family. He spoke about the many business courses he took just out of the NBA about monetizing ideas. But he also spoke about trust.

"Los, we're professional basketball players. If people wanted to know how to become a better basketball player, they would come ask us," he said. "As a businessman, always align yourself with the people that know more than you, so they can teach you how to be successful at it."

I make it no secret that I like how Shaq retired so gracefully, found new sources of income, blossomed into a Renaissance man entrepreneur, and became an example, not just for his own children, but for mine. When my kids' friends asked them what their retired father does all day, I wanted them to be able to rattle off a ton of things.

"Our dad owns real estate and hotels and has a clothing line and a winery," is what they'd say. And this is where I need to thank Shaq, because it was his generosity of time and knowledge on that noisy black couch that made me focus on a couple of obtainable goals, instead of casting a wide net that might not have caught anything.

What Shaq had said about trust reminded me of someone. I'd accrued a lot of lifelong friends, one who happened to be a close friend of the president of Restaurant Brands International (RBI), which owned Burger King, Popeyes, Firehouse Subs, and Tim Horton's. Together, we started a very detailed application process to get approved by RBI corporate, one that took about ten months of due diligence. RBI vetted my partners and me, along with the top management we'd hire to oversee any franchise locations we took over or opened. This was serious business and I felt like I was lining up the game-winning shot. Just like it. When our application was approved, I was incredibly excited. I'd always wanted to own a tangible business. A list of potential RBI opportunities was sent our way, and a familiar name leaped off it.

I'd bit into my first spicy Popeyes chicken drumstick in Fresno during one of my travel-ball summers with Mats and the EBO team. It had quickly become one of my staples, so when I saw the chance to purchase three existing locations on the border of the Carolinas, we went for it. Over a year later, after meetings and visits, it felt surreal walking into a Popeyes, a world-recognized brand with its bright orange logo, knowing I was one of its owners. This would be my first trio of Popeyes, with more to come. *If a Boozer never gets paid to dribble a basketball or smack a baseball out of the park again, this will change the dynamic of my family for generations to come,* I thought.

That family was expanding quickly, too. The apple of my eye, Bloom Boheme Boozer, was born on April 5, 2019. She had Neeka's angelic face and her grandmother's hazel eyes. I held her and just melted. With my fourth child, I'd now completed my team.

Neeka, Bloom, and I settled into our new Miami home, while my "away" schedule continued to grow between NBA TV, ESPN, and the Popeye's deal. I was traveling when I first got wind of the coronavirus pandemic and the worldwide shutdown it would cause in mid-March 2020. Like everyone else, I checked on my parents and my siblings and their families, then hunkered down. ESPN and NBA TV stopped all traveling production, as outlets adapted to having hosts and guests streaming from their homes. Professional sports were also put on hold and with no live events to cover, I had some time on my hands to knock an important item off my to-do list. I reenrolled online at Duke University to finish my sociology degree and graduated after eighteen years away. I had made it through my junior year before leaving for the NBA, and though my parents never stipulated I had to go back, part of me wanted to complete what I'd started there for them. I also did it for myself—I was a business entrepreneur now and I could do it from my home during a pandemic that had basically pressed Pause on the world. I really had no excuses.

One of the courses I selected was "Race, Identity and Power," which focused on Black sports participation patterns from a variety of angles, including physical differences, racial stereotyping, identity development, gender issues, and social influences. I learned about the larger social impact of athletes like Muhammad Ali and Colin Kaepernick—outside of sports. Former San Francisco 49ers quarterback Kaepernick's story was still playing out as I studied about him, when Black Lives Matter protests sprang up across the country in response to the murder of George Floyd by a group of police officers outside a convenience store in Minneapolis.

I'd had my own experiences with racism, though my boys had thankfully been more sheltered from it. Still, one of my sons came home upset from a friend's house, having overheard the father on his phone.

"He used the N-word, Dad," he said, a little shocked. "Why would he use that word?"

"I don't know," I answered because I didn't.

The Black Lives Matter movement had an impact on my life, as I'm sure it did for nearly every Black person in the country. How could it not? It was as if a mirror had been propped up in front of us, revealing the ugly parts of our country's reflection for all to see.

I think everyone took a hard, long look at their lives; Neeka and I were no different. She and I had brought Bloom into this world, a world we wanted to make better for her in our own ways. As my work travel began to pick up again, Neeka and I realized we were heading down different paths. There was no hatred or anger toward one another. We simply knew our journey together romantically had ended. Neeka and Bloom moved back to the west coast to be closer to her family. We amicably worked out every detail of our divorce, including sharing equal time with Bloom. I'm incredibly grateful to Neeka that we've found a way to remain very close to this day.

★ ★ ★

In March 2022, my father and I sat in a high school gym in South Miami, watching his grandchildren on the court. Cayden, now six-foot-three, had just been fouled during a layup run. With five seconds on the clock, he calmly walked up to the free throw line. His eyes stayed glued to the rim, as he lifted his arms and flicked the ball away. The ball swooshed cleanly through the net and we jumped to our feet. Five seconds counted down as the opposing team tried to piece together a final play, but the last attempt bounced away. Cayden's shot secured a 45–44 victory, cinching a state championship for his freshman season. Not to be left out, Cameron, now six-foot-eight, led the team with 17 points and 8 rebounds.

"Make sure you save their jerseys," my father said, as I climbed down the bleachers toward the mass of celebrating players. "I want to frame them." I loved my father for wanting to do this, especially in his seventies.

A couple of months later, Cameron and Cayden's travel team took the Peach Jam, a prestigious tournament that no freshman-led squad had ever won before. It was obvious that Cameron and Cayden had a shot at the NBA, if they wanted it. When Duke University offered both the boys full scholarships to attend and play for them in three years, it was time to get organized.

"We need to find the boys some good management," I told CeCe later. CeCe and I were in a better place than we'd been in years, more united around our boys' futures than we'd ever been. We needed to be: Cayden and Cameron weren't the only ones who had a shot at pro sports.

That summer, sandwiched between Carmani's sophomore and junior years, I accompanied him to a well-known camp in Cape Coral, Florida. The coaching staff were all affiliated with an MLB team, and it attracted a ton of college and pro scouts, much like those early camps I attended that put me on the map.

Carmani was an imposing six-foot-three, two-hundred-pound pitcher on the mound. And he was good. Very good. Better than I ever was at basketball at his age. It was fulfilling to see that Carmani had stuck with baseball long enough to see his dedication start to pay off. I lived vicariously through every strike he threw and every ball he connected with.

I sat with the other parents, taking in the tournament games played by some of the best high schoolers in the country. However, I didn't stay anonymous for long. The coaches recognized me, as did the scouts, and they knew Carmani was my son. It was virtually the same thing that happened with the twins: once the first scout showed interest with Carmani, we exchanged numbers and others followed. Again, my phone blew up all weekend.

That fall, Carmani and I visited Duke and its championship baseball team. We walked along the same paths I took as a teenager and I pointed out the shortcut through the parking lot and across the street to Duke Gardens, where his mother and I had gone to get lost together among the rose beds. I put zero pressure on any of the three boys to attend Duke. Still, we all agreed that it was an incredible option to already have in our back pockets.

In the fall, the cool breeze that sweeps through Miami is heavenly. Sitting on my porch, letting the flow hit me, I nervously dialed my father's number and he picked up cheerfully for our daily conversation.

"Pops," I said, my voice spiked with anxiety. "I wanted to talk to you and mom about something before my book comes out. I'm going to share what happened with Chris."

I paused for his response, but was met with silence.

"I remember," he finally said, almost in a whisper.

Later, I continued the conversation with both my parents. I dragged out my metaphorical attic trunk and they hauled out theirs, wiping off nearly forty years of dust. To be honest, they didn't remember much of the details of Chris's death. Both of my parents were now entertaining their seventies. "We've lived a lifetime since then," as my father put it.

I described what I recalled through the eyes of a six-year-old and saw recognition light up in my father's eyes. The danger we fell into, the fear we felt having to leave—that was all real. As an adult, I now understood why my parents never discussed Chris's death with me, that forcing me to relive those events might tether the trauma to me permanently. They'd made an effort at a clean break. I'm glad they did.

For over thirty years, none of my siblings, including my best friend and older sister, Natasha, knew what had happened to Chris and me on the basketball court that day, nor that it was one of the underlying reasons why our family moved to Alaska. I'd never told a coach, including Coach K. My sons don't know that my best friend bled out in my arms.

Like I said before, the Boozer family has never been one to dwell. Hardships were just obstacles to overcome. We were always pushing forward, though Chris has always stayed with me. I never left him behind. During the summer between my junior and senior high-school years, on the cusp of meeting Coach K and the world opening to me like my own private oyster, I saw Chris's mother at my family's annual Fourth of July barbeque in DC. My career was taking off and the big schools were circling around me. Her face lit up when she recognized the six-foot-nine teenage Goliath who had been her son's best friend. I gave her a long hug. It had been about a decade since I'd last seen her.

"I'm so very proud of you," she said, eyes glistening. I had to let her know in that moment, and I hoped it wouldn't upset her—"Chris is with me," I said, "and he's going to stay with me all the way to the NBA."

She let out a sigh of gratitude. "I know you'll make it," she said, patting my arm. "I know you will."

Years later, as this book came alive on the page, my thoughts went back to her.

"I haven't been able to find Chris's mom," I told Neeka one day, fretting about the book. The pandemic had shattered everyone's regular semblance of travel and human connection.

Still, I wondered if Chris's mom would approve of me including him in my story.

"Do you need to reach her?" Neeka asked earnestly. "You're remembering her son that she lost. A son that many people have forgotten. I think that wherever she is, she'd be okay with this. You're capturing her son in time forever."

I'll also never forget my beloved Utah Jazz coach, Jerry Sloan, who passed away at the age of seventy-eight in May 2020. Coach Sloan had been diagnosed with Parkinson's disease and dementia in 2016. He was a ferocious coach who allowed me to flourish in a family-first environment.

I've made it a point to keep in touch with all of my coaches. I still speak to Coach K at least once a month, and a lot more lately now that the boys are contemplating college ball. Coach Lucas still checks up on me once in a while, as well. Mats, the man who discovered me, remains a fixture of our family.

When I made it to the NBA, Coach Houston and I began hosting an annual summer camp, where I'd bring along bonus players, like Jay Williams and Corey Maggette. Coach Houston and I still speak by phone—always about basketball—every month or so.

When the boys were old enough to make the trip, I started taking them to Juneau. We feasted on crab legs and salmon at one of my high school friend's father's restaurant. When we stopped in the grocery store, nearly everyone in the place was a former classmate. One of them was a Supreme Court judge who had followed in his father's footsteps. Robert Casperson, one of the seniors who took me under his wing, succeeded Coach Houston as the basketball coach. I get why people live their entire lives in Juneau. Those same reasons are why I'll always get back there.

While we try and save Juneau for summer trips, I'm resolute about spending winter breaks in Park City, Utah. As soon as I had the money and enough time, I bought a snowboard to rival any I'd seen in the Foot Locker store window in Juneau. It was worth the wait. Surfing down a mountain of slick, packed snow at forty-five miles per hour is quite a rush.

As we entered 2023, the sophomore twins' high school team won their second state title, unstoppable with the six-foot-nine (and still growing!) Cameron and his six-foot-three cohort out front. Cameron, who ESPN ranked No. 1 in the 2025 class for a second year, had an explosive season, averaging 21.1 points, 11.2 rebounds, 4.2 assists, 2.0 blocks, and 1.3 steals per game.

That March, I stood outside Cameron's classroom door, waiting for five-time NBA All-Star Kevin Love to present him with Gatorade's National Player of the Year Award. Cameron was only the second sophomore to win an award usually reserved for seniors. Past winners include Kobe and LeBron. I saw the surprise on Cameron's face when Kevin entered, making me proud not only for his efforts, but for the poise he showed in accepting the award.

Over the summer, Cameron and Cayden led Team USA's Under 16 squad to gold at the FIBA World Championships in Mexico, the beginnings of their journey to the Olympics. CeCe and I watched the entire tournament together from the sidelines, glancing at one another from time to time with giddy pride. Heading into their junior years, both Cameron and Cayden, also ranked among the top 25 players in the Class of 2025, have earned over 20 college offers. At the moment, Cayden has one more offer than his brother, from a school that fell in love with him. The boys could play together in college, but they also understand that different programs might suit their strengths better. Not to be undone, big brother Carmani has received multiple college offers to play baseball, his eyes still fixed on the MLB.

I'm immensely proud of my sons for their sports accomplishments. My career success made it possible to hire the right coaches and to send them to schools with strong sports programs, but I could never buy the determination they'd needed to stay late on the court or field, fighting through their exhaustion.

It was never required that our children become athletes. Bloom loves to paint for hours. If she wanted to become a professional artist, Neeka and I would get behind her without fail. However, the Boozers are a sports family with just as much framed memorabilia on our walls as family pictures. When our family attends games, we sit together as a cheering unit, our presence known. If my children didn't have an appreciation for sports, I know I could've eventually won them over, but playing was never a requisite.

After my partners and I broke ground on three more Popeyes locations in 2021, we initiated a step-by-step plan to build eighteen Popeyes locations into our portfolio within five years. Our company also purchased seventy-five acres to build a condominium and shopping plaza in Conway, where we'd eventually lease space to companies like Hobby Lobby, Costco, Home Depot, Verizon, and Chase Bank. We'd also started plans to build a Papa John's and a Starbucks on the property we leased.

In 2023, I'd also joined my younger brother, Charles, in earning my real estate license. The name "Boozer Real Estate" flashed through my head—another road to take. I'll walk down it optimistic and hopeful. Whether it be professional or personal (I'm keeping my heart chakra open to fall in love again)—you have to stay positive to yield the best results. Everything that I've enjoyed has come from love.

We all make decisions that send us down different paths, never quite knowing what going the other way might have brought. That's life. I think it's just as important to commit to the road that you do choose or you might never get to where you're going.

My parents taught me to give it my all, a theme that continued with Coach Houston, Coach K, Kobe, and so many others who guided me along the way. CeCe and I have tried to instill that lesson in our children.

Life throws continuous curveballs that only get faster as you get older. Yet, whether I was a moody twelve-year-old bickering with my parents or a forty-year-old man grappling with the sudden loss of his teammate and friend, basketball has always been the elixir that heals me. What a gift it was to discover that throwing a ball into a hoop could cure all my ailments. I've loved everything about basketball from day one. I rose to the challenge. I grinded. I agonized. I celebrated. I agonized some more. But I embraced every moment of it. I made every shot count.

★ ★ ★ ★ ★

# ACKNOWLEDGMENTS

The book was a few years in the making, having traversed a worldwide pandemic that brought life, death and then life again. There was never a question if *Every Shot Counts* would happen, but when, and many assisted us along the way.

First, I thank my collaborator, Loretta Hunt, who tirelessly worked on this project for years (!), going with the flow as my schedule remained an absolute bear, even in retirement. Loretta had Coach K energy from start to finish, bobbing and weaving like a champ, and kept this beast on track, despite some hefty obstacles. We had an absolute ball—Los and Lo!

I'd like to thank my literary agent, Roger Freet, the project's early MVP. Roger made a beautiful pass to our editor, John Glynn, who recognized a diamond in the rough and shined it into a gem. We also thank Eden Railsback for the editorial assist in overtime, a fresh reinforcement when we needed it the most. I'd also like to thank my agent, Gideon Cohen, who lined this project up for me.

Editor Tracy Wilson and Taryn Ortolan were clutch, whipping us into performance-shape. Thank you to typesetters Tamieka Evans and Amanda Roberts, too.

We also thank Emer Flounders for his diligent publicity and marketing work, as well as Dayna Boyer and the rest of the Hanover Square Press team. From our initial Brady Bunch Zoom call, we knew the book was in the right hands.

In the photography department, eternal gratitude goes to Brian Wallace, who had the foresight to capture my early days in Juneau, save the images, then dig them up after so many years.

Thank you to photography extraordinaires Andrew Bernstein and Melissa Majchrzak, who caught so many marvelous shots that the insert could have been refilled many times over with theirs alone. Michael Klein, with Getty Images, was a saint in helping find them, while Natasa Hatsios miraculously resurrected pictures I'd thought long gone and unusable. Pure magic!

Thank you to Jason Probst, who lent transcription and research support, and to sports proofreader Bryan Graham, who caught a correction here and there, as he always does.

From my collaborator: To David and Susan Dottin, together forever on the page. To my unmatchable husband, Shane, and to my best friend, Lisa, who I thought of often during this project. I love you all.

# BIBLIOGRAPHY

"Appendix A: A 30-Year Review of Homicides in the District of Columbia (1972–2002)." *DC.gov Office of the Chief Medical Examiner,* https://doh.dc.gov/sites/default/files/dc/sites/ocme/publication/attachments/APPENDIX%20A%20-%2030%20year.pdf.

Beck, Howard. "A Twosome Reminiscent of the Stockton-Malone Era." *New York Times,* May 28, 2007. https://www.ny-times.com/2007/05/28/sports/basketball/28spurs.html.

Ciccarone, Daniel. "Heroin in Brown, Black and White: Structural Factors and Medical Consequences in the US Heroin Market." *International Journal of Drug Policy* 20, no. 3 (May 2009): 277–82.

Keech, Larry. "Boozer Continues Alaskan Tradition/Duke Freshman Carlos Boozer Picking Up Where Fellow Alaskan and Fellow Blue Devil Trajan Langdon Left Off." *Greensboro News & Record,* February 25, 2000. https://greensboro.com/

boozer-continues-alaskan-tradition-duke-freshman-carlos-boozer-is-picking-up-where-fellow-alaskan-and/article_89c494f6-ac63-5dcd-941f-84f23c3a6c57.html.

Neel, Eric. "Fearless Love." *E:60, ESPN*. http://www.espn.com/espn/eticket/story?page=boozers.

Williams, Van. "Carlos Boozer: Grizzly Bear." *Alaska Sports Hall of Fame*. https://alaskasportshall.org/inductee/carlos-boozer/.